Developing Competent Youth and Strong Communities

Through After-School Programming

Edited by Steven J. Danish *and* Thomas P. Gullotta

D1565381

GIMBEL CHILD & FAMILY SCHOLARS

CWLA Press • Washington, DC

CWLA Press is an imprint of the Child Welfare League of America. The Child Welfare League of America (CWLA), the nation's oldest and largest membership-based child welfare organization, is committed to engaging all Americans in promoting the well-being of children and protecting every child from harm.

CHILD WELFARE LEAGUE OF AMERICA, INC.
440 First Street, NW, Third Floor
Washington, DC 20001-2085
E-mail: books@cwla.org

CURRENT PRINTING (last digit)
10 9 8 7 6 5 4 3 2 1

Cover design by Tung Mullen
Text design by Peggy Porter Tierney

Printed in the United States of America
ISBN # 0–87868–796–3

Library of Congress Cataloging-in-Publication Data
Developing competent youth and strong communities through after-school pro-
gramming/edited by Thomas P. Gullotta, Steven J. Danish.
     p. cm.
   Includes bibliographical references.
   ISBN 0-87868-796-3
   1. Social work with youth--United States. 2. Social skills--Study and
teaching--United States. I. Gullotta, Thomas P. II. Danish, Steven J.

HV1431 .D48 2000
362.7'083'0973--dc21
                                                      00-057911

Issues in Children's and Families' Lives
An Annual Book Series

Senior Series Editor
Thomas P. Gullotta, *Child and Family Agency of Southeastern Connecticut*

Editors, The University of Chicago At Illinois Series on Children and Youth
Arthur J. Reynolds, *University of Wisconsin-Madison*
Herbert J. Walberg, *University of Illinois at Chicago*
Roger P. Weissberg, *University of Illinois at Chicago*

Drawing upon the resources of the Child and Family Agency of Southeastern Connecticut, one of the nation's leading family service agencies, **Issues in Children's and Families' Lives** is designed to focus attention on the pressing social problems facing children and their families today. Each volume in this series will analyze, integrate, and critique the clinical and research literature on children and their families as it relates to a particular theme. Believing that integrated multidisciplinary approaches offer greater opportunities for program success, volume contributors will reflect the research and clinical knowledge base of the many different disciplines that are committed to enhancing the physical, social, and emotional health of children and their families. Intended for graduate and professional audiences, chapters will be written by scholars and practitioners who will encourage readers to apply their practice skills and intellect to reducing the suffering of children and their families in the society in which they live and work.

Thomas P. Gullotta
Chief Executive Officer
Child and Family Agency of
Southeastern Connecticut

Contents

Tables

Figures

Introduction

What does it mean for a young person to be socially competent? Do sports, wilderness, and art activities help or hinder the development of prosocial behaviors and resiliency? What are the rituals that mark the passage from childhood to adulthood? How do communities celebrate events, and can those celebrations be used to encourage the development of community-interested youth? What is the role of the charitable giving community in supporting after-school activities? These are just some of the questions this book addresses.

Renewed attention has been given to undertaking those efforts that would encourage young people to grow into healthy productive citizens. The reemergence of violent gangs, the continued use of illicit drugs, and the tragic killing of young people by other young people, whether on a city street or in a suburban school, has American society wondering how it might better use its resources to address these issues. Appropriately, this interest has extended beyond the school day and into other than school activities. Given the reality that schools are in session about half the calendar year and, on average, classes occupy less than six hours of each weekday, this concern is deserved.

Modern American society does not have in place the means to effectively monitor its youth. Historically, apprenticeship and an agrarian lifestyle offered this supervision. With industrialization, these methods dissolved to be replaced, after the passage of child labor laws, with public education. This worked successfully in stable communities with at least one parent or other responsible family member providing after-school care. Times, however, have changed. Consider that the nuclear family is overwhelmingly comprised of two wage earners, and that most single-parent families are stressed to meet its financial needs. Both are pressed to meet basic child rearing obligations not, we believe, out of a lack of interest but out of a lack of time and, in many cases, resources. At another level, our communities are no longer designed for community intimacy but for individual privacy. In many metropolitan areas, subways like BART, METRO, and the MTA or other means make it possible for youth to

1

roam freely and widely across communities. Thus, the neighborhood monitoring of youth that older generations, including our own found so common, is all but absent.

Most Americans are not comfortable with leaving young people to video games, music television, and graphically violent films. Most Americans are uneasy with leaving their children alone. Most Americans are concerned about who their children associate with and where those meetings occur. Americans are not looking for a police state; rather, these concerns are expressed in recent calls for improving the availability and the quality of after-school programming.

This collection of essays on the promotion of youth social competency through after-school programming is a contribution toward achieving that purpose. It represents the scholarship of a select group of individuals chosen in some cases for their skilled practice experiences and in other instances for their academic scholarship in this area. This unique group of practitioners and scholars represents the third class of Gimbel Child and Family Scholars.

For nearly a decade, the Gimbel Foundation has supported Child and Family Agency of Southeastern Connecticut in the funding of this program. Previous learning communities have explored the prevention of violence in America [Hampton et al.1996] and approaches to bridging the disparate fields of substance abuse and child welfare [Hampton et al. 1998]. Through independent study and two meetings over two long weekends, the authors of the chapters in this book sought to strengthen their programs and their knowledge in a learning community devoted to exploring ways in which young people's lives can be enriched and personal competencies developed.

The book divides into three untitled sections. The first three chapters provide a backdrop for the volume. In the first chapter, Gullotta places in historical context the evolution of play as work in America. He attributes the rise of after-school activities to the decline of young people in the labor force and the interest American society has on promoting individual change. Chapter two by Bloom undertakes an examination of the meaning of social competency. Martin examines the scant research literature on the contributions of various activities to social competency and concludes by offering several observations about key program factors that appear to optimize youth development. In chapter three, Blumenkrantz examines the concepts of play and rites of passage. He also describes a program he has developed to assist communities in helping young people make the transition from childhood to adulthood.

The next four chapters represent a variety of perspectives for engaging young people in competency-promoting after-school activities. For example chapter four, by Petitpas and Champagne, explores the contribution of sports to the development of social competency. Their review points out that the literature is mixed on the value of sports activities toward promoting social competency. As others note in this volume, it is not the activity per se that encourages youth competency, but the context and with whom the activity is undertaken that promotes healthy development. Toward this end, the authors describe the National Football Foundation's Play It Smart program. In chapter five by Stemmermann and Antonellis, the authors discuss the importance of programming for young women. Living in a society still striving for sexual equity, the issues of promoting the healthy development of females are different than they are for males. Using an experiential approach, the authors describe Circles of Courage, a model adventure program for girls. In chapter six, Chris Gullotta and Bert Plant offer practical advice in how the arts can be used to encourage social competency. Again, the authors stress the reoccurring theme that the process matters much more than the activity. This section concludes with a chapter that revisits one of the earliest forms of play—that being the festival. Porter repeats another familiar theme in this book, that healthy youth live in healthy communities. Public celebrations can be used to build healthy communities.

The next two chapters focus on the community planning that needs to be undertaken to successfully implement these activities. Chapter eight by Edmundson provides a broad overview of the problem issues facing communities and funding bodies in the development of quality after-school programming. In chapter nine, Fukuzawa with the Detroit Skillman Foundation provides a case study of how one national foundation undertook to increase the quality and availability of after-school programming in a large urban American city. In the final chapter, Danish reviews the contributions made to this volume and the themes that emerged.

In this book, readers will find a starting point for their own work toward developing quality after-school programming for youth. We believe the value of this effort has been made clear. The complexity of doing it well is also very clear. Suggestions both programmatically and organizationally have been offered. As with all suggestions, they will need to be tailored to fit with the values and beliefs of the local community. It is our hope that readers will use this book in those local efforts to design youth programs that nurture young people toward a healthy and productive adulthood.

Steven J. Danish
Thomas P. Gullotta

References

Hampton, R. L., Jenkins, P., & Gullotta, T. P. (1996). *Preventing violence in America*. Thousand Oaks, CA: Sage.

Hampton, R. L., Senatore, V., & Gullotta, T. P. (1996). *Substance abuse, family violence, and child welfare*. Thousand Oaks, CA: Sage.

1

From Idle Amusements to Leisure Activity as Work for Youth

Thomas P. Gullotta

Time was in North America that a young person's labor was needed by the family for survival. The occasional free moments to be found in the day were spent resting after the strenuous work that would be found on the farm. On Sundays, across much of this land, the day was devoted to religious activities. The concept of leisure time for any but the youngest child was alien to these early American settlers. Indeed, leisure activities in this new and expanding world were viewed with fear that idle habits would develop. Gradually, with the rise of manufacturing and the decline for the need of child labor, play became the work of the younger generation.

In this introductory chapter, I'll briefly review our early social history and trace the evolution of the social event to the acceptance of leisure activities as legitimate behavior for youth. Drawing from early children's books, school primers, and period writings, my understanding of U.S. social history leads me to conclude that the social activity which accompanied the hard physical labor that developed this land gradually evolved to stand-alone leisure activities. In turn, these leisure activities have developed into the new work of young people. If successfully completed, it is believed this work results in a socially competent and productive young person. One final observation—unlike today when equal opportunity between the sexes is both desired and more common, the past was inequitable. Expectations for males and females were different and nearly always favored the male. Using historical sources as I am, this inequitable condition is clearly reflected in this paper.

Work and the Social Event

For the early citizens of the United States, words like leisure, recreation, and social activities which were grouped under the heading "amusements" had unhealthy undertones as the following passage taken from *Letters on Practical Subjects from a Clergyman of New England to his Daughter* [Anonymous 1822] suggests:

> There are, perhaps, few greater chances of danger to young females, than an excessive love of amusement...[Activities] which are fitted to inflame the passions, to lessen the sensibility of conscience, to invest worldly pleasure with new attractions, or merely to kill time, must of course, be condemned [Anonymous 1822, pp. 47-49].

Failure to heed the good clergyman's advice by reading novels, engaging in gossip, or, worse still, playing cards had disastrous results, as this moral lesson found in an early school primer details:

> In a dirty, ruinous looking house, that stood in one of the back streets of a smoky town there lived an elderly man of the name of Smith...Smith was apprenticed [as a teenager] to an honest trade, and he wanted not ability to become more than ordinarily expert in it. But whenever his master's back was turned, he thought it more agreeable to gossip over the fire with his fellow apprentices, to crack a pocketful of nuts, to play a game of whist, to read a dirty novel, or even to sit resting his head on his hands, over the bench, than to go on with his work. Thus, at the end of seven years, he left his master with an imperfect knowledge of his business, an indifferent character, and worse than all, with desultory and idle habits...Having as before hinted, read a great many worthless novels during his apprenticeship, his indolent mind was often occupied in the injurious habit of castle building....Little acts of indulgence commonly introduce strong habits of intemperance...[and] Smith quickly lost one of the great advantages of honest poverty—health [Hall 1843, pp. 76-77].

In a new land that needed to be cleared, crops planted and harvested, and tools made, idle habits could be ill afforded. Having said this, it would be deceptive to say that young people in the past had no free time. Life, no matter how difficult, did include time for social events—the forerunner of today's activities for youth [Kett 1977; Earle 1899]. Even our anonymous clergyman [1822, p. 48] conceded that, "the mind should occasionally unbend from a posture of severe effort. The only legitimate end of amusement is to restore the mind to its native elasticity, and thus prepare it for prosecuting its useful pursuits with more vigour." Even given what would be the vehement protestations on the part of New England's Puritans, I think it useful to point out that their weekly religious gatherings served more than a religious purpose. This group gathering acted as a social glue, binding members to the larger community. It served as a means of establishing acceptable behaviors and, when necessary, correcting those who wandered from the teachings of the day. Strong among those teachings was the importance of work— regardless of age.

With time and the growth of religious diversity in the United States, events beyond those tied directly to religious activities emerged. Understanding the barn dances, the quilting parties, and the military regiments that comprised social life in this young nation demands an appreciation of the fluidity with which the child moved from the status of consumer to provider. Consider for a moment that adolescence did not exist, and that young people moved quickly from dependence to independence, from occasional schooling to work, and that the median age of the population in 1800 was 18 [Kett 1977]. In this setting, social activities served a different function than, say, the school dance of today. For example, the barn dance of the 1800s was typically the climax to a work event like haying, husking corn, or a barn raising. Yet, in its time it could be seen as recreation—that is, a refreshment of mind and body from the grueling labor of the day. Social activities, like the quilting sessions that built community networks, and the young males' involvement (down to age 12) in military regiments, acted to create a sense of community in a new and rapidly developing land.

It would be deceptive to state that life was filled with social events for the young person. Rather, visits to neighbors, the old swimming hole, and even school were sandwiched in between the realities of hard physical labor beginning at an early age. Adulthood was in most cases reached before age 16. Adulthood in the sense I use it here refers to being a productive, useful member of society. Interestingly, adulthood in this sense does not necessarily mean marriage or separation from the family. In our early colonial history, young males often remained subservient to their parent(s) for many years. In those early days, sons equated to social security. To illustrate, most young men did not marry until after their 25th birthday. In large part, the reason can be traced to the unwillingness of their parent(s) to provide them with land to enable them to achieve economic independence. Since, in this era, the amount of manpower available dictated the size of the crop planted and harvested, it was in the parents' interest to continue a young person's servitude as long as possible. Without the money to purchase land elsewhere, the young lad of the 1600s in Massachusetts had little choice but to work for his father in the hope of someday being given the family farm.

Even when a father granted land to his son, parental authority did not end. By searching through early land records, Greven [1973] found that many parents retained legal ownership of the property. This tactic effectively continued the sons' dependence on the family until the father's death, when the land was divided among the male heirs.

Social activities in this period served the function of extending a sense of community in a new land and binding neighbors more closely together. As time passed, social activities would undergo a transformation from an occasional amusement to the work of youth.

With Time On Their Hands

The events leading to the transformation of social activities from community glue to the social work that contributes to individual social competency can be found in the changing status of the young person in a rapidly growing and industrializing nation. In 1880, with more than half the U.S. population no longer living on farms, the growth of athletic activities like sports or scouting to occupy young people's time begins to accelerate. This development coincides with growing concerns about non-English speaking immigrants, especially youth, living in cities [Gullotta et al. 2000].

Consider the time. Rapid change brings opportunity, not only for growth but also economic and political turmoil. From the 1880s to the First World War, reformists, like Jane Addams. the founder of the Chicago social settlement Hull House, and socialist author Sinclair Lewis, decried the treatment of the working class, particularly immigrants.

To illustrate, in *The Jungle*, Sinclair Lewis [1906] describes abuses in the meat packing industry toward both workers and consumers. The central figure in this story is Jurgis Rudkus, a Slav immigrant, working in the stockyards. Mistreated by his supervisors and beaten into sickness and depravity by the poverty that surrounds him and his ill-fated family, Jurgis emerges from the loneliness of facing modern society alone to embracing socialism as a means of returning dignity to the faceless worker.

For those who might doubt the severity of conditions at the time, consider this. While some citizens marveled at the new industrialization, owners of the New York City-based Triangle Waist Company used the laissez-faire attitudes of the day concerning labor to exploit a mostly young, female immigrant labor force anxious for work at any price. Sewing garments on a piece-work basis from 7:30 in the morning to 6:00 in the evening, these young women worked six days a week. With luck, the fast worker might earn $18 a week. More likely, she would earn $6 to $8 a week. Literally a sweat shop lacking ventilation and ignoring all fire safety precautions, the Triangle Waist Company routinely packed several hundred young women into three upper storied floors where doors were kept locked lest an employee attempt to steal an item of clothing. On April 20, 1911, the inevitable happened. A fire broke out that spread quickly among the oil-soaked rags that littered the sewing room floors.

Within moments the building was engulfed in flames. An estimated 145 young women died that day.

Imagine the consternation that "capitalists" of the day must have felt reading Lewis, watching the labor movement develop in response to tragedies like the Triangle Waist fire, and recognizing (perhaps for the first time) that languages other than English filled the streets of this nation's major ports. Real and fictionalized events like these drew the attention of labor organizers and social reformers. Solutions ranged from macro-level changes to the system, like the passage of child labor laws, to micro-level changes concerned with the individual. At the micro-level, by expanding individual opportunity to better educate and develop one's spiritual, intellectual, and physical body, the citizen's life can be improved without fundamentally redistributing wealth or reordering the economic structure of the United States.

As one might imagine the micro-level view of individual effort leading to social and economic prosperity found widespread support among the established classes and the foundations they established. Writing for the Russell Sage Foundation, Perry [1913] in *The Wider Use of the School Plant* provides an example of this position. The author's premise is simple enough. Representing a large capital investment, school facilities should be put to wider use. Evening school, public lectures, and social activities, including sports and dances, would help address America's new plights. Perry [1913, p. 361] sees these plights, as do other reformists, as outgrowths of industrialization, which, among other things, virtually eliminated apprenticeship:

> To become the [operator] of a machine takes only a few months practice, but after this training the man is not so well equipped even for this labor as was the craftsman of old who had to learn the whole trade.[The craftsman] acquired agility and skill, and coping with a wide range of situations cultivated self-reliance that gave him the power to meet with success whatever change of circumstances fate might bring him...the operator of [machinery] is stunted intellectually and physically by his work.

Further, this fundamental labor production change, "tended to break up the old social solidarity." Perry [1913, pp. 365-366] continues:

> Within the past ninety years a score of different countries have sent us...over twenty-six millions of people, and today the persons of foreign parentage among us form over a third of the whole population. Machinery sliced us into horizontal layers, and immigration, by cleaving us vertically, has chopped us up into isolated chunks.

These concerns were especially felt in regards to children. Unemployed, poorly educated, and potentially (physically and politically) dangerous, these factors led reformers in several directions.

The most dramatic approach to the problem of "street arabs," "gutter snipes," or "waifs" was practiced by the minister Charles Loring Brace [1880], who established the New York Children's Aid Society in 1856. After several failed attempts to use prayer meetings to reform these unruly and rebellious youth, Brace developed several industrial schools and homeless shelters to serve young people barely managing an existence by selling penny newspapers and other wares on street corners. Brace initially saw education as the means to redirecting this "dangerous" class into respectful employment. However, the sheer numbers of children in need or suspected to be in need led Brace to other more radical solutions. Taking literally Frederick Jackson Turner's [1892] remark of, "Go West Young Man," from 1853 to 1882 Brace placed over 67,000 young people on trains headed in that direction. In many cases, these children were homeless and destitute. In other instances, overly zealous caseworkers literally swept up and packed off children to new homes, whether they had caring families or not [Levine & Levine 1992]! Once out of the city and in the countryside, the children and their caretaker would stop at train stations and disembark. Working with local religious leaders who were notified in advance of their arrival:

> There was usually a dense crowd of [farm] people at the station...The sight of the little company of children of misfortune always touched the hearts of a population naturally generous...[The next day] the [caretaker would

address the community] stating the benevolent objects of the Society, and something of the history of the children. The sight of their worn faces was a most pathetic enforcement of his arguments. People who were childless came forward to adopt children; others who had not intended to take any into their families, were induced to apply for them; and many who really wanted the children's labor pressed forward to obtain it" [Brace 1880, pp. 231-232].

This practice of "placing out" illustrates for this author two recurring themes in American lore. The first is that the city is the center for depravity, and that in rural (or at least suburban) America young people can be cleansed of its corrupting influences. The second is the value of rigorous physical activity toward purification. Life on a farm and the rigors it entails would accomplish both. However, not all children can be removed from the city or for that matter from their parents. This gave rise to second solution— recreational activities. These are activities that are intended to encourage the healthy development of the mind, the body, and the spirit in the absence of work.

Recreation as the Work of Young People

It should not be surprising, then, that the recreation movement began in the city. Reynolds [1977] sees this movement as a first attempt to stem crime, not by individuals, but by whole groups of people. First intending to neutralize the sinful influences of dance halls, pool rooms, and theaters, the supporters of the recreation movement believed that these diversions polluted young people's bodies, minds, and souls. As Perry [1913, pp. 374-375] describes it:

> In the days when the family lived in the country the children were able to stretch their limbs and expand their chests by roaming the hills and pastures. The attic and barn allowed them plenty of room for that rehearsal of the roles of grown-up life...But play finds small opportunity in rubbish-cluttered alleys and the diminutive areas which surround the city tenement. If boys attempt in our streets

even a weak imitation of the freedom enjoyed in the farmer days, we arrest them and deprive them of liberty. But exercise of body and discipline of mind and mind and temper which come from play and competitive games are necessary to the development of strong men and robust women.

Supervised recreation was seen as a tool for promoting the individual competency of individuals once obtained through labor as an apprentice if a male or in the domestic sciences if a female. It could train young people to be team *America* players, not immigrants. It could teach responsible citizenship and instill democratic values in young people. It could even prevent criminal behavior.

The following incident [related by Miss Whitney to Mr. Perry] selected out of "scores of incidents" that came to notice demonstrates clearly...[the] belief that no matter how bad a young man may be, the acquisition of "the athlete's code of honor is a triumph over lawlessness, the beginning of a citizen's conception of duty." One club of street loafers organized last winter, seemed as unpromising as any we ever attempted to reform. The leader, a swaggering, unclean fellow, fortunately had "the vulnerable heel." He began to observe expert performances, then to obey instructions, until pride and skill were so developed that...he outranked all the athletes in his center and made his club equal with the best [Whitney cited in Perry 1913, pp. 234-235].

Not only was this true for boys but also for girls:

One of the marked instances of the year was the rescue of what police designated one of the worst gangs of girls on the East Side. In a club of twenty young women, now tamed and decent, one would not recognize the hoydens of a few months ago [Whitney cited in Perry 1913, p. 235].

In a society in which boys no longer worked beside men, recreational activities such as those offered by the Boy Scouts could reintroduce young men to their proper role models. Indeed, the original purpose of the Scout movement was to counteract the "threatened...development of manliness" [Hantover 1978, p. 185] occurring as a result of smaller, female-dominated families in an increasingly industrialized nation that saw father working away from the home. If you believe I am belaboring this point—of the influence industrialization had on promoting recreation—consider this claim for scouting made by its founder in 1914:

> The Wilderness is gone, the Buckskin Man is gone, the sainted Indian has hit the trail over the Great Divide, the hardships and privations of pioneer life which did so much to develop sterling manhood are now but a legend in history, and we must depend upon the Boy Scout Movement to produce *men* of the future [Beard, cited in Hantover 1978, p. 189].

Beard's remarks bring us full circle. Work—whether as an apprentice in a trade or beside a mother learning the domestic sciences—had become legend. Where daily life was integrated, it was now separated. Where work was home-centered and an all-family event, it was replaced by a new industrialized society that compartmentalized the manufacturing of parts and lives. These changes redefined the way in which young people moved from childhood through adolescence (which became popularized as a life stage at the turn of the century) to adulthood [Hall 1904]. These changes moved idle amusements to leisure activity as work for youth. How and whether social competency is promoted through the use of after-school activities is the subject for the remainder of this volume.

Notes

1.   Consider, that in order to develop "new" land, not only was a grant from the authorities necessary, but access to a minister was required—which explains why in New England new communities developed from old. Settlers in outlying areas would petition for permission to retain a minister and build a meeting house because travel to religious services was too long. Thus, a new incorporated town would develop from an older community.

2. Recall that most of these illustrations occurred before the advent of the Federal personal income tax - this nation's primary means of redistributing income.

3. A hoyden is a girl exhibiting boyish behavior.

References

Anonymous. (1822). *Letters on practical subjects from a clergyman of New England to his daughter*. Hartford, CT: Huntington and Hopkins.

Brace, C. L. (1880). *The dangerous classes of New York and twenty years' work among them* (3rd ed.). New York: Wynkoop and Hallenbeck.

Earle, A. M. (1899). *Child life in colonial days*. New York: Macmillan Co.

Hall, J. (1843). *The reader's manual*. Hartford, CT: Gurdon-Robins.

Kett, J. F. (1977). *Rites of passage: Adolescence in America 1790 to the present*. New York: Basic Books.

Greven, P. (1973). Family structure in 17th century Andover, Massachusetts. In M. Gordon (Ed.), *The American family in social-historical perspective*. New York: St. Martin's Press. [need page numbers for chapter]

Gullotta, T. P., Adams, G. R., & Markstrom, C. (2000). *The adolescent experience* (4th ed.). New York: Academic Press.

Hall, G. S. (1904). *Adolescence: Its psychology, and its relations to physiology, anthropology, sociology, sex, crime, religion, and education* (Vols. 1–2). New York: Appleton-Century-Crofts.

Hantover, J. P. (1978). The Boy Scouts and the validation of masculinity. *Journal of Social Issues, 34,* 184–195.

Levine, M. & Levine, A. (1992). Helping children: A social history. New York: Oxford University Press.

Lewis, S. (1906). *The jungle*. New York: Modern Library

Perry, C. A. (1913). *Wider use of the school plant*. New York: Survey Associates / Russell Sage Foundation.

Reynolds, J. (1977). Two hundred years of children's recreation. In E. H. Grotberg (Ed.), *200 years of children* (Publication No. OHD 77-30103). Washington, DC: U.S. Government Printing Office.

Turner, F. J. (1893 / 1960). *The significance of the frontier in American history*. El Paso, TX: Texas Western College Press.

2

The Uses of Theory in Primary Prevention Practice: Evolving Thoughts on Sports and After-School Activities as Influences of Social Competency

Martin Bloom

For my grandchildren, play is hard work and they go at it with great gusto, without a thought as to what they are doing or why, and without the knowledge that Aristotle saw play as cathartic, or that Herbert Spencer [1855] considered play as a discharging and recharging of psychic energies. They would be amused to learn that Groos [1898] thought that children's play was a way of learning about and preparing for adult life, or that Piaget [1962] considered play part and parcel of human development. They are too busy at play to waste time on adult musings. But musing is my business, and I would like to share these evolving thoughts on the nature of play—or, more specifically, on sports and after-school activities as they influence social competency, which is the general subject of this book. My way of musing about this topic involves casting a big net, and then trying to tie up what I catch into usable packages. My preferred net is a theory concerning primary prevention. Let me lay out this net and you will see what kind of fish I hope to catch.

Primary prevention may be described as the simultaneous actions that seek to prevent a predictable problem, protect an existing state of health (or healthy functioning), and promote some desired goal for the party involved. If we seek to understand how to augment social competency in young people, then we have to address the issues of prevention, protection, and promotion viewed in a systematic or simultaneous perspective. Specifically, this primary prevention net suggests that we should (so far as these factors are relevant) seek to *increase* individual strengths, sociocultural supports, and physical environmental resources, while at the same time, we should also *decrease* individual limitations, sociocultural stresses, and physical environmental pressures in order to facilitate social competence in young people [Bloom, 1996]. In what ways do sports and after-school activities increase the individual's natural and learned strengths with regard to becoming a more competent person? How do these activities increase the social support this individual experiences? What does the physical environment contribute by way of resources to help the individual? All of these we use to promote and protect, so far as we can. However, the individual may have some personal limitations, may experience some social and cultural stresses, and may be oppressed by his or her physical environment— all of which may interfere with that individual gaining social competence, and all of which we therefore seek to prevent, to whatever extent is possible and feasible. So the net of primary prevention seeks to catch specific ways that have been shown to be effective in promoting and protecting specific factors leading to social competence, while at the same time, using the same literature in preventing specific factors that interfere with this goal. These are going to be abstract musings— sorry, but it is unavoidable—yet my concern is always: How can we use these ideas from primary prevention to facilitate social competency in youth? In back of (or behind, or underneath) every abstraction is a pragmatic proposition aching to come out. Let's meet it halfway.

Kurt Lewin, the great social psychologist, made what is probably the most famous remark in all of the social sciences—that there is nothing as practical as a good theory. Lewin's idea of a good theory involves a small number of clearly defined terms that can be combined into logical propositions, the set of which describe, explain, and predict some significant aspect of human behavior, and from which, empirical tests of deduced hypotheses of social importance can be made. Unfortunately, there are very few such behavioral science theories, and what I will present here are a series of stepping stones toward a strategy, that is, a network of terms set within a context of values that can be used to guide measurable professional efforts with regard to a significant aspect of human behavior. This is a long way from the logical precision that a Lewinian theory implies, but I hope will be helpful is sorting out many of the terms of the topic of this book: In what way and to what degree can sports and extracurricular activities promote social competence in youth?

As a kind of road map to this chapter that will discuss many specific concepts and variables, I will identify a cluster of independent or causal factors, which I will then link to a cluster of dependent or outcome variables. In fact, life is not that simple; a systemic or ecological model is more realistic—but complex in its presentation. I will explore these complex interactions after I have defined the separate components. Table 2-1 shows the map (and the chapter outline that begins with the dependent variable complex).

Dependent or Outcome Variables: Health, Social Competency, Resilience, Life Skills, Conventional Bonding

Health is the larger context for the present discussion of social competency because it is assumed to be present in order that social competency may exist. Health includes several broad domains: physical health, psychological health (both cognitive and emotional health), social (or sociocultural) health, at minimum. Some might wish to add spiritual or philosophical health. These various forms of health are notoriously difficult to define satisfactorily, and so I will offer this working definition: that *health* refers to the expanding and/ or self-sustaining operation of the system of which it is a characteristic. So, to take the easiest example, a physically healthy body has all of its components operating singly and in coordination as part of expanded growth of the young person and/or as part of sustaining functioning of the mature individual. What constitutes sustenance of the body is a value-laden decision, made differently by the gourmand and the ascetic, the athlete and the couch potato, people

Table 2-1. Links Between Variable Complexes

Independent Variable Complex:	Dependent Variable Complex:
Sports:	Health:
Sports	Physical Health
Games	Psychological (cognitive and emotional) Health
Play	
Exercise	Social (socio-cultural) Health
Lifetime Activities	Spiritual or Philosophical Health
After-School or Extra-Curricular Activities:	Social Competency:
Community Services	Working well
School Services	Playing well
School-related Recreational	Loving well
Clubs	Thinking well
Mentoring as a general factor in any	Serving well
independent variable used to	
promote competency in youths	Resilience:
	Personal competence dimension
	Environmental support dimension
	Life Skills
	Conventional bonding

living in the culture of superabundance and the culture of bare survival. However, it is the combination of these broad health domains that constitutes the context for any discussion of significant human behaviors. A well-wrought physical, psychological, sociocultural, and spiritual health is the ultimate goal of humankind, differently expressed according to local values and norms. Whatever these local values and norms may be, they all represent *good things to have in this culture at this time.* Any proposed social program ultimately has to conform to this cultural truism: a good thing to have.

Social competency is a "good thing" for children and youth (and the rest of us) to have, and to this end countless conferences and papers have been constructed to figure out how to promote social competency. Interestingly, social competency is not at the same conceptual level as the several domains of health. Indeed, social competency seems to share some aspects of physical, psychological, and sociocultural health. To paraphrase a popular saying, social competence involves "a healthy mind in a healthy physical and sociopolitical body." This aphorism fits comfortably with common sense, even when some uncomfortable truths may be extracted from it, such as the fact that social competence intrinsically involves both the person and the social and physical environment. One cannot adequately discuss this concept without always taking into account the individual and his or her environments [Lewin 1951; Germain 1991]. The following discussion is intended to explicate what this implies.

Social competence is an extraordinarily useful concept, and yet is very difficult to define. Here are some examples of the ways different theorists have conceptualized the term:

> Evidence from a variety of sources suggests a high level of agreement concerning the domains that reflect social competence [Commission on the Prevention of Mental-Emotional Disabilities 1986; Consortium on the School-Based Promotion of Social Competence 1994; Lickona 1991; Westchester County Social Competency in the Schools Task Force 1990]. Socially competent children, at least as defined in mainstream American culture, are those who:
>
> * possess a positive sense of self-worth;
>
> * feel capable as they interact with others and take on new developmental tasks and challenges;
>
> * behave ethically and act responsibly toward others;
>
> * appreciate the benefits of a multiracial society and respect the value of others;
>
> * are skilled in interpersonal encounters and communication, get along with others, and develop long-term interpersonal relationships;

- develop sound work habits, motivations, and values;

- engage in health-enhancing and health-protective behaviors;

- are motivated to become productive citizens by serving as positive, contributing members of their peer group, family, school, and community; and

- avoid engaging in behavior that may lead to negative consequences such as substance abuse, unwanted teen pregnancy, AIDS, social isolation, serious physical injury, school dropout, depression, suicide, unemployment, or criminal prosecution.

[Elias, 1995, pp. 14-15]

Here is another definition of social competence, from Weissburg et al. [1995, p. 272]:

According to social-information-processing models, individuals who behave competently in particular contexts have the capacities to (a) control impulses and manage affect in order to engage in responsible problem solving; (b) perceive the nature of a task and the feelings and perspectives of the people involved; (c) feel motivated to establish an adaptive goal to resolve a situation; (d) feel confident in their ability to achieve a goal successfully; (e) access or generate goal-directed alternatives and link them with realistic consequences; (f) decide on an optimal strategy and when necessary, develop elaborated implementation plans that anticipate potential obstacles; (g) carry out solutions with behavioral skill; (h) self-monitor behavioral performance with the capacity to abandon ineffective strategies, try alternative plans, or reformulate goals as needed; and (I) provide self-reinforcement for successful goal attainment or engage in emotion-focuses coping when a desired goal cannot be reached.

Actually, I quoted these two definitions of social competency by highly esteemed theorists in part to give you a feeling for the nature of the concept, and in part to make my own simplistic definition seem pleasantly uncomplicated and easily remembered in comparison. I will get to my definition by thinking about social competency along with other things that are "good to have."

However, we have to specify what portion of the life course we are discussing, because the social competency of a child would be different from the social competency of an adolescent or an adult. In this chapter, I will focus on youth, which includes puberty to young adulthood, and thus is somewhat fuzzy on both the beginning and endings of the age group. Let's say ages 10 to 21, just for the sake of discussion, depending on the gender and maturation rate of the individual involved.

Now that we "know"—that is, we have conceptualized some common sense experiences—that social competency is some combination of physical, psychological, and sociocultural health (and maybe spiritual health); that it is socially desirable and possibly individually desired; that it has an individual and a social environmental component; and that we will focus on social competence in youths, what do we have? Frankly, not much. We would be very hard pressed to try to promote this vague conceptualization by means of some specific program. This is a critically important statement that is all too often ignored by program developers: *Whatever concepts we construct for both the desired outcome and the preventive means to attain them, there has to be a clear conceptual relationship between potential causes and possible effects, as well as a clear empirical pattern of results linking causes and effects.* This is the only base on which we can build a valid and reliable applied social science.

It is this lack of clarity in the present situation that requires a continuing conceptualization of the meaning of social competency, or, as I will now characterize it, as *psychosocial competency* to emphasize the person-environments unit. Fortunately, we have many guides: Sigmund Freud, Alfred Adler, Jean Piaget, among others. These founders of modern psychology provided us with the conceptual hints that I will combine as a rough working version of social competency. To paraphrase these theorists, I will tentatively define *psychosocial competency as the ability to work well, play well, love well, think well, and serve well.*

These are five goals to be approximated throughout life, each appropriate to the age of the individual. I now have to specify what forms these goals take in the lives of youth, so as to provide enough operational clarity to guide programs and practice.

1. *Working Well.* What does "working well" mean in reference to youth? In the real world, one would ask experienced individuals, such as parents, youths, employers, and helping professionals, as well as consulting research studies. In the artificial world of social science essay writing, I draw on a slender sampling of the literature and some common sense, and subtly change these modest experiences into weighty abstractions: Working well for a youth might involve performing household chores adequately [Werner & Smith 1992] or actually working to the level of expectation of a boss in some paid capacity, usually in a nonhousehold situation.

   These two operational definitions of working well are reasonably self-contained. We can know whether a youth works at household chores or for paid employment, and at what level of adequacy these activities are performed. We also know from research that if a youth who is still at school is working ten or more hours a week, this work may be well performed, but at a detriment to his or her school work, which is ordinarily viewed as the major task of a person this age [Greenberger & Steinberg 1986; Bracey, 1982]. So, any operational definition of a term has to be put into context of other terms as well, that is, the person: environments unit.

2. *Playing Well.* What is "playing well" in the youth context? I think the underlying meaning of this concept is the experience of having fun, of enjoying a given activity for its own sake, not what it can do or achieve. We would have to ask the individual if he or she were having fun as the basic way of operationalizing this term. A second major meaning of "playing well" involves knowing the rules and

the roles of the game involved. Playing often involves group activities where rules and roles are a necessary part of the play. Individual play, such as swimming alone just for the sake of the experience, also has implicit rules such as the kinds of strokes that are possible, the safety context, and keeping time. We can often infer how well a person knows the rules and roles by observing him or her in context. So, giving empirical meaning to some conceptual terms require that we ask the participant directly, while other terms might involve us as observers—unfortunately, never purely objective observers, but that is another issue.

3. *Loving Well*: What is "loving well"? While it might involve the Freudian implication of sexual intimacy, at least for the million or more pregnant teenagers for each year for the past twenty or so, to say nothing about the millions of other teenagers who engaged in the same intimacy but were planful enough or lucky enough not to become pregnant. However, for most youth most of the time, loving well might be operationalized as having strong positive personal attachments to a variety of people—family members and peers. This would include "best friends" or "role models." Second, loving well might also involve group affiliations or pride, such as being strongly attached to a team, a school, or an ethnic group. And third, loving well might also involve a goodly amount of self-love, or self-esteem, as the basis for being able to reach out to others to form intimate or affiliative contacts. These operational definitions of the components of loving well seem reasonably clear and measurable, although I must add that there are dozens of operational definitions of "self-esteem," which means that people do not easily agree on the right definition. Again, conceptual definitions are arbitrary, and ultimately, we use our common sense as judge of their adequacy.

4. *Thinking Well*: What is "thinking well"? The cognitive aspects of youth include a number of important features, such as problem-solving skills, anticipating the future and remembering the past, and also planning for a desired future.

The category might also include thoughts on how to manage anxiety or how to resolve conflict. I am going to focus on effective problem solving as being the core ingredient. Problem solving may include short-range challenges or long-range life and career topics. Using just one operational definition has the advantage of being able to make use of a number of well-conceptualized and empirically-supported programs for improving problem solving in young people of a wide range of ages, including youth [Shure & Spivack 1988; Shure 1997]. But having only one operational definition is not likely to please all readers because this one leaves out someone's other favorite, a risk every conceptualizer faces.

5.   *Serving Well.* And finally, what is "serving well" in the context of youth? This component brings in a moral or ethical component to social competency that is missing from the other definitions, but is age-appropriate as young people begin to take their place in adult society. "Serving well" would seem to have at least these components: First, the young person should become increasingly dependable, as people begin to depend on his or her contributions in the family, the school, the peer group, and then beyond. Second, the young person should exhibit a sense of care and concern for others, as he or she has been exhibiting that same sense of concern for him or herself. This is an expectable part of being a mature adult, and youth is the important transition period. Third, the young person may begin to exhibit actual but unpaid contributions to others, such as in the form of being a peer tutor, a candy striper in a hospital or nursing home, or a worker in soup kitchen.

To summarize this definition and expansion of the term, "psychosocial competency," as the outcome for the primary prevention services, let me offer the following: Psychosocial Competency consists of five major categories, and eleven possible operationalized subcategories, as shown in Table 2-2. All of the categories and subcategories are required for an ecological definition of psychosocial competency except the two phrases in brackets, which may or may not be present.

Table 2-2. Components of Psychosocial Competence	
Conceptual Categories:	**Operational Definitions (for Youth):**
I. Working well:	1. Chores at home
	2. [Possibly having a paid job not at home]
II. Playing well:	3. Having fun
	4. Knowing the rules and roles of the game
III. Loving well:	5. Having good friends
	6. Having strong group affiliations
	7. Having a strong sense of self-esteem
IV. Thinking well:	8. Problem-solving skills
V. Serving well:	9. Being dependable
	10. Exhibiting care and concern for others
	11. [Possibly serving others (without pay)]

Having given this degree of operational specificity has several effects. It becomes much easier to see whether or not a particular primary prevention program is doing things that will affect these specific goals. And second, it sets one up for criticism because inevitably one has left out some facet or another that the critic believes is central to social competency. But this is the nature of applied social science, and we only make progress in our thinking and programming through the critical appraisal of others.

Resilience

The hot topic of the 1990s has been "resilience," a late bloomer in the obvious recognition that sometimes healthy competent youth and adults emerge out of unhealthy disadvantaged childhood environments. There have been a number of empirical explorations and theoretical discussions of the term [Benard 1992; Werner & Smith 1992]. I want to emphasize the ecological aspect of resilience, which is intrinsically composed of person and environment elements.

Why should some individuals (about a third of the high-risk group) be able to emerge as reasonably healthy adults when many others of their peers do not? Surely we must find something in these individuals—and indeed, there are many personal correlates associated with children and youth who become resilient into adulthood.

(But these personal correlates should not blind us to the available environmental supports.) On the other hand, there are other individuals who share some of these same personal traits that do not develop into resilience. In these cases, we are quick to blame the inhibiting social and physical environment. (But, again, these environmental correlates should not blind us to the other personal qualities that may be operative.) Given the larger paradigmatic context for this chapter, an ecological systems approach, I will assume that both personal and environmental elements have to be present to produce the resilient individual.

Let me diagram this assumption in Table 2-3 by assuming three levels of personal competence and three levels of environmental support, and then making observations about the cells formed of their combination.

First, levels of personal competence refer to both the intrinsic traits of the person, such as energy level, physical appearance, and temperament; and the learned characteristics, such as communication skills, problem-solving abilities, and social graces. (Some factors are not as easily classified, although are important, such as sense of humor, personal warmth, and empathy.) A "high" level of personal competence would involve having many intrinsic and learned characteristics that are socially valued; a "low" level would reflect having few of such socially valued characteristics.

Second, levels of environmental support refer to both the physical and sociocultural environments. Having a "high" level of environmental support would mean that both the physical surroundings and the sociocultural context in which the individual lived were conducive to that individual's healthy growth and development. For example, living in a pollution-free setting, with very low crime rates (such as not having drive-by shootings) would be two of many possible elements of a high level of environmental support for the growth and development of youths. Likewise, living in a chemically polluted setting where there was a high incidence of youth violence would indicate two instances of a low level of environmental support for healthy growth and development. The main point about environmental factors is that they are subject to social forces to make changes as directed by social values and social-political will. It is

Table 2-3. Three Levels of Personal Competence and Environmental Support

		Levels of Personal Competence:		
		Low	Middle	High
Levels	High	1	2	3
Of				
Environ-	Middle	4	5	6
Mental				
Support	Low	7	8	9

equally difficult, in a different way, to make changes in individuals, as this is usually a matter of increasing knowledge, skills, motivation, and self-efficacy beliefs with regard to some socially desired ends through socially approved means. Sometimes the individual is self-initiating in learning about some objective, obtaining relevant skills, feeling appropriate motivations, and believing in him or herself that he or she can do it. At other times, it requires a social jump-start.

The two dimensions are combined in Table 2-3. My point with the creation of this figure is that resilience is always a combination of these two dimensions. Consider the cell combinations, essentially viewed in diagonal slices:

- Cell 3 [High Competence (C), High Environmental Support (ES)]. This is the cell combination where we are most likely to find "resilient individuals"—or, rather, "resilient individuals in resilient-supportive environments." These lucky people are not to be neglected merely because of their double good fortune; rather, promotive services may make it possible to encourage outstanding leaders for, and contributors to, society. There are costs to encouraging these kinds of people—especially when others are obviously hurting and needing aid—but civilizations often make significant progress from the contributions of highly talented people in highly supportive environments.
- Cell 2 (Middle C, High ES) and Cell 6 (High C, Middle ES). These would be the cell combinations being next most likely to exhibit "resilient individuals" because presumably the strengths

of the high level of one factor could facilitate the mid-levels strength of the other factor. In these cases, either the individual or forces in the environment would have to work harder to compensate for the weaker factor, but together, there would likely be ample capacity to generate a resilient person. This might be the site of optimum payoff for primary prevention programs, other things being equal.

- Cell 1 (Low C, High ES), Cell 5 (Middle C, Middle ES), and Cell 9 (High C, Low ES). This slice of the figure contains the next most likely sites for resilient individuals in supportive environments, but they are very different instances. Cells 1 and 9 require very large compensations of one factor for limitations in the other, while Cell 5 with its middle ranges of both personal competence and environmental support probably represents the statistically normal condition. There are many reasons why a person might be "low" in personal competence, but I am most concerned with the lack of learned competence because these may best be compensated for through a planned prevention program. There are doubtless many reasons why an environment provides low levels of support, but some of these reasons are theoretically surmountable by vision and collective action. It may be most difficult to change the normative situation, as some decision-makers may question any need for change for these "good enough" conditions—whereas, in primary prevention theory, such "normal" situations make ideal points for promotive services, where so much more is theoretically possible.

- Cell 4 (Low C, Middle ES) and Cell 8 (Middle C, Low ES). This combination represents a democratic challenge. If we accept the equality of opportunity ideal for all persons, then we are obliged to work toward achievable goals. These cells probably reflect the cumulative effects of oppressive sociocultural environments on the long-term miseducation of large numbers of persons with various minority statuses. There is considerable experience of the difficulty of providing these people with treatment for ingrained problematic behaviors; yet, in the democratic ideal, it is important that services be provided. Primary prevention seems to offer the best resolution of this social dilemma by building on the *strengths* of people and cultures, especially when working with infants and young families over whatever periods of time are necessary for moving them into a different resilience category—such as high levels of environmental supports and at least middle levels of personal (learned and innate) competence. Having faith in the innate abilities of people and their abilities to learn, along with the natural supportiveness of some environments, we seek to facilitate both in combination.

- Cell 7 (Low C, Low ES). This represents the category of person and environment combination in which society has failed in a number of respects in the past, and where the compensatory efforts will be difficult, expensive, and long-term. A short-sighted, tight-fisted society will suffer many long-term expenses and potential social contributions unfulfilled if people in Cell 7 continue as usual. Primary prevention often offers surprises that may be relevant to category 7; for instance, in Spivack & Shure's interpersonal cognitive problem solving model, it turns out empirically that the children most strongly affected are those who are either most shy or most aggressive—exactly the kinds of individuals one would hope to influence in positive directions [Shure, 1997]. We must not promise primary prevention miracles because there is no such thing as a free lunch in nature or society. Yet, we can build on prior research findings to put together programs that appear to be optimally effective in the most difficult of situations [cf. Weikart & Schweinhart 1997; Nettles & Pleck 1994].

Life Skills

A number of theorists and researchers discuss "life skills," some set of learned cognitive/affective/behavioral skills that permit the individual to accomplish whatever tasks the society sets for admission to adulthood [Botwin & Tortu 1988; Schinke & Gilchrist 1984]. Ordinarily, most people learn these life skills in the process of growing up in a family, a neighborhood, with peers, in school, and on the job. Levenstein [1988] called this the hidden curriculum in the normative middle class home so as to fit into a middle class-dominant society. However, there is nothing inevitable about these learned lessons, especially constructive and effective ones, and they don't happen by accident. Young people may learn the wrong lessons and persist in having problems throughout life. There may be a spiraling effect, and the incorrect social skills may cause larger and larger problems as the individual grows up and enters new social domains.

Life skills seem to be linked to resilience as the portion of personal competence that can be learned—or presumably, trained through the planned actions of teachers, parents, and others. Different theorists propose different packages of life skills and training programs associated with them, such as Botwin and Tortu [1988]; Schinke & Gilchrist [1984]; Danish [1997]; and Weissberg, Barton & Shriver, [1997] which seek to incorporate vital life skills in individuals at some risk of not obtaining them "naturally" to the extent needed in today's complex and difficult world.

One particular life skills program merits special mention in the context of the central theme of this book: the use of sports and extracurricular activities in promoting competency in adolescents. Danish [1997] and his colleagues developed a program, Going for the Goal (GOAL), which won the 1996 Lela Rowland Prevention award. They used sports as a means to an end and a metaphor for the overall life skills program. Because youth, especially adolescent males, spend so much of their free time and energy devoted to sports, play, games, and exercise, the GOAL program can use this motivation to help teach adolescents the various skills needed to succeed in the family, school, neighborhood, and community. Briefly, this ten-session, ten-hour program taught to middle school-aged youth is designed to facilitate a sense of personal control and confidence in their own future, so they can make better decisions which, we hope, will lead to a more efficacious maturity.

Values are clearly embedded throughout the GOAL program, but they are not imposed. Rather, participants choose their own dreams and reachable goals—"a goal is a dream they work hard to reach" [Danish 1997, p. 19]—by planning the steps toward that goal. Participants also learn about roadblocks to reaching their goals—such as drug abuse, teen pregnancy, and violence—and they learn problem solving methods in order to address these pressures. Later, they are taught how to deal with setbacks as well as how to reward themselves for their accomplishments. Leaders are trained, and there is a participant Activity Guide. Research on the effectiveness of GOALs is very encouraging. So far, a limited number of schools have participated in the program because Danish [1997, p. 307] believes that it is better to facilitate its use by working with communities, schools, even diving clubs, and soon, mental health associations nationally, to deliver a high fidelity program.

The interesting thing about these life skills programs is their degree of overlapping ideas and their distinctive ones, because the programs are not identical. Each demonstrates some degree of empirical success. What this suggests at the moment is that programs seeking to promote resilience may in effect "plug in" some reasonably efficacious programs to achieve reasonably definable objectives for relatively predictable costs. This is an enormous advantage to planners and program directors, even though they must maintain eternal vigilance that these "standard" programs can be individually tailored to fit the unique contours of new people and settings.

Conventional Bonding

Hawkins & Weis [1985], Hawkins [1997] and their colleagues, have advanced an important theoretical model and have conducted (or stimulated others to conduct) relevant research studies. The essence of this *social development model* is that children sequentially form bonds of involvement and attachment to the family, to the school, to peers, and eventually, the community, given the right supporting circumstances. There are three types of processes that each of these institutions must use if youths are to develop bonds of attachment and commitment to, and belief in, conventional society as organized by law and following a common moral code. These processes include opportunities for interacting with conventional or mainstream people, the level of social skills these young people have in obtaining reinforcement for their conventional behaviors, and consistent reinforcement for conventional social actions.

Primary preventions can construct situations and/or teach relevant adults in these areas to encourage prosocial bonds or psychological linkages, especially in the face of anti-social groups that subvert the conventional social world. (The term "conventional" does not mean mindless conformity; it refers to the range of acceptable social actions and values in a given community.) For example, bonding in the family may be facilitated by training parents to give children age-appropriate participatory roles as contributors to the family (and thus a stakeholder in it), to use good communication skills (active listening) with their children, and to provide clear and consistent expectations and sanctions for given kinds of behaviors. Probably all parents do some of these actions some of the time, but there are other parents who may need prompting for optimal effectiveness with their children—as in Cells 4, 5, and 6, but especially Cells 7, 8, and 9.

As with all primary prevention program ideas, the question arises about the natural rights of parents to do as they wish with their children (within legal limits), in contrast to organized but voluntary efforts to promote personal and public health. To what extent can these "good ideas," that are presumably offered by humane and benevolent helping professionals, be forced onto people or propagandized through mass media, educational and religious institutions, and other places to "convince" people that it is "all for their own good" to do as we say (and hopefully, as we ourselves do)? This is a question beyond the scope of this paper, but it is a lingering assumption underlying any helping strategy that "we know best" [Bloom, 1976]. Do we?

The importance of this social development model is that it offers one programmatic mechanism by which to connect various life skills programs to various points in the resilience paradigm so as to achieve some types of a healthy social competence.

Independent or Causal Factors: Background Characteristics, Natural Happenings, and Programmatic Events

So far, we have discussed only the outcome variable. Now we have to do the same sort of conceptual analysis of the input variables, the presumed causal factors, some of which we may be able to influence or control, and others that we cannot. The terms of the theme of this book call for an investigation of the effects of sports and after-school or extracurricular activities on psychosocial competence. So what are sports and after-school activities? Or rather, what are the active ingredients in sports and these other activities which we can conceptually link to desired outcomes and for which we can seek relevant empirical confirmation? To answer this question, we have to look at these terms and find their components so that we can study which, if any, is empirically associated with positive changes in social competency. Just because a boy or girl is on a sports team does not necessarily mean he or she will be aided in becoming more psychosocially competent; likewise, because a boy or girl is a nonathlete or team member does not mean that he or she will become psychosocially *incompetent*.

Clearly, there are many background factors in the physiology and psychology of the individual, as well as in the social, cultural, and economic contexts, that will also influence the development of psychosocial competence. Unfortunately, these other factors such as social class, ethnic background, and family structures and dynamics, are beyond the scope of this chapter. This means that any principles I suggest as emerging from my reading of the literature have to be qualified as dependent on these other powerful factors in real world situations. Such is the limitation of any social science analysis that focuses on one topic.

I think it is also useful to distinguish natural happenings like physiological and psychological changes in puberty or the psychological and sociocultural changes that occur at a religious confirmation, from the constructed events that influence changes as we introduce primary prevention programming. All of the former are background factors, while the constructed programs are the only areas where we may actually intervene. We may pretend that our tiny program will be a great influence, moving participants toward some glorious goal. In fact, our tiny program is set within the context of gigantic structures and forces, and we have to be, as Mark Twain noted, as lucky as the Christian with four aces in order to feel moral superiority for winning a hand at primary prevention blackjack.

The background characteristics (like gender, intelligence, social class, cultural background, etc.) clearly interact with the natural happenings (like puberty, confirmation, etc.) or constructed events (like a pregnancy prevention program). All of life is essentially made up of these interactions, which involve individuals, families, peer groups, neighborhoods, community institutions, and larger societal units. What theorizing does is to select some subset of these for particular analysis. In this case, we want to look at the possible effects of sports and after-school activities on psychosocial competency (as defined in terms of those five categories and eleven operational subcategories discussed above). So, let's begin to test the luck of our draw:

Specific Independent Variables: Sports, Games, Play, Exercise, and Lifetime Activities

First, let's consider the term "sports." Unfortunately, everyone "knows" what sports are, even though we all may have different meanings in our mind, like the visually-challenged men of Hindustan and their phenomenological elephant, which makes any modifications from preconceived notions difficult. However, let me offer some distinctions that may be useful as we look for critical ingredients that may be employed to promote social competency.

First, I distinguish four parts of the sporting territory. There are (a) *sports* in the narrow sense of the term—a socially structured, competitively organized team activity that is governed by known rules often involving intra-group cooperation and is time-limited in terms of the participation of the particular members. Winning involves hard effort. For example, paid baseball players play professionally on a named team, although for only a few years before they are "too old" to compete. Likewise, the senior members of the high school team eventually graduate and cease playing on the team; there is no salary involved, but the payoff may be in prestige or possibly the team experience itself.

In contrast to sports, there are (b) *games*, a socially structured, frequently competitive, but not organized aggregates of people engaged in irregularly-occurring activity that is governed by consensual rules, and is without time-limits as to who can be in the games. For example, grandparents will play "catch" with their grandchildren at odd times when they get together and the collective mood is favorable. Or, some exam-period college students will spontaneously strike up a game of tag football, just for a break from their studies. The rules of the game are relatively flexible, depending on who is playing and for what purpose. These kinds of games are played for the sheer fun of it.

In contrast to both sports and games is (c) *play*, a personally or socially structured, noncompetitive activity engaged in irregularly-occurring segments, often with no rules or made-up-on-the-spot rules, for the pure sake of having fun. For example, a child will make a chalk hopscotch diagram on the sidewalk and play alone or with a friend. Or a teenager will spend hours trying to glue the balsa wings on a toy glider that she will attempt to launch with the aid of a friend. The hopscotching child may find the glider-making activity utterly dull, while the glider-maker may also enjoy vigorous cross-country skiing as well. Play is idiosyncratic and is likely to be environmentally opportunistic.

Finally, in contrast to sports, games, and play is (d) *exercise*, defined as individually structured, noncompetitive, but purposeful activity intended to strengthen one or another portion of the body and mind. Exercise is not intrinsically fun, as is play or games, but may be made enjoyable by connecting them to social situations, such as jogging with one's buddies. Exercise is definitely a learned or acquired taste; youth are not born to pump iron, but come to feel the need for this quasi-masochistic activity for greater values—an attractive physique, a healthier body, and/or to participate in group activities as part of the gang.

Readers may fairly object to my definitions of terms, for example, finding exercise as intrinsically pleasurable, rather than agree with my masochistic definition. I have no divine anointment that makes my definitions better than anyone else's, but I try to provide the basis of my reasoning. For example, with exercise, I think a reasonable definition is patterned exertion against resistance such that muscles are stretched to a level of stress, at which point the wise exerciser stops and gives relief to his or her muscles, lest they be damaged by excessive exertion. I find it difficult to believe that this is "fun" except as we make ourselves believe it so, by its beneficial effects, or by the company we keep. Or, possibly because exercise feels so good when we stop. So, too, with my other procrustean definitions; readers may disagree. Perhaps more important than mere arbitrary definitions is the methodology employed, as a suggestion for how to find some orderliness in a field of vague and slippery terms, in order to guide preventive/promotive practice.

Lifetime physical activities: Some of the activities defined above may be engaged in over one's whole lifetime; others are usually time-limited. Given that these activities are health-promotive, then it would seem useful to enable people to move through the spectrum of activities such that by the time they leave the structured school environment, and they have essentially free choice as to whether they will engage in any of these activities, they should be thoroughly introduced to the lifetime physical activities that can give them pleasure as well as forms of health over nearly the whole life span.

Organized sports are mostly a youth/young adult phenomenon, although there are notable exceptions as when precocious acrobats and mature adults participate in competitive sports. The golf player may slice and slam throughout his or her life. But bruising football is definitely for the testosterone-suffused youth. What about the young and less-than-young women and men who make up the serious basketball or football league players? While many a youth, especially minority youth, dream of being in the big leagues, in fact only one in 10,000 will come any where close [Fotheringham, 1997]. So, while we pay some men (and a few women) considerable money to bash their bodies and brains to provide the Saturday couch potato a vicarious thrill, in fact, very few people consider organized sports for the lifetime of actual engagement.

On the other hand, games and play, as well as exercise, have the potential for lifetime activities. Games, to the extent they mimic sports, become increasingly difficult, as a middle-aged man discovered after a few minutes on the basketball court with players half his age. Play is always possible, but it may be difficult to rule-bound adults to give up rules for some period of time—to be come childish?—even though it is fun. Rather, adults get their fun in different ways, through *adult play* (or possibly, *adult recreation*)—adventure travels, hiking, camping, canoeing, biking, and the like. These are very different from competitive sports; they usually involve social or cooperative activities, and are fun for the sheer sake of the experience, rather than for the results per se. Adult play or recreation differs from exercise in being more irregular in times and players, but may share some of the health-promotive consequences—and may be done over much of the adult life span. For example, the person who swims for the pure enjoyment of swimming may do it alone or with others literally over a lifetime. (Older people may come to enjoy swimming additionally for the contribution it makes to reduce or forestall arthritis.)

I have characterized these four aspects of sporting activities with six broad polar dimensions that seem adequate to characterize their distinctive features. Others might see additional polar characteristics, but these will do for present purposes. The polar dimensions were selected because these may be manipulated in designing primary prevention practice so as to create a program that most closely links the conceptual form of sporting activities with the conceptual form of competency. My choices were, necessarily, arbitrary, but hopefully in keeping with a common sense understanding of all of these activities. Of this, the reader must be the judge. Now, we will examine the polar dimensions.

1. *Competitive versus cooperative activities.* What is the lesson learned from "beating" the other team versus participating in, and abiding by, the rules of the game? What are the effects of being in a piano duet performing at a school assembly, versus being on a debating team striving to persuade judges of the merits of their argument over that of their opponents? Competitive and cooperative activities are not pure types, but researchers have long observed their differential effects [Lewin 1951].

2. *Team versus individually organized activities.* Individual versus organized efforts were among the first variables studied in social psychology at the turn of the century (on rope pulling—it turned out that a group pull involved more energy that the sum of the energy exerted by players individually). Lewin also enabled us to understand that there was an emergent force associated with group activities, and yet other researchers have pointed out the value

of "working alone" on creativity (as contrasted to the larger number of potential creative ideas generated by groups). Is the team phenomena a healthy experience for youngsters or a controlling influence in ways that parents and other agents of society disapprove? [Fine 1988].

3.   *Short-term versus long-term activity.* The effects of any learning experience are subject to the laws of massed or distributed learning, along with the intensity of the experience at any period of time. Team sports directed by a trainer tend to provide long-term learning, extensive practice (and thus overlearning), and various reinforcements under a context of uncertainty: Will I be cut from the team? Will I make a terrible error and be humiliated? In short-term situations of known duration, many of these uncertainties are not present, nor are the intensive learning experiences and the time to build the esprit de corps of a cooperative team. In their place are the freedom and fun of the activity itself.

4.   *Intrinsically pleasurable versus not intrinsically pleasurable.* The use of the body in natural ways is often a nonconscious experience; so long as no pain is involved, nor any intense pleasure (like an orgasm), the natural actions of the body and concomitant feeling states go unnoticed most of the time. When we begin to pay attention to "feeling well" or "stretching our muscles" or "becoming aware of the sights, sounds, scents, and pressures around us," then we begin to enter pleasurable or nonpleasurable experiences. The expression "no pain, no gain" is a gross error in exercise, including the exercise that is part of the training in sports. Pain is always an indication of exceeding the natural function of some body component. Gradual expansion of what one can do before reaching the painful stage is the correct way of expanding athletic capacities. The more one exercises to that (moving) point, the greater the range of strength and mobility one can obtain. Fundamentally, having fun (or pleasure) is the name of the game, and when it becomes less than fun, or when the activity interferes with others that are more pleasurable or more socially rewarding, then we reach a stage in which "fun things"

become nonfun or comparatively nonpleasurable. It is at this stage when youth move away from team sports to games or exercises, as well as nonsports activities.

5.   *Purposive versus no particular purpose in mind.* Why do we engage in a sporting activity? Initially, young people are inducted into games as socializing devices—from the universal peak-a-boo game, to various ball games involving some skill—and presumably learn to enjoy the social camaraderie, prestige, and physical benefits from the activity. Michener [1976, p. 16], writing about *Sports in America*, laments even a quarter of a century ago that children were being introduced into highly organized sports too young. He goes on to state [pp.10-11] as his primary principle regarding sports is that "Sports should enhance the health of both the individual participant and the general society," a strong purposiveness criterion. Others emphasize the noncognitive, nonplanned nature of sports. There is a physiological high that comes from attaining muscle tone and the state of mind of the Zen archer; maybe it is also a spiritual high (albeit nonreligious). But most human activity is purposive, even when there is no explicit mission statement or written goal objectives. It is difficult to be nonpurposive, just as it is difficult to clear one's mind of annoying daily preoccupations. Yet this is exactly what Zen and other mind-clearing philosophies propose as the purposeful nonpurpose.

6.   *Compatible with contemporary social developmental tasks versus not compatible.* The question here involves the timing of a sports activity in relation to one's whole life course development. To paraphrase the Biblical expression: "When I was a child, I played like a child. When I was an adult, I ...." Yes, what does the adult or adolescent or aged person do in his or her time of life? There are indeed social developmental concerns or obligations for each section of the life course, but unlike the rigid stage models of Freud or Erikson that define set tasks for each age, the facts of the matter are that life is much more flexible and fluid, and what is required of a person at a given section of the life span depends to a considerable degree on the sociocultural

context. Young children put away their toys when the family needs an extra hand in harvesting the crop, or caring for even younger children. The mature adult is now urged to "play" so as to reduce the stresses of a pressure-cooker life.

Now, the subjective part: I herewith propose to characterize the four sporting activities on the six polar dimensions. Then I will likewise characterize the five categories of psychosocial competency on the same polar dimensions. And finally, I will compare how many of the same polar types sporting activities and competency share.

My choices of the polar dimensions on the four categories of sporting activities:

- Sports: competitive, team-oriented, short duration, may be pleasurable with considerable pain, purposive, and temporarily compatible with stages of social development
- Games: noncompetitive, individual or team, short duration (but over a long possible span of time), pleasurable, nonpurposive, usually compatible
- Play: noncompetitive, team or individual, short duration, pleasurable, nonpurposive, and compatible (even though it takes very different forms from childhood to adulthood)
- Exercise: noncompetitive, individual, long duration (possibly), nonpleasurable, purposive, and compatible.

My choices of the polar dimensions on the categories of psychosocial competency:

- Working well (chores/job): noncompetitive, team or individual, long duration, may be pleasurable but often not, purposive, and usually compatible
- Playing well (fun/rules of game): noncompetitive, individual or team, long duration, pleasurable, may be purposive, and usually compatible
- Loving well (friends/group affiliations/self-esteem): noncompetitive (except self-esteem in a capitalistic country may require economic competition for positive self-esteem), team, long duration, pleasurable, may be purposive, and compatible
- Thinking well (problem solving): may be either competitive or noncompetitive, may be either individual or team effort, long

duration, pleasurable (but also possibly frustrating), purposive, and compatible

- Serving well (dependable, caring, serving): Noncompetitive, team, long duration, pleasurable (but possibly not), purposive, and compatible.

Now the big question is, what theoretical linkage, if any, is there between them? I have counted the frequency when the same polar term applies to both a sporting activity and a component of competency. For example, sports and work both share four polar terms: they both involve a team activity, mainly pleasurable (but with some nonpleasurable aspects), both are purposive in the sense of "winning" or being economically "successful," and both occur in a compatible stage of the life span. They differ in that sports are competitive, while work is more likely to involve a cooperative venture, and sports involve a short duration, while work is for the long haul. In a similar manner, I counted the number of exact shared components, presented in Table 2-4.

At first look, there is no exact equivalent pattern between sporting activities and psychosocial competence, meaning that no one of the sporting activities alone will be an exact learning experience for all of the components of psychosocial competency. (Maybe combinations of sporting activities would compensate for what each lacks individually.) What this table does suggests is that exercise is most nearly compatible theoretically with the analytic components of psychosocial competency, followed by a distant cluster of games, play, and sports. Surprisingly, sports in the narrow sense is in fact least likely to be compatible with psychosocial competency, having the lowest total number of "shared characteristics" with competency (11), while exercise had the most similar pattern (20 out of a possible 25 points). Looking at the column totals, it appears that four out of five components of competency are in the same range of shared traits with the four sporting activities; interestingly, only thinking is literally and figuratively "out of the ballpark."

From this limited and arbitrary kind of conceptual analysis, I would not expect a lot of strong empirical connections between sporting activities and psychosocial competency. The next step of the analysis was to scan the current psychological literature seeking

Table 2-4. Shared Components of Sporting Activities and Psychosocial Competence

| | Number of (exact) shared components | | | | | |
	Work	Play	Love	Think	Serve	**Row Totals**
Sports (narrow def)	4	1	2	2	2	11
Games	3	4	3	1	3	14
Play	2	3	3	1	3	12
Exercise	4	5	4	3	4	20
Column totals	13	13	12	7	12	

empirical studies that made connections between some types of sporting activities and some times of competency. This proved to be a difficult task because the language in which I have framed this paper was not the common language in psychology. In place of psychosocial competency I used the available language of physical and mental health. In place of my four categories of sporting activity for youth, I could only find appreciable literature on sports in the narrow sense. With exercise, the age group was mainly adults; and with play, research tended to deal with children. Games was not easily identified in the literature. So, although I still find meaning in my four sporting activities, this report will essentially focus on connecting sports (in the narrow sense) with physical and mental health (the closest match I could attain for social competency).

What does the literature tell us about the causal connection between sports and health? Unfortunately, the literature sometimes speaks in a muffled voice and requires, like the Greek oracles of old, that we interpret its grunts and murmurs. Here is my interpretation of some specific studies or reports of programs from the psychological literature from over the last decade regarding the positive or negative effects of sports on the health of participants.

The good news is that there have been many reports of positive effects of sports on youth, and in particular, on young women. More of that in a moment. The bad news is that there are a number of reports on the negative effects of sports on youth, particularly on young men.

I will give a sampling of some of these studies to illustrate the general points I just made. First, there is an interesting local theory on the benefits of competitive sports; it is termed the iceberg profile (by W. P. Morgan in the early 1980s) and hypothesizes that outstanding athletes exhibit a better profile of mental health than regular athletes and presumably nonathletes. When Newcombe & Boyle [1995] tested this hypothesis with 184 males and 128 females (Australian) adolescents, they found support for the model: competitive sports players were less anxious, less neurotic, less depressed, less confused, and more extroverted and more vigorous than nonparticipants or nonelite players. Sounds encouraging. Unfortunately, Rowley, Landers, Kyllo, and Etnier [1995] also studied the iceberg profile using the meta-analytic techniques, that is, they examined the findings of 33 studies, using statistics that reduced these findings to standard statistics, and found that there was very little evidence in favor of the iceberg profile. That is, in this comparative study, successful athletes exhibited only a very small advantage over less successful athletes, enough only to account for 1% of the variance between them.

On the other hand, Biddle [1993] found that having a *quality* experience in sports can have beneficial effects in terms of reduced negative affect and increased self-esteem. Likewise, Vilhjalmsson & Thorlindsson [1992] studied 1,131 Icelandic adolescents with regard to their team participation in contrast to individual sporting activities. They found that team (sporting clubs and informal groups) participation was inversely related to smoking and alcohol use, while individual sport is unrelated to alcohol use (and has only a small negative correlation with smoking). In general, they report that team sport has an integrative effect when predicting positive aspects of mental health. However, this effect is limited only to urban communities, a variable I had not considered in my conceptualizing.

The literature is, however, more upbeat on the effects of sports for young women. For example, girls who play sports are 92% less likely to use drugs, 80% less likely to have unwanted pregnancies, and are three times more likely to graduate (high school) [Intercollegiate Sports 1994]. Fortunately, the numbers of young women participating in sports has climbed dramatically, as the cultural bias toward men in sports has shifted—to some degree. The amount of funding men's and women's sports is moving toward equality to some degree—with a long way to go.

The literature also indicates that these positive findings are to be found among young people who have sustained disabling injuries [for example, Greenwood et al. 1990]. Disabled persons who are active in sports show indicators of better mental and physical health than those who are not active.

On the other hand, there are a number of reports of negative affects of sports, such as the increased use of anabolic steroids. Boys are more at risk of wanting to gain weight using drugs than girls, and thus would be more likely to put themselves in a compromising position with regard to their future health [Wang et al.1994]. Rozin [1995] reported that the University of Michigan's "Monitoring the Future" study of high school and college aged youth in America showed that 200,000 high school males nationwide had taken steroids within the year. Other estimates are even higher, with reports of boys starting as young as 10 years old [see also WHO Press, June 25, 1992].

Likewise, athletes have been reported as users of alcohol and cigarettes [Bush & Iannotti 1992] and chewing (spitting) tobacco [Durbin 1997], perhaps reflecting the masculine or macho image of the athlete. There is also an association with sports involvement and pathogenic weight control in swimmers, gymnasts, and other athletes—especially among women [Biddle 1993]. And predictably, there are many sports injuries and emergency room visits. One-third of all sports injuries are found in the five-to-fourteen year group. There are 4 million emergency room visits and another 8 million visits to the family physician for such sport injuries [McEwin & Dickinson 1996].

One major problem that doesn't show up directly in broken bones or artificially enlarged muscles, and that is in regard to the prestige of big-time sports heroes and their multimillion dollar salaries and perks. The truth of the matter is that about 1 in 10,000 high school athletes will make it to the pros, and only 1 in 50,000 high schoolers will make it to the NBA [Fotheringham 1997].

However 66% of African American boys between the ages of 13 and 18 believe that they can make a living playing in pro-sports. [Fotheringhom 1997]. Thus, sports as a life career may be a long false lead to thousands of youngsters who may perceive few other ways to fame and fortune, especially fortune. What this does to their social competency is not yet studied, and may be an important area of investigation. It may be that this impossible dream energizes minority youth in ways that few other legal activities may do.

On the other hand, millions—literally millions—of youth are engaged in sports as part of school classes or games after school and at family outings. Many of them gain a sense of accomplishment (even with some frustration), get reinforced by peer admiration and parental support [Fine, 1988], and for whatever else they may be able to do or not do (like succeed in academic work), sports becomes a significant part of their lives. However, for millions of youth, there comes a time when sports become less compelling, in favor of other activities including academics, socializing with the opposite sex, and working for pay; moreover, the reality emerges that they will never be stars or professional athletes regardless of how much they like their sport. With a sigh of regret, these millions of youth put away their heavy equipment in favor of the occasional game or play, or possibly exercise—and get on with their lives. For those youths who hang on too long, who become overly preoccupied with dreams of sports and lives in sports, if only in college, there is a secondary frustration that occurs because they have lost time and energy needed for the reality of their life careers. A. E. Houseman's poem, "To the athlete dying young," might be read as well for the would-be athlete who does *not* die young, and yet must face life demands.

After-School Activities or Extracurricular Activities

A second component of the theme for this book is after-school activities or extracurricular activities. This term needs clarification as many vital activities occur before school, immediately after school (in that critical 2:00 p.m. to 5:00 or 6:00 p.m. period), in the evenings, on weekends, and in the summertime or holidays when school is not in session. Basically, I will use the same conceptual approach to analyze what is the nature of the various activities, from

4-H clubs; to theater groups; musical associations; outdoor adventure groups; service clubs; social clubs; gender, ethnic, or cultural groupings; and the like. And then I will relate their underlying dimensions with those of psychosocial competency to see if there is any conceptual linkage supporting the hypothesis that a certain amount or kind of extracurricular activities can lead to development in psychosocial competency. Many of the conceptual tools and strategies we used in analyzing sports will be carried over to this discussion of after-school activities.

The phrase "after-school activities" includes lots of apples and oranges and bananas, making it hard to analyze. With the chutzpah of a theoretically-inclined chapter writer not obliged to undergo a blind review process, I unhesitatingly suggest three subcategories, excluding any sports-type programs, which I will describe and analyze below: (a) community service; (b) school service; (c) school-related recreational groups.

Community service: Adolescents may become involved with voluntary community services in which they serve others (rather than being served themselves as they have been for most of their lives), away from their parental or family monitoring—so babysitting your younger sister does not count here. The adolescent generally has to be "better at" or "more knowledgeable or skillful than" the persons they are serving, but not necessarily a lot more advanced. An example would be an eighth grader who is poor at math tutoring a third grader, but is still a lot better at math than the third grader. The service must activate and use the knowledge and skills the adolescent has, thus promoting overlearning. The service activity will necessarily involve an adolescent and some adult monitor who may become a role model or at least a confidant in this context. The adolescent becomes involved with some organization, even to an elementary degree—perhaps his or her first autonomous experience beyond family and school—and may become bonded to this larger unit of conventional society (as in the social development model). When involved in community service work, the adolescent is necessarily away from other temptations that may lead to self-harming or antisocial behaviors. There will be various reinforcements for these services, some social or community recognition, as well as self-feelings of pride of accomplishment. When dealing with people with limits, the adolescent may begin to learn the principles of caring and empathy, and may see role models for their own future careers.

School service group: A second category of extracurricular activities may be termed "school service groups" such as choirs or orchestras, theater groups or debating teams where the participants in some ways represent the school to outsiders. These are almost exclusively group or team structures in which youths work together, on relatively equal footing, to make their individual contributions to what is necessarily a collaborative effort. They gain a kind of temporary identity as member of the group, and share the group's norms and values. Yet, these are not exclusive groups; essentially anyone may try out for a part in a play or choir, and it would be unusual if they were completely turned away from some role or other. Each of these groups shares some school symbols with other groups, the sum of which represents the school's service component, a source of pride for the administrators and community, as well as the students, teachers, and parents. Coming together for positive and constructive activities further develops the sense of (school) community. That some individuals shine more brightly than others is inevitable—perhaps leading to further training or academic careers—but the democratic amateurism of the whole is most prominent so that few are embarrassed by their limited performances.

Walsh-Bowers [1992, p. 143] observes that in the creative drama approach to social skills training, the students develop, through experiential learning, the basic skills—taking turns, listening to others, trying to understand their feelings, negotiating conflicts—because they need to work together to create the play. There is a play within the play going on, by which participants learn far more than the lines and procedures of putting on the manifest drama.

School-related recreational clubs. A third category of school-related extracurricular activities would be those engaged in primarily for personal gratification, since they do little to enhance the school as community (except that these recreational programs exist along with educational or sporting ones). These groups may not be official school-sanctioned activities, even though they are permitted to use school facilities. One thinks of D & D clubs (dungeons and dragons), recreational outing groups (such as going to the beach or sunbathing), and pure socializing groups. These groups may involve collective efforts, but they may also involve personal hedonism performed in group settings. I would guess that these groups would appeal more to people on the fringe of alternative school activities that are more normative, if not more productive. No school symbols are involved, and the presence of these groups may be something of an embarrassment to administrators and parents.

Next, I will attempt a similar analysis of these three categories of extracurricular activities in order to compare them with a similar analysis (above) of psychosocial competency:

- *Community Service Activities:* Cooperative (noncompetitive), team (even in a one-to-one setting, it is a group affair), short term, pleasurable (although it may be an acquired taste), purposive, and compatible with contemporary social developments.
- *School Service Groups:* Cooperative, team, short term, pleasurable, purposive, and compatible.
- *School-related Recreational Groups:* Cooperative, team or individual, short term, pleasurable, nonpurposive, compatible.

Now I can construct another table, Table 2-5, showing the number of shared polar attributes between components of psychosocial competency and extracurricular activities:

What these arbitrary and limited data suggest is that there is no exact match between extracurricular activities and psychosocial competency, but that both community and school service most closely approximate the competency variables, with recreational experiences a distant third. I want to note that community service and school service scored as well, as did exercise in the sporting category, while recreational experiences scored on a level with games, play, and sports.

From this limited analysis, I would expect a moderate correlation between extracurricular activities and psychosocial competency in the empirical literature. However, there isn't a very large literature on extracurricular activities, compared to sports. So, I will report mainly on community service where several well-designed

Table 2-5. Shared Components of Extracurricular Activities and Psychosocial Competence					
	Work	Play	Love	Think	Serve	**Row Totals**
Community Service	3	4	5	3	5	20
School Service	3	4	5	3	5	20
Recreational	3	3	3	2	3	14
Column Totals	9	11	13	8	13	

Number of shared attributes

studies are available. I will quote from the Moore & Allen [1996] review of this literature because they so aptly summarize the themes I have developed above. I will number each quotation, so that I can refer back to it quickly:

1. For example, Newmann and Rutter proposed that community service may aid adolescents' development into competent, independent adults and promote the growth of reasoning skills, abstract and hypothetical thought, and problem-solving abilities [1983]. [Moore & Allen, 1996, p. 233]

2. In addition, volunteering may increase self-esteem and reliability, influence social and personal responsibility, impart a sense of personal worth, and increase adolescents' capabilities for leadership and getting along with others [Harrison, 1987; Kirby, 1989]. [Moore & Allen, 1996:233]

3. By enhancing these competencies in adolescents, volunteering may also increase adolescents' resistance to other problems, such as teenage pregnancy, school drop-out, and delinquency [Allen, Philliber, & Hoggson, 1990; Newman, 1983]. [Moore & Allen, 1996, p. 233]

4. Volunteering has also been seen as a mechanism by which adolescents gain mastery over their affairs, increasing their sense of personal control and concern with social influence, and thus as a way of empowering adolescents [Allen et al. 1990; Rappaport, 1987]. These goals may be accomplished through adolescents' changed perceptions of them-

selves from "help-receivers" to "help- givers." [Moore &
Allen, 1996, p. 233]

5. Increased contact between teenagers and adult supervi-
    sors, who can serve as role models, may also help adoles-
    cents to identify more with prosocial values. Such identi-
    fication is related to social competence and negatively
    related to problem behaviors [Allen, Aber, & Leadbeater,
    1990]. [Moore & Allen, 1996, p. 233]

6. "Thus the idea that community service may reduce feel-
    ings of alienation for adolescents, at least during the period
    of service, is supported by this research...." [Moore & Allen
    1996, p. 238]

7. Program students increased significantly more than com-
    parison students on specific questions from this measure,
    including sense of competence in communicating effec-
    tively to groups, starting conversations with strangers,
    persuading adults to take their views seriously, and making
    plans and organizing group activities. [Moore & Allen
    1996, p. 240]

8. Students expressed enthusiasm for the program, praising
    its contribution to personal growth in communication
    skills, patience, taking responsibility, and in facilitating
    constructive relationships with others. They indicated
    that the most rewarding aspects were feelings of accom-
    plishment with other people and being successful in teach-
    ing a task. [Moore & Allen 1996, p. 240]

I could find no empirical results from community service work
that were inimical to psychosocial competency. Rather, except for
the Working Well category, I was able to connect the specific
operational statements with the results summarized in Moore &
Allen. This is documented in Table 2-6, by listing the 11 operational
components of psychosocial competency defined above, and connecting one or more of the 8 quotations from Moore & Allen. This
micro-analysis adds further empirical weight to the previous conceptual analysis hypothesizing moderate correlations between community service and competency.

There are a variety of outcome measures that speak to this linkage, some of which have received an encouraging degree of support, in well-designed programs that have been repeated in many places across the country. For example, the Teen Outreach Program has been used in 237 sites around the nation, with about 8,000 students (half experimental, half control). Findings show that Teen Outreach Program participants have "significantly lower levels of suspensions, school dropouts, and pregnancy" after controlling for levels of problem behaviors in the teens at entry and other significant demographic factors [Allen et al. 1990]. These are particularly hard indicators of the logical consequences of having greater psychosocial competency.

With school service groups, I would expect about the same level of moderate correlation between these service experiences and psychosocial competency on the logical grounds that they share the exact pattern of polar characteristics as did community service programs. However, there is very little strong research on evaluating these programs. I would call this a gold vein waiting to be discovered and mined.

The third category, school-related recreational clubs, might be expected to show a weaker correlation with psychosocial competency, given the pattern of logical matches with my definition of the competency term. Unfortunately, I could find no research on this category in relation to competency.

General Independent Variables: Mentoring, Coaching, and Advocating

One of the chief components cutting across both sports and after-school activities as well as other significant sites of youth socialization is the mentor, coach, or advocate. There is an extensive literature on this topic, from the point of view of educators [Clark 1991; Ramsey, Thompson, & Brathwaite 1994]; developmentalists [Mech, Pryde, & Rycraft, 1995; Muri, 1996]; people in the business world [Thomas, 1993]; practitioners in religion and social services [Mowrey 1994; Collins 1994; Zippay 1995], as well as in sports and after-school activities [Rizzo et al. 1997; Sinclair & Vealey 1989; Pierce & Singleton 1995]—to mention only a few. The one consis-

Table 2-6. Shared Components of Psychosocial Competence and Research on Community Service

Operational Components of Psychosocial Competency	Moore & Allen Quotations (by number)
A. Working well:	
1. Chores at home	No mention
2. Paid job	No mention
B. Playing well:	
3. Having fun	8
4. Knowing rules, roles	7
C. Loving well:	
5. Having good friends	2, 5
6. Having group affiliations	2, 8
7. Sense of self-esteem	2, 4, 7
D. Thinking well:	
8. Problem-solving skills	1
E. Serving well:	
9. Being dependable	2, 4
10. Caring and concern	4, 7, 8
11. Serving without pay	8

tent finding within these areas is that a supportive older or wiser person may contribute to the development of the younger or less experienced person, especially in the context of a hazardous or stressful environment [Rhodes 1994, p. 187]. Reissman [1965; 1976] might also suggest the corollary that the helping person might also be benefited from the very act of engaging in a helping relationship as much as the helpee benefits from the content and context of the helping. Yet, as Rhodes [1994] notes, there are many conceptual and practical issues remaining, not the least of which is a clear definition of the terms.

So what I present here is a small subset of this larger domain, but one that is crafted to fit the issues of mentoring in sports and after-school activities.

First, there is a plethora of words associated with this territory—mentoring, coaching, advocating, teaching, parenting, socializing, advising, guiding, and many more. My classification is arbitrary, but I hope useful. I will use the term *mentoring* as the general category, as this seems to reflect the current conventions in the several fields using like terms. Within mentoring are several dimensions. It may be useful to distinguish important subtypes, as well as to indicate commonalities across sub-types:

1. The mentor is "older and wiser" (more experienced) relative to the younger or less experienced mentee.

2. There is a relatively sustained and long-time relationship, often over the period of some social event, such as a semester, a season of some sport, the length of production of a play, etc.

3. Generally, mentoring involves unrelated individuals, but under certain circumstances, a relative might play the mentoring role with regard to some specific topic, in one of the following subcategories:

    a. with some specific content goal in view, along with some specific intermediary objectives—such as facilitating the mentee's academic competence by assisting in developing reading skills;

    b. and/or some specific goal involving the mentee's personality or feelings, thoughts, and behaviors, such as interacting so as to support the mentee's growing sense of self-esteem;

    c. and/or providing some ethical or valuational guidance.

4. Over time, a limited psychological relationship develops that is generally pleasant for both parties, although with growing closeness may come the expression of negative feelings as well. The important point is that the emotional bonds are relatively circumscribed around the mentoring task, and are not diffuse bonds such as occur between parent and child, where every significant aspect of the relationship is subject to intense emotional meaning. In addition, the mentor may gain secondary benefits (as in Reissman's Helper Principle) by the very act of engaging in helping, such as overlearning some content area, feel appreciated and praised, feel vicarious pleasure at the accomplishments of one's mentee, and so forth.

5.   This is an unpaid relationship (although the mentor may
     be paid for other, possibly related work, as when a teacher
     goes out of her way to provide special support for a given
     children, she is still being paid to teach).

6.   Sometimes, the mentor may take independent action on
     behalf of the mentee, in order to augment the mentee's
     needs or development, such as in writing a letter of
     reference, or taking class action with regard to shared
     problems.

Now I can distinguish among the major contenders for the
mentoring role: The *mentor per se* is described by all of the above
aspects, but generally with less of the direct content instruction
component (#3a) and with less of the independent action on behalf
of some group (#6). The major emphasis of the mentor is the
emotional bonding (#3b), a positive and intense but focused connection between two people, which may be the critical dimension of the
mentor.

The *coach* would have all of the above, but generally with a focus
on the direct instructional component (#3a) and less on the emotional and ethical connections (#3b and #3c) and probably none on
the independent action (#6). The coach is more likely to receive pay
for the service because it is connected with delivering a product, but
reading or math coaches may also be volunteers, and a drama or
debate coach might perform these duties as part of the overall
teaching role.

The *advocate* would have all of the above, but most importantly,
the independent action (#6), and probably less of the personal
involvement with any one mentee (#3a), in favor of collective
ethical or valuational action on behalf of a group.

There are other related roles that should be mentioned—and
distinguished. The *role model* is someone that a youth "looks up to,"
"admires," or "wishes to be like" because of some specific traits; it is
not necessary that the role model be aware or, or interact with, the
youth, whereas mentor, coach, and advocate all have sustained
contact with the mentee over some extended period of time. A
practitioner may mobilize the interest in some celebrity, such as a

football star, to promote some cause, but youth will more likely come to see the star, rather than believe the message per se. There is rarely any two-way communication, which seems central to the mentoring context.

Parents are not mentors in this definition because they have widely diffuse personal relationships with their children over extended periods of time. They may provide the mentoring support, the coaching directions, and the advocates helping initiatives, but within the context of an intimate relationship that is concerned with every significant aspect of their lives. What mentors offer is a small and focused approximation of the parents offer in general. However, more distant relatives may take on mentoring roles, like taking a child camping with the relative's family, etc.

Teachers are not mentors in the strict sense, as they occupy prescribed positions vis-à-vis the student. Teachers, of course, may go beyond these formal roles and offer personal support, extra coaching, and advocacy on special occasions—and it is these that make some teachers memorable to students. No teacher is memorialized for conveying the rules of grammar. Maintenance staff, service people (at local stores, or mail carriers on their daily routes), religious workers, and others may also provide important mentoring services as the personal chemistry between adult and child takes place.

Whether or not therapists are mentors, coaches, or advocates depends on the particular brand of therapy being conducted, as some approaches indeed to provide mentoring-like support, direct coaching of behaviors to be changed, or social advocacy. But by and large, therapists seek to help clients see themselves as they are so as to solve problems as they exist—these would be beyond the scope of mentors, coaches, and advocates as defined above.

The major point of this discussion is that it is reasonably clear that when adults form strong personal relationships with children on relatively focused areas for reasonably long periods of time, something important happens, probably for both child and adult. Werner & Smith [1992; Werner 1993, 1995] have documented the association between children and youths who exhibit resilience and having a teacher, a caring neighbor, or an elder relative, among others, as mentors—particularly when the parents of these young people may not be able to provide the necessary long-term support and nurturing. My reading of this literature, along with the mentoring, coaching, and advocacy literatures, is that a powerful ingredient in any kind of competency-promoting program is the long-term availability of a responsible adult able and willing to provide personal support, possibly behavioral coaching, or social advocacy for a young person who is receptive to these efforts—or, as Werner shows, actively reaches out to obtain mentoring, coaching, or advocacy. This is clearly a point that needs further investigation, but as a point of departure for any program seeking to promote competency, it seems highly useful to find staff who deliver "themselves" along with their direct service, who can be that caring and supportive adult, along with providing some behavioral coaching as needed and social advocacy at the critical moments. Merely being present is not necessarily the same as *being there* for the child, and we musers and teachers had better be clear on what to do about the difference.

Autobiographies are replete with examples of that special schoolteacher, a favorite neighbor (often the parent of one's friend), or someone who comes along at just the right time when the child is seeking some mentoring. So, it isn't just the sporting activity, or the school play, or even going to the nursing home to help out—there has to be some mature feedback, teaching self-reflective understanding and actions, offering rewards appropriate to the levels of success. We cannot expect even the most resilient child to make it without some supportive environment, but we can expect that by increasing the supportiveness, stimulation, and monitoring, that even children who are personally not highly resilient may be enabled to make it.

How Shall We Promote Psychosocial Competency in Youth?

Given the preceding theoretical discussion and the reviews of the available empirical literature, how shall we promote psychosocial competency in youth, using sporting activities and extracurricular events? This is a delicate question, as you can see in the chapters of this book, because different authors will have different takes on this question. My overall response to the question would be use of community services (and probably school service involvement), along with exercise (probably viewed in the context of lifetime activities), as being the best components of sporting and extracurricular activities as general categories. I think, both logically and empirically, the present evidence favors this position, which involves clear-cut programs with caring and nurturing adult monitors (that is, who are mentors and/or coaches and advocates) along with reflective discussions, so that the young people consciously think about the issues and make mental decisions that become part of their life strategies.

The major exception to this position may be the new hybrid program that combines the massive appeal of sports with the reflective feedback and connection with adults and peers in cooperative activities that underlies extracurricular work. Danish and his colleagues have constructed and implemented such programs, and their empirical results are most encouraging. Botwin & Tortu [1988] and Schinke & Gilchrist [1984] have general life skills programs with some demonstrated success, but without any connection to sports or extracurricular activities. The main question is whether the common sense appeal of sporting activities and the empirical documentation will be sufficient to generate a mass movement to help very large numbers of adolescents move toward psychosocial competency. We have not a moment to lose, for each day we continue to "love our children" by means of our current benign neglect, we will lose more and more of them to the modern morbidities and their associated mortalities—unwise sex, drugs, alcohol, cigarettes, violence, suicide, unwanted pregnancy, STDs, and AIDS. The list is long; time is short.

Summary and Speculation

By means of an arbitrary conceptual analysis and a brief review of the literature, I suggested that *some* of the domains of sports and after-school activities appeared to be relatively useful in increasing competency in adolescents: exercise, community service, and probably school service. With adolescents, exercise should probably begin in the service of sports—one of the great attractants of millions of youths—to build up strength, endurance, and the aerobic capacity to perform sporting activities as ably as possible. In order to cash in on the near universal interest in sports, I would suggest universal intramural activities where all levels of skilled players are brought together in mixed-skill teams, such that each participant has to help the others play as well as possible so that the team may prevail in games—not necessarily competitive sports as such. These games can blend into lifetime exercises, as well as helping to prepare individuals for a diverse world.

Sports-based growth-promotive programs (such as Danish's Going for the Goal) offer a promising avenue for enhancing competency in youth, albeit currently in small numbers. The next step would be to deliver such programs to large numbers of youth, particularly minority youth who erroneously believe that sports will be their path to a golden future.

Again, sports may be a near universal "hook" to interest youth in team work, then in team service to the school, and then perhaps to community service. Role models should be employed, and not as one-shot contacts. The use of "sports awards" to help youth remain in high school should be used, payable in college scholarships in their future. Indeed, as a 21st century replacement of job corps, there may be "sports institutes" where school dropouts and unemployed youth can learn the basics of education as needed, foundation classes (for the GED) as possible, and advanced skills as desired for specific career options—all in the context of going for the goal. Service occupations in gerontology, preschool and day care, are all going to be growth industries in the next century. If society can dignify these services and pay them accordingly, then these could be the specific career options for the sports institutes.

Sports for high school women is generally a big plus. All efforts should be made to continue this push toward equality in sports. The next research step would be to understand why sports are so beneficial for young women—and perhaps apply this solution to young men.

Likewise, there appear to be some negative factors associated with young men in sports. The next research step would be to understand these untoward dynamics and to prevent them, both for young men now, and for young women before they succumb to these problems.

No sports or after-school activities are perfect as leading to competency. If they have the different kinds of components as my analysis suggested, it may be that some combinations of sports and extracurricular activities might be optimally effective. I proposed various kinds of mixed skill-level teams as ways to build on interests in sports, but also as services for the players to learn to participate together with diverse classmates. It may also be possible that these teams could perform before audiences of elders, the handicapped, and parent groups, both for the stimulation of these audiences, and for the rewards to the players themselves. These kinds of games would be service activities, and potentially blendable with other kinds of services that would increase competency.

We must not forget that the topic of this book, although very broad, is only one element in the larger community and society. Sports and extracurricular activities are the beginning points, not the endings, to encourage youth in pro-social, general life- long activities: work, play, love, thinking, and service.

References

Allen, J. P., Philliber, S., & Hoggson, B. (1990). School-based prevention of teen-age pregnancy and school dropouts: Process evaluation of the national replication of the Teen Outreach Program. *American Journal of Community Psychology*, *18*(4), 505–524.

Bernard, B. (1992). Fostering resiliency in kids: Protective factors in the family, school, and community. *Prevention Forum*, *12*(3), 1–16.

Biddle, S. J. (1993). Children, exercise and mental health: Special issue : Exercise and psychological well-being. *International Journal of Sport Psychology*, *24*(2), 200–216.

Bloom, L. Z. (1976). "It's all for your own good:" Parent-child relationships in popular American child rearing literature, 1820–1970. *Journal of Popular Culture*, *10*(1), 191–198.

Bloom, M. (1996). *Primary prevention practice*. Thousand Oaks, CA: Sage.

Botwin, G.J. & Tortu, S. (1988). Preventing adolescent substance abuse through life skills training. In R.H. Price, E.L. Cowen, R.P. Lorion, &

J. Ramos-McKay (Eds.) 14 ounces of prevention: A casebook for practitioners. Washington, DC: American Psychological Association.

Bracey, G. W. (1992). Achievement and employment. *Phi Delta Kappan*, 73, 492–493.

Bush, P. J. & Iannotti, R. J. (1992). Elementary schoolchildren's use of alcohol, cigarettes and marijuana and classmates' attribution of socialization. *Drug and Alcohol Dependence*, 30(3), 275–287.

Clark, M. L. (1991). Social identity, peer relations, and academic competence of African-American Adolescents. *Education and Urban Society*, 24(1), 41–52.

Collins, P.M. (1994). Does mentorship among social workers make a difference? An empirical investigation of career options. *Social Work*, 39(4), 413–419.

Danish, S. (1997). Going for the goal: A life skills program for adolescents. In G. W. Albee & T. P. Gullotta (Eds.), *Primary prevention works* (pp.291–312). Thousand Oaks, CA: Sage.

Durbin, R. J. (1997, May 6). Major league baseball players say "no" to spit tobacco. (Web links). *Congressional Record, Daily Edition*, 143(57), S4035.

Durlak, J. A. & Wells, A. M. (1997). Primary prevention mental health programs for children and adolescents: A meta-analytic review. *American Journal of Community Psychology*, 25(2), 115–152.

Elias, M. (1995). Primary prevention as health and social competence promotion. *Journal of Primary Prevention*, 16(1), 5–24.

Fine, G. A. (1988). Good children and dirty play. *Play and Culture*, 1, 43–56.

Fotheringham, A. (1997, April 14). Lionizing athletes is a disservice to blacks. *Maclean's*, 110(15), 64.

Galton, L. (1980). *Your child in sports: A complete guide*. New York: Franklin Watts.

German, C. B. (1991). *Human behavior in the social environment*. New York: Columbia University Press.

Germain, C. & Gitterman, A. (1995). Ecological perspectives. In R.L. Edwards et al. (Eds.), *Encyclopedia of social work* (19th ed.). Washington, DC: National Association of Social Workers.

Greenberger, E & Steinberg, L. (1986). *When teenagers work: The psychological and social costs of adolescent employment*. New York: Basic Books.

Greenwood, C. M., Dzewaltowski, D. A., & French, R. (1990). Self-efficacy and psychological well-being of wheelchair tennis participants and wheelchair nontennis participants. Special Issue: Wheelchair sports. *Adapted Physical Activity Quarterly, 7*(1), 12–21.

Groos, K. (1901). *The play of man* (E. L. Baldwin, Trans.). New York: Appleton. (Original work published 1898)

Hawkins, J. D. (1997). Academic performance and school success: Sources and consequences. In R. P. Weissberg, T. P. Gullotta, R. L. Hampton, B. A. Ryan, & G. R. Adams (Eds.). *Enhancing children's wellness.* Thousand Oaks, CA: Sage.

Hawkins, J. D. & Weis, J. G. (1985). The social development model: An integrative approach to delinquency prevention. *Journal of Primary Prevention, 6*(2), 73–97.

Hodge, K. & Danish, S. (In press). Promoting life skills for adolescent males through sport. In A. Horne & M. Kiselica (Eds.), *Handbook of counseling boys and adolescent males.* Thousand Oaks, CA: Sage.

Intercollegiate Sports. Hearings, 1994.

Levenstein, P. (1988). *Messages from home: The mother-child home program and the prevention of school disadvantage.* Columbia: Ohio State University Press.

Lewin, K. (1951). *Field theory in social sciences.* (D. Cartwright, Ed.). New York: Harper.

McEwin, C. K. & Dickinson, T. S. (1996, March/April). Placing young adolescents at risk in interscholastic sports programs. *Clearinghouse, 69*(4), 217–221.

Mech, E. V., Pryde, J. A., & Rycraft, J. R. (1995). Mentors for adolescents in foster care. *Child and Adolescent Social Work Journal, 12*(4), 317–328.

Michener, J. A. (1976). *Sports in America.* New York: Random House.

Moore, C. W. & Allen, J. P. (1996). The effects of volunteering on the young volunteer. *Journal of Primary Prevention, 17*(2), 231–258.

Mowry, D. D. (1994). Mentoring among the Hmong: A practice outlet for teaching faculty and a possible community development tool. *Journal of Community Practice, 1*(1), 107–112.

Muri, S. (1996). A study of the impact of early socialization factors on self-efficacy, self-confidence, and autonomy in women. Unpublished dissertation, Boston College.

Nettles, S. M. & Pleck, J. H. (1994). Risk, resilience, and development: The multiple ecologies of black adolescents in the United States. In R. J. Haggerty, L. R. Sherrod, N. Gamezy, & M. Rutter (Eds.), *Stress, risk, and resilience in children and adolescents: Processes, mechanisms, and interventions*. Cambridge, UK: Cambridge University Press.

Newcombe, P. A. & Boyle, G. J. (1995). High school students' sports personalities: Variations across participation level, gender, type of sport, and success. *International Journal of Sports Psychology, 26*(3), 277–294.

Piaget, J. (1962). *Dreams and imitation in childhood* (G. Gattegno & F. M. Hodgson, Trans.). New York: Norton.

Pierce, W. J. & Singleton, S. M. (1995). Improvisation as a concept for understanding and treating violent behavior among African American youth. *Families in Society, 76*(7), 444–450.

Ramsey, D. E., Thompson, J. C., & Brathwaite, H. (1994). Mentoring: A professional commitment. *Journal of National Black Nurses Association, 7*(1), 68–76.

Riessman, F. (1965, April). The "helper" therapy principle. *Social Work,* 27–32.

Riessman, F. (1976, September/October). How does self-help work? *Social Policy,* 41–45.

Rizzo, T. L., Bishop, P., & Tobar, D. Attitudes of soccer coaches toward youth players with mild mental retardation: A pilot study. *Adapted Physical Activity Quarterly, 14*(3), 238–251.

Rhodes, J. E. (1994). Older and wiser: Mentoring relationships in childhood and adolescence. *Journal of Primary Prevention, 14*(3), 187–196.

Rowley, A. J., Landes, D. M., Kyllo, L. B., & Etnier, J. L. (1995). Does the iceberg profile discriminate between successful and less successful athletes? A meta-analysis. *Journal of Sport and Exercise Psychology, 17*(2), 185–199.

Rozin, S. (1995). Sports business: The drug trade: Steroids: A spreading peril. Business Week, June 19, pp. 138–141.

Schinke, S. P. & Gilchrist, L. D. (1984). Life skills counseling with adolescents. Baltimore: University Park Press.

Schweinhart, L. J. & Weikart, D. B. (1988). The High/Scope Perry Preschool Program. In R. H. Price, E. L. Cowen, R. P. Lorion, and J. Ramos-McKay (Eds.), 14 ounces of prevention: A casebook for practitioners. (pp. 53–65) Washington, DC: American Psychological Association.

Schweinhart, L. J. & Weikart,D. B. (1992). Early childhood development programs: A public investment opportunity. In M. Bloom (Ed.), *Changing Lives: Studies in human development and professional helping* (pp. 97–105). Columbia, SC: University of South Carolina Press.

Shure, M. B. (1997). Interpersonal cognitive problem solving: Primary prevention of early high-risk behaviors in the preschool and primary years. In G. W.Albee & T. P. Gullotta (Eds.), *Primary prevention works* (pp. 167–188). Thousand Oaks, CA: Sage.

Shure, M. B. & Spivack, G. (1988). Interpersonal cognitive problem solving. In R. H. Price, E. L. Cowen, R. P. Lorion, & J. Ramos-McKay (Eds.), *14 ounces of prevention: A casebook for practitioners* (pp. 69–82). Washington, DC: American Psychological Association.

Sinclair, D. A. & Vealey, R. S. (1989). Effects of coaches' expectations and feedback on the self-perceptions of athletes. *Journal of Sport Behavior*, *12*(2), 77–91.

Thomas, D. A. (1993). Racial dynamics in cross-race developmental relationships. *Administrative Science Quarterly*, *38*(2), 169–194.

Vilhjalmsson, R. & Thorlindsson, T. (1992). The integrative and physiological effects of sports participation: A study of adolescents. *Sociological Quarterly*, *33*(4), 637–647.

Walsh-Nowers, R. T. (1992). A creative drama prevention program for easing early adolescents' adjustment to school transitions. *Journal of Primary Prevention*, *13*(2), 131–148.

Wang, M-Q., Yesalis, C. E., & Fitzhugh, E. C. (1994). Desire for weight gain and potential risk of adolescent males using anabolic steroids. *Perceptual and Motor skills*, *78*(1), 267– 274.

Weikart, D. B. & Schweinhart, L. J. (1997). High/Scope Perry Preschool Program. In G. W. Albee & T. P. Gullotta (Eds.), *Primary prevention works* (pp.146–166). Thousand Oaks, CA: Sage.

Weissberg, R. P., Barton, H. A., & Shriver, T.P. (1997). The social-competence promotion program for young adolescents. In G. W. Albee & T. P. Gullotta (Eds.), *Primary prevention works* (pp. 268–290). Thousand Oaks, CA: Sage.

Werner, E. E. (1993). Risk, resilience, and recovery: Perspectives from the Kauai longitudinal study. *Development and Psychopathology*, *5*(4), 503–515.

Werner, E. E. (1995). Resilience in development. *Current Directions in Psychological Science*, 4(3), 81–85.

Werner, E. E. & Smith, R. S. (1992). Overcoming the odds: High risk children from birth to adulthood. Ithaca, NY: Cornell University Press.

WHO Press. (1992, June 25). *Drugs and sports*, pp. 1–2.

Zippay, A. (1995). Expanding employment skills and social networks among teen mothers: Case study of a mentor program. *Child and Adolescent Social Work Journal*, 12(1), 51–59.

3

Let's Play: Initiating Youth Into the Healthy World of Play

David G. Blumenkrantz

How do we help children make a healthy transition through adolescence and become successful and happy adults? This is the $64,000 question to which billions of dollars and countless strategies have been devoted over decades. Two constructs essential to our species' successful growth and development have been overlooked in our recent quest to answer this question: rites of passage and play, which were created by our species long before formal education and social science.

First identified in 1906 by the French Anthropologist/Sociologist Arnold van Gennep [1960], the *rites de passage* was designed to meet the challenge to the homeostasis of a community following an individual's change of status at critical points in the life cycle, i.e. birth, initiation to adulthood, marriage, and death. Many of history's prominent scholars and social intellectuals, including Plato, Aristotle, Homer, Kant, Nietzsche, Freud, and Piaget [Spariosu, 1989], debated the meaning and importance of play and prompted Frederick Schiller to write that "man is human only insofar as he plays, thereby replacing homo sapiens and homo politicus with homo ludens: For, to mince matters no longer, man only plays when he is in the fullest sense of the word a human being and he is only fully a human being when he plays" [Spariosu, 1989, p. 59].

These organic constructs were the way our species transacted the business of becoming human beings long before our attempts to describe and define the phenomenon through language. The language of social competency, however, has been gaining currency in describing the essential processes that contribute to adolescent growth and development. Its utility lies in its comprehensive consideration of adolescent development [Gullotta et al. 1990] and moves beyond seeing adolescents as a distinct set of problems in need of mending [Bloom, 1990]. Numerous approaches [Albee & Gullotta, 1997; Price et al. 1988; Weissberg et al. 1997] have been developed to meet this challenge in a range of areas, such as life skills training [Botvin, 1988], social problem solving [Weissberg et al. 1997], cognitive problem solving [Shure & Spivack, 1988], transitional events [Felner & Adam 1998] and rites of passage [Blumenkrantz & Reslock 1981; Blumenkrantz 1992, 1998].

This chapter presents an overview of the salient features of rites of passage and play and their relationship to community development and social competency. It attempts to expand our thinking about after-school and positive leisure time activities and recast their use within the historical constructs of rites of passage and play.

The first part, Play Ground: Play and its relationship to social competency, addresses the historical perspectives and biological imperatives of play and its relationship to social competency within the context of community. The second part, Initiation as a Pathway to Play, will explore the concept and contemporary application of rites of passage and will discuss the Rite Of Passage Experience©, ROPE®[1] [Blumenkrantz & Reslock 1981] approach. This six-year three-phase approach establishes a process that builds a community context for guiding youth to explore and experience the elements of play and fun.

Play that promotes health and contributes to the egalitarian evolution of our species should be an important consideration in crafting after-school activities. It is a component of a contemporary initiatory process and can foster transcendence, thereby promoting a greater sense of community, through guided experiences. ROPE helps communities take play seriously, and treat it as an essential element in the survival of our species and an important part of a well-balanced healthy life. It is discussed here as a case example of how a community can collaborate to set forth clear expectations that youth will make a commitment to "experiment" with after-school and positive leisure time activities and how they systematically increase opportunities for and guide youth into these health promoting activities.

This chapter considers how rites of passage can be used as an architectural structure for creating community programming that systematically initiates adolescents into the world of healthy play. It explores the historical considerations of play and its implication for the evolution of our species and the development of social competency in our youth.

Play Ground: Play and its Relationship to Social Competency

Recent scientific inquiry [Brown, 1994] coupled with historical perspectives [Spariosu, 1989] recognize that "play may be as important to life—for us and for other animals—as sleeping and dreaming. Play is key to an individual's development and to its social relationships and status" [Brown, 1994, p.8]. Play is the natural way a species prepares itself to function within its culture and the physical world. Anthony Stevens [1993, p. 104] writes: "Play is nature's high school. It is a preparation for living out the relationship in adult life. " It is part and parcel of life. "Life must be lived as play" [Plato, 1950]. Fred Donaldson [1993, p. 38], one of the foremost authorities on play, laments that play has been "adulterated" and undergone a profound "fundamental shift from a life process to an act in service to culture." As Paul Hogan [1978, p. 14] wrote: "Our playgrounds are designed by adults and destroyed by children." For Freud [Spariosu 1989, p. 178], "The child's play is determined by his wish to grow up. Through it, he imitates what he knows of adult life, and he has not reason to hide his wish. The adult, on the contrary, has suppressed his wish, which is, ironically, that of becoming a child again. The poet, like the intoxicated man or the neurotic, is one of the few adults who may behave like a child without shame: here the phrase poetic license assumes its full antithetical sense."

Within a historical context, play is treated as a very serious subject. It is linked to power, social and behavioral learning, transformation, and no less important than contributing to the evolution and survival of a species [Spariosu, 1989]. "Beneath all the studies and comments about animal and child play runs a central, if unrecognized, thread: Play serves survival," [Pearce, 1977, p. 141]. How can after-school and positive leisure time activities be designed within a community context to maximize the utility of play (as reflected in the historical discourse), and promote social competence, positive youth development, and a psychological sense of community that contributes to the egalitarian evolution of our species? In play we find three elements that relate to and support the foundation of rites of passage. They are: (1) the creation of a community context to build social competency in youth; (2) the promotion of a psychological sense of community; and (3) its transformative potential.

After-school and positive leisure time activities offer constructive opportunities for youth to develop competencies in both intrapersonal and interpersonal domains. Play [Caplan& Caplan 1973; Donaldson 1993; Pearce 1977; Neumann 1971], sports, and games [Danish, Petitpas, & Hale 1990] present opportunities to build competency in adolescents. Across the country there has been a recent increase in attention to after-school activities [Carnegie Corporation 1989; Lefstein, Kerewsky, et al. 1982; Lipsitz 1986]. Federal and state grant programs [Connecticut State Statute 10-266t. (e) 1–9] have been established for the creation and implementation of community-based after-school programs. One philanthropic organization (The Open Society Institute) has announced its commitment of $1 billion to after-school activities in New York City alone.

Although consideration is given to the health promotion benefits of these activities, a primary goal of after-school programs appears to be occupying young people's time to keep them out of trouble. "The devil finds work for idle hands" [p. 72, Flavell, 1993] may be the overarching theme of public support for after-school programs. But are we missing an opportunity? Does this present thrust to engage youth in after-school activities consider the historical dialectic on play of so many philosophers, scientists, and social commentators?

Play is one of the most powerful ways children build their social competency [Neumann, 1971]. Yet, we tend to underutilize it in the service of promoting a more egalitarian evolution of the human species. Consider how organized youth sports and activities have been made available to younger and younger children. What is the impact on the development of 5- and 6-year old children who are, in growing numbers, engaging in organized soccer, football, baseball, and basketball?

I overheard an 11-year-old telling a friend that a classmate had freely shared her candy with him. In utter amazement he said, "Why would she just give me the candy? No one just gives anyone something." When 5- and 6-year-olds are pitted against each other in games and sports, isn't it predictable that a youth is astonished when one of his peers shows compassion and altruism? Are compassion and altruism important qualities we would like our children to acquire? By immersing youth in sports at an early age, are we compromising their acquisition of skills and attitude necessary for compassion and altruism? To what end are we organizing sports for young children? This has implications for the training of all coaches, especially those who establish the early foundation for children's entry into play through organized sports.

What are the cultural implications and the future evolution of our species when the important work of children's play has been adulterated and usurped by adult-created, goal-oriented, competitive, skill-building activities? What may be called for is a greater attention to the balance between child-created play, play that promotes a sense of balance and connection, with play that promotes mastery of skills and social competency as defined in a majority of the literature.

Spiel to Speilraum

In his expansive work, *Dionysus reborn: Play and the aesthetic dimension in modern philosophical and scientific discourse*, Mihai Spariosu [1989] reaches back to antiquity to weave a historical perspective of the phenomenology of play. Spariosu references dozens of scholars, philosophers, physicists, educators, psychologists, and sociologists who consider play to be serious business. Typical of such consideration are the Caplans' [1973] comments: "We believe the power of play to be extraordinary and supremely serious" [p. xii]. It is the symbolic representation of our intrinsic desire for life—Eros—and transformation and the mediation of negative forces—thanatos—power and control over our environment and others.

Spariosu's [1989] exhaustive search for the quintessential definition of play led him to the simple declaration:

> Despite an ever-growing interest in play and countless attempts to explain its nature and function, the play concept remains today as elusive as it was two thousand years ago. We all seem to know what play is and can recognize it as such, but find ourselves at a loss when confronted with the task of conceptualizing this knowledge. In other words, play seems to belong to what the Germans call *das stumme Wissen* (tacit knowledge), involving intuition rather than the rational faculty. There are hundreds of definitions of play, but none seems satisfactory. [p.1]

Immanuel Kant [Spariosu, 1989] uses the German word for play or game, *Spiel,* in his discussion of play. Yet he does not consider play as a concept but rather, an "anticoncept, or that which resists all conceptualization and which renders the critiques of pure Reason and the power of judgment necessary" [p. 33]. Erikson introduces the notion of Spielraum which he translates as "leeway of mastery" [Spariosu, p.186]. "Erikson observes that Spielraum connotes something common also for the 'play' of mechanical things, namely free movement within prescribed limits. This at least establishes the boundaries of the phenomenon: where the freedom is gone, or the limits, play ends [Spariosu, p. 186].

"Play is older than culture, for culture, however inadequately defined, always presupposes human society, and animals have not waited for man to teach them their playing" [Huizinga, 1996, p. 59]. All play means something. It is a paradoxical paradigm that eludes definition and parameters. Noted authority on play, Fred Donaldson wrote, "I'm only playing well when I am not playing" [p. xv,

Donaldson 1993]. Play is the phenomenology of our creative inter-action with the world and ourselves in order to extract meaning and pleasure from the world. "With Nietzsche," Spariosu writes, "Human play, especially the play of the child and the artist, becomes the 'conceptual key to the universe' or a 'cosmic metaphor'" [p. 128 Spariosu, 1989]. Play informs work in its mediating relationship between intuition, imagination, and understanding. Through play we expand our consciousness unveiling potentiality residing within the gaiety of experience. Play helps us to step out of real life and real time to experiment with the world. Scientific inquiry is a sophisti-cated form of play with facts, axiom, and ideas. Letting the mind play with concepts allows us to uncover essential meaning. In a sense, play is one of our earliest forms of scientific inquiry. It is the unfolding expression of our inquisitive nature. "Play is experimenting with chance" [Fideler/Novalis, 1996].

McCullagh [1978] considers play across the ages and also suggests it parallels and prepares youth to engage in culturally sanctioned and useful activities. "Most of the games of the Middle Ages were real-life sports, such as riding, hunting, hawking, tilting at the quintain on a wooden horse, etc. As through most of history, children's play was a preparation for the rigors of adulthood" [p. 5]. This supports a contemporary context for rites of passage to be linked to play.

Spariosu's translation of Gadamer's [1989, p. 141] work on play recognizes the relationship between festivity and play and its contri-bution to creating and maintaining a community. "For Gadamer [1977], festivity is the experience of togetherness par excellence: 'Festivity means community and is the representation of community itself in its perfect form' [p. 52]. Celebrating means coming together over something, and festivity exhibits the same common purpose that play does. What is essential is not 'simply the coming together as such, but the intention which unites all participants and prevents them from lapsing into individual conversations or splitting into individual experience" [p.54]. The celebratory events that mark a rite of passage illustrate its utility to promote a sense of community.

Play satisfies psychic needs that cannot be satisfied by work. It helps to mediate and purge violent and destructive emotions and assimilate unpleasant experiences, limiting them to socially acceptable events, such as popular games or sports. Caplan [1973] speaks to this when he writes: "A young child stretches the boundaries of his world by means of make believe" [p.80]. "Children are usually most co-operative when engaged in satisfying play together. They can turn rivalries into make-believe play instead of open conflicts. Social learning takes place in relation to the resolution of conflicts as well as in co-operative play" [Caplan, p. 85]. Considering perspectives from both the historical and contemporary dialectic on play has substantial implications for sports and after-school activities. While some may consider these considerations of play to be folly (intellectual play!) play's importance in the evolution of species should inform us, more than it presently does, about building social competency in children and youth.

Frank and Theresa Caplan [1973] write: "Take any book on the philosophy of education and check the index to see if it contains the word 'play.' You may find 'Plato,' but rarely 'play.' Many philosophers have assumed that man's ability to survive has been a tenacious context. Actually, man has prevailed because he was more playful and steadfast than other creatures" [p. xx]. Caplan cites Eric Hoffer [1967] who suggests that "whenever you trace the origin of a skill or practices which played a crucial role in the ascent of man, we usually reach the realm of play" [p. xx].

Like Brown [1994, 1998] Caplan also ascribes great importance to the role of play in the development of life skill in almost all species. Life skills has been discussed as containing some constellation of cognitive, affective, and behavioral skills that help the person accomplish what they need to in order to become adults who lead happy and fulfilling lives [Botwin & Tortu, 1988; Schinke & Gilchrist, 1984]. In theory these skills are integrated and enable the person to perform well in the "conceptual categories of work, play, love, thinking, and service" [Bloom, 1999].

Playtime aids growth by helping a child assimilate the outside world in support of his ego [Caplan, 1973]. Caplan reviewed the classic work of Harlow [1962] on social deprivation in rhesus monkeys, which demonstrated the impact play deprivation had on the gross abnormalities monkeys showed in their adult sexual and social roles. Even when compared with monkeys that were separated from their mothers, those deprived of play showed far greater lack of social development. Hogan [1978] shares similar reports from a research study in Czechoslovakia. "A child who lives on the twentieth floor of a Prague housing complex generally has greater mental problems than one who lives on the tenth floor, who in turn has more than the child living on the first floor. Distance from a playground was proved to be an important determining factor in the child's mental heath" [p.13].

Following the 1966 University of Texas at Austin sniper attack, which killed 13 people and wounded 31, Stewart Brown [1994] conducted a study of 26 convicted murderers in Texas. The profiles of 90% of these men showed "either the absence of play as children or abnormal play like bullying, sadism, extreme teasing, or cruelty to animals" [p. 12]. Like Harlow's classic experiment, Brown's qualitative investigations revealed the importance of play.

Brown, [1998] a neurophysiologist, contends that the preponderance of the evidence draws a direct relationship between the amount of REM sleep (rapid eye movement sleep is correlated to a level of sleep, just below consciousness, associated with dreaming) a species is engaged in and its concomitant requirement for play. Humans average about 45 minutes of REM sleep a night, and therefore, we need to play for about 45 minutes each day. When sleep is interrupted for two weeks, health is compromised, and life-threatening symptoms begin to appear. Interacting with the environment through play, myth, ritual, and storytelling, all essential parts of human play, fosters adaptability and flexibility. The process of maturation through play is a necessary component to wholeness [Brown, 1998].

Work in the 20th century took on a superior position to play. Yet, modern theories of play underscore what Plato said: "Play is the noblest activity of Reason" [Spariosu, 1989, p. 54]. "The most recent theories attempt to dissolve the opposition between play and work, but they retain play's biological usefulness; they actually come to favor play over work as a learning and arousal-seeking activity, or as a motor in the individual's physical and psychological development" [Spariosu 1989, p. 167]. The motivating element in play may be directly related to the transformative properties. Winnicot [1971] wrote of play's potential to help humans transcend the world of the mundane and unveil that which is sacred. Plato refers to this directly when he declares that man is the "plaything of the gods" [Spariosu 1989, p. 59].

Play has an intrinsic potential to engage children, as well as adults, at a very deep level of their human beingness. It can facilitate transcendence that fosters a connection with the spiritual dimension—a dimension that professional athletes describe as "being in the zone" [Cooper, 1998], where time and space are transmuted, and performance rises to another level of beauty and artistry. Performance for that one moment becomes "ephemeral" and helps to focus your full attention on being present in the moment.

Victor Turner [1969] and Joseph Campbell [1988a, 1988b] suggest similarities within a ritual process. Play, sports, and games are a ritual in the way that they help "pitch the individual outside of him or herself" and achieve a heightened sense of awareness, enhancing a sense of connection with all one's surroundings, and achieving ecstasy. Bellah [1972] writes, "In the ritual the participants become identified with the mythical beings they represent. The mythical beings are not addressed or propitiated or beseeched. The distance between man and mythical being, which was at best slight, disappears altogether in the moment of ritual when everything becomes now. There are no priests, congregations, mediating representatives or spectators. All present are involved in the ritual action itself and have become one with the myth" [p.41]. When immersed in play, as with ritual, transcendence becomes possible. For Sarason [1992], this was a prerequisite for the creation and maintenance of a psychological sense of community. Sarason writes:

> Transcendence is the need to feel that what one is, was, or has done will have a significance outside the boundaries of one's personal place and time. Put in another way, it is a belief that one is part of a larger scheme of things in two respects: that scheme of things impacts on you and you somehow do or will impact on it. Whether that belief is empirically right or wrong is irrelevant. What is relevant is that you believe there is a larger scheme of things in which your life makes or will make a difference. [p. 5]

Almost every sport has its commentators that wax eloquently on the ephemeral qualities of sport. None may have done it better, or with more authority, than six-time National Basketball Association champion, Phil Jackson, [1995] who recently wrote: "On the surface this may sound like a crazy idea, but intuitively I sensed that there was a link between spirit and sport" [p.3]. He claims that the "most effective way to forge a winning team is to call on the players' need to connect with something larger than themselves" [p. 5]. According to Jackson, creating any successful outcome that requires the collaboration of people is "essentially a spiritual act... because it requires people to surrender the self-interest for the greater good of the collectivity so that the whole adds up to more than the sum of its parts" [p. 5]. Peter Gent [1996] offers another description to the same phenomenon when he speaks about the power of sports to bond people together and lift one's sense of self and place in life as intimately connected and related to an individual's relationship with others.

Fostering a transcendent experience for youth adds another dimension to the term "psycho-social competency" not frequently discussed, the ability to live well with others. Bloom's chapter begins to touch on this when he sets forth five categories to consider psychosocial competency that profile qualities for working, playing, loving, thinking, and serving well. Living well with others was one of the chief goals of traditional rites of passage and is one of the most important aspects of a contemporary model. Building a play ethic [Meeker, 1997] that is explicitly oriented to this is no less important. The initiatory experience can effectively use play as one of the vehicles that promotes transcendence, which leads to living well with others.

Is the experience of those who write on the esoteric and spiritual realm of sport—Jackson [1995] in basketball; Gent [1996] in baseball; Millman [1980] in sports in general; Murphy, [1972] Wallach [1995], & Fisher [1997] in golf; Strickland [1997] in bicycling; Gallwey [1994] and Jennings [1995] in tennis—unique and unavailable for a majority of people? Why is the potential for spiritual awareness achieved through sport and other leisure time or recreational activities like art, untapped as a resource in the health and social competency promotion of our children and youth? Could we consider sport, games, and play to be related to and promote a secular spirituality?

"Games hold a mirror to civilization" [Grunfeld 1975, p. 10]. Many times they are echoes of our ancestors' rituals and have "profound similarities in their fertility rites and their sun and moon worship. Many games appear to have common property to human beings everywhere" [p.10]. Sport is play within cultural parameters that places constraints on its violent and aggressive tendencies. In 1872, Spencer [Spariosu, p.169], has related it to power, compensation, catharsis, and a way to give off surplus energy.

Sutton-Smith [Spariosu, 1989] also recognizes the reflective qualities of play to mirror sociocultural life: "More collaborative cultures have more collaborative kinds of games, more competitive cultures have more competitive kinds of games" [Spariosu, 1989, p. 201]. Sutton-Smith's [1983] anthropological perspective sets forth a polemic of play within the domains of either "instability and conflict" or conversely, one of "communitas and unity" [Spariosu, 1989, p. 202]. Sutton-Smith links all the cultural interpretations of play with their universal tendency to have "some systematic pattern of social relationships and mythic beliefs." For Sutton-Smith and Grunfeld [1975], the play of a culture is so important that it defines its reality. The direct sponsorship of sport at both the professional and amateur level by corporations defines this reality of western culture.

Playing sports could be considered an oxymoron since play is related to freedom of movement and spontaneous imaginative acts, while sport is an activity within a set of clearly defined parameters for a final goal-driven outcome. Play has been considered to be virtuous and desirable for its own sake. The player achieves self-satisfaction and internal rewards through greater understanding of and connectedness with the world, and although sport can be engaged in for these esoteric pursuits, it is more likely to be undertaken to achieve some goal related to mastery and conquest.

Meeker [personal communication, October 10, 1998] suggests that it is important to have some definition of play. He writes: "I quite understand your reluctance to nail down a definition of play, and I agree that it is virtually impossible. However, in the absence of a working definition, it becomes almost impossible to distinguish among play, games, and sports. I prefer to use a rough definition that defines play as non-goal-oriented and spontaneous behavior that is gratifying in itself without further rewards. That permits discussion of games and sports as goal-oriented activities that have rules and judges presiding over them, as play does not. To be sure, those lines blur sometimes, as when athletes become so absorbed in their sport, they forget the goals and enjoy their participation in a fully playful way. Still, games and sports generally work more closely to the rules of war than to the principles of play."

The reader may be struck by the presentation of both sides of the argument of sports and its contributions to youth development and social competency. The motto of many coaches is; "the only thing that matters is winning." This could be the guiding principle that sets the conditions in which sport aligns itself with social competency in the arena of mastery. Humanitarian growth-producing components center around the concept of sportsmanship where a person behaves generously in either defeat or victory. How to win and lose well, sportsmanship and compassion, all comprise areas underrepresented in youth's early exposure to organized games and sport. A balance needs to be struck between helping youth develop skills for mastery of a particular sport and helping them appreciate and experience the transcendent potential of sport. As discussed earlier, this has important implications for the training of coaches, especially those engaged in guiding young children into the arena of sports. Wouldn't it be interesting if the guiding motto of coaches became, "It's not whether you win or lose, it's how you transcend the game."

Play is "adulterated" into the domain of sport through an overlay of cultural attitudes, beliefs, and behaviors. In this way, it is a lot like art in that there are cultural sanctions and values placed on "good" art and "bad" art. As with art, play is subjugated within the construct of mastery and the quality of play is related to the quality of its proficiency. Similarly, there are cultural values placed on good and bad art, art that reflects proficiency and art that does not. Again, the value-laden concept of mastery can inhibit the esoteric potential of play to emerge in the service of achieving a more desirable egalitarian evolutionary pathway. What would the result be if we intentionally guided youth to play's transcendent potential that enabled them to have an expanded and perhaps even esoteric and playful relationship to sports? What could happen to youth development and communities, for that matter, if we overtly talked about and had as a goal "playing in the zone" rather than scoring goals or other measures of proficiency?

This consideration is taken up at some length in Seymour Sarason's [1990] book, *The Challenge of Art to Psychology*. He articulately compels the reader to consider what happens to artistic ability, present in every young child and systematically extinguished as they progress through elementary school. He writes: "Artistic activity is extinguished relatively early in life in large part because of the individual's feeling of inadequacy in representing reality, the belief that artistry is a talent or gift that few possess, and intimidation by the perceived gulf between what the individual can do and what great artists have done. The result is a form of learned helplessness or inadequacy" [1990, pp. 4-5].

James Michener [1976] alludes to this as well in his book *Sports in America*. He considers the potential peril of sport as an agent of complicated cultural values such as competition, materialism, and commercialism, where most participants are inferior and only some are superior, that could be detrimental to the development of adolescent competence [Michener, 1976]. "Even the highly successful black athlete runs the risk of establishing himself as a destructive behavior-pattern for younger blacks who cannot hope to emulate him" [Michener 1976, p. 195].

At one end of the spectrum, play helps to re-create and nourish the soul and has the potential for enabling transcendence and connection with the world outside of one's ego, a necessary prerequisite for contributing to a sense of community. It has the capacity to direct aggressive instinct in socially sanctioned ways that accommodate violence and conquest. At the other end of the spectrum, play— when mediated by cultural values—may become violent and preoccupied with the singular needs of the ego for dominance and mastery. A dynamic tension between these polar opposites of play presents challenges as well as opportunities. It also adds to the complexity of how to guide a young person in their relationship to play. It illuminates a deep-seated societal belief in the separation of the spiritual life from the secular life. The questions need to be restated again. Why is the potential for transcendence achieved through sports untapped as a resource in the health and social competency promotion of our children and youth? Could we consider sports, games, and play to be related to and promote a secular spirituality?

Transcending cultural values such as winning is good, losing is bad, mastery over a skill vs. a sense of balance, that predominate participation in sports and play may be at the root of a partial answer to these complex questions. I am reminded of my own struggles with this and will use a personal story in the hopes of illuminating the point. While infrequent, it has not been uncommon that I have found myself on the sixth tee of my favorite golf course at even or one under par. For those uninitiated to golf, "shooting par" is the ideal number of strokes in which a hole, or the course, should be played by a professional or "scratch" golfer. This is unfamiliar territory for me. In every instance, up until the moment of "conscious awakening," I am completely unaware of my score or how I got to achieve that level of play. I do remember having had a sense of disconnection from the game of golf and those with whom I was playing. I was enjoying a walk on a beautiful day in a state of grace, feeling blessed to be able to be in that wonderful place. The condition of being at one with that place consumed my consciousness. I was not thinking about the game from the perspective of performance, but was immersed in a state of rapture, interrupted for only a moment by the physical transaction of the golf swing. My body tacitly knows how to perform the golf swing, more or less, without my mind's mediation. In this state, I am truly *playing* golf. This state, referred to as being "in the zone," is quickly obliterated when my play is brought to my conscious attention and shifted into the realm of sport. It is done when one of the members of my foursome begins to notice that I am playing "over my game" and says something like, "Hey, you really are playing well." Or, "Hey, you've got a great score going." Through the same internal narration I have also brought this level of play into consciousness. In either instance, I have supplanted play through the cultural value of performance, mastery, and competition, and moved it into the realm of sport. When my play was interrupted by the reality of the sport, I typically had to fetch my next golf shot out of the bushes!

As a society, we seem to be more comfortable with the symbolic representation of play as it relates to mastery and conquest, indelibly linked to sports, than to consider its utility in affirming the importance of the spiritual life of children. Spirituality appears to be the "S" word of the 1990's as "sex" was the unmentionable "S" word of the 1950s and 1960s in educating children. It is just beginning to emerge as an important consideration in the overall development of youth [Coles et al. 1995].

For the reader not familiar with golf or experienced in "playing in the zone," the prospect of transcendence through sport or even the relevance of transcendence to a sense of community and psychosocial competency will not resonate, and you may be inclined to have the "so what" or "I don't get it" response to the chapter thus far. Perhaps these readers would relate better to two other experiences that contain an element of transcendence. First, we have all had the experience of getting out of bed in the morning. Have you ever found yourself dressed without any apparent recollection of the events that transpired between sensing your awakened state and being dressed? The entire experience in between being awake and getting dressed had been practiced so frequently that performing the task was not in your conscious mind. In fact, most of us have had a similar experience during the day. We are immersed in something and before you know it, you say, "Where did the time go?" Everyone I know who "surfs the Internet" has had this experience. Second, have you ever driven a car to a destination to which you have frequently driven and not remembered the ride?

In these situations your familiarity and mastery of the performance, or immersion in an activity was so keen that you did not need your conscious mind to mediate and guide the satisfactory completion of the task. While neither experience would engender a blissfully satisfying experience nor a sense of connection with the universe typically associated with transcendence in areas related to play, the psychological and physiological phenomena are relatively similar.

If one has little appreciation of the significance of transcendence usually achieved through direct experience, then the arguments contained throughout this chapter will not be sufficient to convince the reader of the relevance of the relationship between play, transcendence, sense of community, after-school and positive leisure time activities and social competency. In fact, while we are all "hard-wired" [Borysenko, 1998] for transcendence, the phenomenology of each of our transcendent experiences may be markedly different. What may be one person's transcendent experience may be little more than another mundane part of life for someone else. Who has the time to smell the flowers (some would suggest this metaphor is an expression of transcendence) on the high-speed super highway of life?

While Meeker's [1997] attempts to define play are useful, I return to Spariosu's position that finding a definition of play, even its interpretation within biological, psychological, physical, and natural domains, eludes meaning. As Huizinga [1996] wrote: "If we call the active principle that makes up the essence of play 'instinct,' we explain nothing; if we call it 'mind' or 'will' we say too much" [p. 59]. Play, as with transcendence, may fall into the unexplainable phenomenon, tacitly known but eluding language's ability to adequately define and describe. It is like Sarason's [1994] definition of the psychological sense of community, which, like hunger and starvation, is best known only when you have it and when you don't.

When I first began to explore the concept of play several years ago, I had no idea of the serious historical discourse associated with it or of its importance in the evolution of a species, especially the human species. Over the years, I have found this limited understanding of play to be the norm rather than the exception for a wide range of youth development professionals. For some, what preceded this may be familiar ground. For many, however, this overview was offered to set forth the "playground" as a foundation for exploring play and its relationship to transcendence, sense of community, and building social competency in children and youth. It also builds a foundation to address these questions: What is the potential impact of play and sport if it could ascend to a form of secular spirituality?

How can we initiate youth into the world of play in a way that unveils its full potential for transformation and contributes to a more peaceful, harmonious, and balanced human evolution?

Social Competency

The idea of social competency was first related to "mastery" [White, 1959, 1963] and considered an individual's abilities that fostered functional capacities to interact successfully with one's environment. Competence is a basic desire to feel capable. When one feels capable, one can experience a sense of accomplishment, satisfaction, and joy. The concept has been used to discuss health promotion [Gullotta et al. 1990; Weissberg et al. 1997] and the prevention of problems in children and youth. It primarily focuses on the acquisition and mastery of skills to engage successfully in manipulating and controlling the environment to satisfy one's individual needs.

Social competency approaches have been built upon a more holistic and ecological view of adolescent development. A youth development approach [U.S. Department of Health and Human Services (HHS) 1997] proposes that youth "development occurs through reciprocal and dynamic interactions that take place between individuals and various aspects of their environment" [p.xi]. Positive developmental pathways are fostered when adolescents have developed the following: a sense of industry and competency; a feeling of connectedness to others and to society; a belief in their control over their fate in life; and a stable identity [HHS 1997].

The interactional model parallels the social development model [Weis & Hawkins 1981], which proposes that youth development occurs through sequential interactions with four key environments or "units of socialization." Healthy development is promoted when youth "bond" with the four environments: family, school, peers, and community. The primary focus is creating a commitment, attachment, and belief among young people to each environment. Positive youth development is promoted when youth achieve a sense of competence, power, attachment, and commitment within the four key environments [Hawkins & Weis. 1985].

Danish, Petitpas, and Hale [1990] suggest that understanding competency is difficult because it lacks a definition on "which theorists and researchers can agree and that has validity across the life span" [p. 170]. Originating in part from the work of White [1959, 1963], competency is related to an "innate need of infants to master their environment that exists independent of the instinctual drives for food, sex, or avoidance of pain [Danish et al. 1990, p. 171].

Thomas & Carver [1990] use the concept of competency to refer to "the degree that an adolescent develops the relevant attitudinal and behavioral repertoire that a given social order sees as good and desirable" [p. 195]. They conceptualize competency as it relates to "socially valued dimensions defined by such characteristics as self-esteem, academic achievement, intellectual development, creativity, moral behavior, and/or an internal locus of control" [p. 195].

Building a sense of competency is inextricably tied to having sufficient abilities and skills to achieve a sense of adequacy in meeting one's needs within the four key environments in which one interacts. Skills training, including social skills and problem-solving, coupled with opportunities for personal growth that meaningfully connect youth with a spiritual awareness, and the major environments that affect them offer the building blocks for healthy development. A central key to the promotion of competence in adolescence includes opportunities for them to practice newly acquired skills in supportive situations where they are able to receive rewards and reinforcement [Hawkins & Weis 1985].

However, another important element of competence revolves around a child's metaphysical understanding and sense of connection to the world and others. It plays itself out in a sense of wonder and awe at the enormous mysteries that unfold as they live in an awakened state. In other words, promoting social competency in youth should not only focus on the mastery of skills but a sense of balance, harmony, and connection with a universe of immense size, mystery, and beauty. This sense of connection builds their confidence in their abilities to obtain meaning, purpose, and identity in their lives. The concept of competency appears to be influenced by the Judeo-Christian belief in dominion over the earth and plays itself out through the construct of mastery.

Robert Coles and colleagues [1995, p. 21] point out that "our fundamental human nature is to wonder about the meaning of life and to try to figure it out. And by no means to be always satisfied so doing." Our lives are enriched by this wondering. For Coles as well as others [Borysenko, et al. 1998], wondering about the mysteries of the universe is the "essence of spirituality." The consequence of not including program elements that address this area is to leave youth adrift in a sea of confusion, blown by the winds of change and the complex and contradictory messages of a diverse society.

Part 2. Initiation as a Pathway to Play

In play we have an innately human capacity that can help us join together, transcending cultural, economic and political boundaries. It affords us the opportunity to be in joy with others and be merrily human. Play can be the maypole around which we celebrate our common innate desire for fun and joy, which helps us move toward transcendence. As discussed previously, transcendence is one essential element prerequisite to the formation of a sense of community. Given the historical discourse on play and its importance in the formation and maintenance of community, how can we guide children and youth into more humanitarian forms of play that contribute both to social competency and, through transcendence, to a greater sense of community? One answer may be found in the traditional structure and elements of initiation rites or rites of passage.

The remainder of this chapter will focus on rites of passage and its relationship to the promotion of positive youth development and a psychological sense of community. A contemporary application of theory will be described through the 19-year accomplishments of the nationally recognized Rite Of Passage Experience, ROPE community-based strategy. A case will be developed that encourages program designers to consider the context in which youth engage in after-school and positive leisure-time activities and to craft a more productive process, through contemporary rites of passage, that engages more youth in these activities and with more humanitarian outcomes.

Various authors have theorized, with equal conviction and authority, that the absence of contemporary rites of passage plays a major role in the problems of youth and families [Blumenkrantz, 1992; Campbell & Moyers, 1988a, 1988b]; Cohen, 1991; Eliade, 1958; Foster, 1980; von Franz, 1972; Lincoln, 1981; Mahdi, 1987; Mead, 1993; Somé, 1993; Turnbull, 1983; Turner, 1969]. This consideration has neither been widely recognized nor included in intervention strategies by mainstream social science and human services [Blumenkrantz & Wasserman, 1998]. Rite of passage strategies may exist in relative obscurity because the province of ritual has been considered to be the domain of religion and not relevant to social science. It may also be related to the deterioration of psychological sense of community. How can contemporary rites of passage initiate and guide youth into a world of play that promotes social competency, a sense of community and the altruistic and egalitarian evolution of human beings?

Back To The Future

At long last science is catching up to history! During the past decade, increased attention has been given to the importance of rites of passage and the consequences of its absence [Mahdi 1987; Mahdi et. al. 1996; Somé 1993; Mead 1993; Campbell & Moyers 1988a, 1988b]. The history of our human experience is rich with accounts of rites of passage [Human Relation Area Files, 1976]. The rites served as a useful way for villages to come together and help children successfully transition to adulthood. The rites present an opportunity to use a common language in crafting a vision for promoting healthy youth, families, and communities. An increasing number of social scientists, commentators, and youth specialists have noted that the absence of contemporary rites of passage and sense of community have contributed to many problems with youth, their families, and communities [Blumenkrantz, 1992, 1996; Blumenkrantz & Wasserman, 1998; Campbell & Moyers, 1988a, 1988b]; Cohen, 1991; Eliade, 1958; Foster, 1980; Lincoln, 1981; Mahdi, 1987; Mead, 1993; Somé, 1993; Turner, 1969; Zoja, 1989]. They suggest that youth engage in drinking, drugs, violence, gangs, delinquency, and many other behaviors as their rites of passage. A rite of passage is an essential ingredient in youth development. It addresses the real needs of youth for transformative experiences. Building contemporary rites of passage focuses on helping young people obtain meaning, identity, and purpose, while building a sense of community and connection between significant people in their lives.

One of the primary challenges in any community-based strategy, is creating a foundation of broadly accepted values for a diverse and multicultural society. The literature on play, discussed previously, illuminates play's utility in promoting prosocial values that may be broadly accepted among diverse cultures. Employing the vehicle of play and its potential to promote transformation and transcendence may serve to establish rites of passage that will promote prosocial community values.

Since 1981, the Rite Of Passage Experience, ROPE approach has been intentionally used to build partnerships between parents, schools, community agencies and institutions that contribute to raising healthy and socially competent childrenand effectively employ the resources of a community. It has helped people build connections and relationships through their awareness of the importance of rites of passage and the consequences of its absence. People have used rites of passage as the common ground for developing their community's collective vision. It is a strategy that builds upon the ancient proverb, "It takes a whole village to raise a child." This approach has had significant achievements [Hawkins, 1986, 1989; Woodard, 1996; Child Welfare League of America, 1992; Kyle, 1987; State of Connecticut Office of Policy and Management, Bates 1986] because it promotes a collaborative evolutionary process within a setting. It does not embrace a paradigm that promotes adoption of a "program" to "fix" a host of problems facing our children and their families. Rather, it offers members of a community a transformative experience, essential to the formation of a psychological sense of community [Sarason, 1992], from which they find ways of integrating and deploying their resources within the context of rites of passage. It is not about anything new. Quite the contrary, it is about everything old that already exists as assets in a community and how they can be tied together through ROPE. The goal is to empower communities to create and implement their own rites of passage through a combination of contemporary social science technology and traditional wisdom.

The paradigm for the Rites Of Passage Experience is a three-phase six-year process that has specific principles to guide practices that will produce particular outcomes advantageous to positive youth and community development. It presents a new way, perhaps considered a paradigm shift, to build a community's capacity to sustain collaborative efforts on behalf of raising children. One measure of its unique capacity may be the perception of both a theoretical and programmatic paradox. One paradox is that a set of activities that could be considered a program help create the vehicle in which a community process unfolds. The programmatic elements are orchestrated by a community and unfold in a rich array of patterns of initiation that reflect the community's unique cultural and social values and resources. A paradox exists because the program is the process and the process is the program.

The second paradox is the use of structured activities to help youth "re-search" the fundamental elements of play. Given the previous discourse on play, how could we provide structured activities to learn how to play? We will return to the subject of play later in the chapter to put the answer in the context of a community strategy.

In Julian Rappaport's 1980 presidential address to the community psychology division of the American Psychological Association, he discussed the paradoxical nature of social/community problems and the implications for viable intervention, which may also be paradoxical. He said; "The point is simply that much of what underlies the substance of our field requires us to recognize that we are being pulled in two ways at once and that we often need to pay attention to two different and apparently opposed poles of thought."[1981, p.3]. His comments were in the context of discussing empowerment as a more viable approach than prevention and the apparent paradox between providing a concrete set of activities within the context of what we call program and the need to promote activities that will empower communities through a process.

There are a number of paradoxes that exist in working with contemporary rites of passage. This is not unwarranted, especially in light of the need for community interventions to seek out and work with paradox [Rapapport, 1981] One paradox that I will address here is whether a contemporary rite of passage strategy (or any really effective community strategy) is a program with a plan or sequence of things to be done or a process relying on a series of acts that proceed from one to the next? Can the process be a program or the program be a process?

Since a portion of the model with which I work - the Rite Of Passage Experience, ROPE - promotes a sequence of planned activities that have expected outcomes, it could be considered a program. Yet, it requires a community process to refine, build, implement, and sustain a contemporary rite of passage. The process does have a set of interconnected principles that offers rationale, methods, examples, time frames, and expected outcomes to help guide the community process for the creation, implementation, and sustainment of contemporary rites of passage. In this way, the process acts as a program to help structure community action that builds relationships, a psychological sense of community, and their capacity to use rites of passage.

One shortcoming of human service approaches is a belief that a "program" is the delivery mechanism for the human service work, not unlike a "pill" is the delivery mechanism for many medicines. Policymakers and administrators look for the magic program (pill), as if the problems that human services works with are like a strep throat that will clear with a simple antibiotic prescription. Look at the "pill" Americans were asked to swallow in response to the drug "epidemic" in the early '80's: "Just Say No." It's not that simple.

The following principles, which build upon each other although not necessarily in a linear manner, guide practice for communities to work in the art of rites of passage.

Principle 1. Orientations.

Statement of Principle: Engage diverse segments of the community in a series of orientations to facilitate their comprehensive understanding and gain broad support of the theoretical underpinnings of the rites of passage paradigm and its practices.

Rationale. A common understanding of and commitment to the essential theoretical and program elements of any community approach builds constituents who are willing to engage in an ongoing process to create, implement, and sustain the approach.

Method. Large- and small-scale presentations with project "expert," community leaders, and others provides information and encourages participation in experiences that give participants a glimpse of the utility of rites of passage and offers an opportunity for transcendence. The presentation includes multimedia presentation on rites of passage and community building, experiential activities, and finally a core group retreat [see Blumenkrantz 1992 for description of core group].

Example. Planning meetings with interested and influential citizens set the foundation for subsequent meetings with larger groups of parents, school personnel, police, members of clergy, youth and others. Meetings, including good food and snacks, use experiential techniques that are fun and promote positive rewarding social interactions.

Expected Results. Expected results are increased understanding of theory and specific details of rites of passage, greater enthusiasm and commitment to select one or more tasks related to supporting the implementation of ROPE. Begin the process of building relationships between diverse representatives of the community

Principle 2. Relationship Building

Statement of Principle. Build relationships to identify and share community and individual assets and precipitate the potential for transcendent experiences.

Rationale. Programs don't help people. People, through their relationships, help people. Transcendence and shared emotional experience are several key elements that contribute to a psychological sense of community.

Method. Convening groups (good food and snacks again!) with "mixers" and "ice breakers" engage citizens in activities that uncover areas of mutual interest, and individual and community assets that can be used within the project. Helping citizens connect with each other on a personal level builds a foundation for the project. Retreats offer opportunities for in-depth encounters that strengthen the bonds between people, and facilitates transcendence and transformation through play.

Example. In the beginning of a group gathering, participants are asked to generate a list of ten questions that people could ask to learn something about each other. Questions like: What is the funniest situation you have encountered during the last two months? What do you do to have fun and relax? In this illustration, the second question can be used as a springboard to discuss play and serve as a foundation for identifying positive leisure-time activity resources in the community and people who can link youth to them. Subsequent activities may include overnight retreats that offer initiatory experiences like vision quests, ropes course, etc. Arranging for groups to share a meal and have fun together are important ways to build relationships.

Expected Result. The relationships will bring an increased sense of community as measured by participants' sense of belonging, a sense of personal relatedness, influence, a sense of mattering, of making a difference, integration and fulfillment of needs, and shared emotional experience. These elements of a psychological sense of community [McMillian & Chavis, 1986] contribute to more community involvement at greater levels of commitment and activity. A felt sense of community fosters an identification and utilization of community assets.

Principle 3. Integration

Statement of Principle. Integration of the rites of passage paradigm and activities with other community and school initiatives and models.

Rationale. Rites of passage is not a panacea. Its utility is in both responding to youths' needs for prosocial, contemporary rites of passage, and as a vehicle to facilitate experiences propitious to increasing the capacity of a community to collaborate on behalf of promoting positive youth development. Using existing community resources and assets helps to create connections between diverse groups and fosters their commitment to the process. It promotes the community's use of common language and shared experiences.

Integration of existing assets, resources, and program approaches builds on and values the community's history. It is not about bringing into a community another "program" to replace existing efforts.

Method. Early in a community's consideration of rites of passage they should identify and examine what models, programs, activities, and resources are directed toward positive youth development goals. Many existing activities in a community offer a piece of a comprehensive community approach and are enhanced through their synthesis within a rite of passage framework. Elements related to a rite of passage approach should be integrated to create a synergy and expand the community's capacity to promote positive developmental outcomes for youth. This is especially important in considering the academic curricula. In-service training for teachers, youth recreation league coaches, clergy, police and other youth workers help to build connections that support the program elements and further the community process of collaboration.

Example. A series of meetings could be held, where open and honest (leave egos at the door!) discussions among key stakeholders identify activities and programs related to positive developmental outcomes for youth. These meetings can be conducted within a context of relationship building (P2) and directed toward identifying common intermediate and long-range outcomes and activities related to these outcomes. Contemporary rites of passage in general and ROPE specifically are compatible with and offer considerable enhancement opportunities to almost all of the present models for supporting positive youth development. Examples include, but are not limited to, Community Recreation Programs, Sport Leagues, Developmental Assets, Resiliency, Character Education, Asset Mapping, America's Promise, and DARE. It can also be easily integrated with all academic curricula. The key to integration rests on the relationship built between key stakeholders in the community.

Expected Result. The community adopts a common language, symbols, and approach in supporting youth development and assessing the results of their efforts. Adults share common (initiatory) experiences that lead to greater understanding and respect for different views and methods. Increased desirable intermediate outcomes, such as youth bonding to family, school and community values and norms, increased youth problem-solving and life skills, and opportunities for youth to demonstrate and be rewarded for using skills. Long-range goals achieved include an increase in developmental assets and resiliency in youth, and a decrease in ATOD use, violence, and other problems associated with adolescent development.

Principle 4. Recruitment

Statement of Principle. Representatives of key constituencies (i.e. community based agencies, community leaders both formal and informal, school administrators and teachers, civic organizations, parents, police, clergy, and youth) to engage in approximately 40 hours of training to build a core group.

Rationale. You can only bring someone as far as you have been yourself. Experiential training is a prerequisite for facilitating, administering and coordinating the resources necessary for experiential programming with students. Have you ever tried to learn how to tie a knot by reading a book? It is very difficult if not impossible. The same situation is true for experiential activities. Building relationships among diverse constituencies within a community helps to tailor the strategies to the specific resources and needs of a community, which engender their ownership and commitment to sustaining the effort.

Method. Following a series of community orientations to the Rite Of Passage Experience a core group representative of the community, including youth and adults, engages in a 40 hour training. The experiential training engages the participants in activities related to the ROPE program and increases their capacity to collaborate to create, implement and sustain all of the phases of a contemporary rite of passage.

Example. During approximately 40 hours of training, 15 representatives of the community collaborate together during experiential activities

Expected Response. The core group develops deep understanding of rites of passage and their contemporary application within the context of the Rite Of Passage Experience. The group has shared their own initiatory experience and has developed intimate connections and a commitment to identify and coordinate the community's resources and thus increase their capacity to successfully implement and sustain their rite of passage. They continue the formation of a "critical mass" of the community with an increased capacity to engage in an ongoing collaborative evolutionary process.

Principle 5. Fidelity

Statement of Principle. There must be fidelity in the core curriculum and program elements.

Rationale. Consistent delivery of skill-building, group-building, community-connecting program elements is critical to establish a common language and framework. This includes at least 90% of the prescribed ROPE sessions as designed and set forth in the program guide [Blumenkrantz 1998]. Particular attention must be paid to the goals and objective of each session, the orientation and celebration events, experiential activities, culminating event and transitional sessions. This comprehensive community strategy includes elements set forth in phases II & III (described in later section).

Method. Activities within the community that promote continuous improvement and focus on the elements of each phase are established. These include adequate training and supervision of new facilitators who are directly engaged with youth, reevaluation of students' sense of connection, and engaging in phase II & III activities. The community monitors results to assess movement toward desired outcomes and allow for ongoing modification to ensure progress to achieving goals through fidelity of the program components.

Example. New ROPE facilitators are linked to seasoned "elders" who provide feedback and support to help their development as ROPE facilitators and community elders. A process for conducting qualitative evaluations will offer important feedback information, from which ongoing refinement of the intervention can be made. Revision of positive leisure time activity and community service opportunity pamphlets by community teams developed through

ROPE community training is ongoing. Frequent meetings of key "players" are scheduled.

Expected Result. When implemented in a community over time substantial change in student behavior occurs and the number of positive community connections increases and are sustained to work toward desired youth and community outcomes.

Principle 6. Feedback

Statement of Principle. Evaluation and Feedback mechanism to provide ongoing information for continuous improvement through adaptation.

Rationale. The viability of a human service strategy depends upon its ability to be informed by changing circumstances and quick adaptation. Techniques that help monitor results of youth, parent, school, and community participation in both the process and program elements are critical to maintain a dynamic, responsive approach.

Method. Both quantitative and qualitative methods may be employed depending upon resources.

Example. In this model, the community members are coresearchers, and they work to establish mutually agreed-upon outcomes and methods to assess how things are going. The following are some of the areas of interest: measures that identify a youth's perception of his or her relationship to the major environments that impact his or her lives, i.e. family, school, peers, and community; perceived social support from parents, peers, and school personnel; measures of perceived peer pressure, delinquent behavior, and substance abuse. A developmental asset community survey could be utilized, as well as results mapping to gauge achievements and create a community process that engages in the use of evaluation and feedback methods.

Expected Result. The community process improves the quality of life for youth, their families, and the community. The process also engages in the creation and implementation of an evaluation and feedback method that engenders greater commitment to researching for the most viable ways to support the objectives of their efforts. The ultimate goal is to implement and sustain rites of passage that promote positive youth and community development. The community will provide ongoing vigilance and be responsible for the continuous improvement to the process.

Three Phases of ROPE

The guiding principles discussed above support a process for creation, implementation, and sustaining the three-phase, six-year process of the Rite Of Passage Experience. The architectural structure for the phases is briefly described below and it has been described extensively elsewhere [Blumenkrantz & Reslock, 1981; Blumenkrantz, 1992; Blumenkrantz & Gavazzi, 1993; Gavazzi & Blumenkrantz, 1993; Blumenkrantz, 1996; Blumenkrantz & Wasserman, 1998; Blumenkrantz, 1998].

Phase I focuses community, parent, student, and school attention on the separation of children from their elementary school experience, on the beginning of their separation from parents, and on the importance of this transitional time in youth development. A core curriculum of life skills training prepares students for the complex challenges ahead and helps build their self-esteem and resiliency. The curriculum, once contextualized to the specific site, also provides a vehicle to introduce important ingredients for having healthy fun, thus setting the stage for the next phase.

Phase II is the transitional phase. It focuses on connecting youth with community resources. It usually occurs for youth in middle or junior high school. Building on the foundational skills for healthy fun acquired in Phase I, students develop a contract with their parents, school, and community-agency representatives to experiment with positive leisure-time activities. These activities are the pathway for youth to experience the transformative potential of play. They can help encourage prosocial values of mutuality, altruism, and cooperation. This view has important implications for the training of coaches and others who guide youth in these activities. Pooled energy and resources of school personnel and community create opportunities for young people to meaningfully participate in positive leisure-time activities, guiding them toward prosocial community involvement.

Phase III focuses on the important adult value of giving of one's self to others through community service. Community cooperation and collaboration make opportunities available for youth to become involved in community service activities. One opportunity involves high school students who mentor younger students as they go through the rite of passage process, functioning as cofacilitators in Phase-I skill-building activities, or mentors for guiding youth into Phase-II positive leisure-time activities. This community service phase continues throughout high school. Phases II and III give youth the opportunity to demonstrate and transfer newly acquired skills to other settings.

Within the framework of these three phases, positive developmental pathways are fostered in adolescents that help them develop a sense of industry and competency, a feeling of connectedness to others and to society, a belief in their control over their fate in life, and a stable identity. Communities using the model have further refined their own contemporary rite of passage within their unique context and culture. The phases function as a vehicle to shape culturally relevant, developmentally appropriate activities for youth and the community. They require that the community inventory its assets and resources necessary to each phase of the intervention.

Throughout the three-phase process, youth, parents, and community members both support and learn from the rite of passage programming. Following are listed only some of each group's opportunities for learning responsibility and community participation [Blumenkrantz & Wasserman, 1998]:

Youth Opportunities for Learning and Community Participation

All youth activities are culturally specific and relevant, developmentally sequenced and appropriate. These activities are designed to increase skills for living, promote good self-esteem, foster a connection with a "spiritual self," promote a shift in consciousness, and a belief in and sense of their own transformation. They include:

- Skill building for positive youth development;
- Positive leisure-time activities and an understanding of the importance of having fun through positive play rather than

more self-destructive activities like drinking, drug use, and sexual experimentation;

- Mentorship relationships and/or peer counseling or other youth empowerment and involvement activities;
- Opportunities for the youth to transfer and demonstrate their newly acquired skills community service, which affords them higher status as an emerging adult in the community;
- Celebration event(s) that mark significant transitions between elementary, middle, and high school, where the initiate demonstrates some form of competency from their initial rite of passage experience;
- Multicultural and ethnically sensitive opportunities for youth to explore and gain an understanding of their own culture of origin; and
- A succession of increasingly difficult physical and mental ordeals or challenges where youth have to demonstrate a competency in skills learned in order to accomplish a challenge and move on to a higher order of ordeal. Youth have an opportunity for self-dialogue and reflection.

Parental Opportunities for Learning and Community Participation

- The importance of rites of passage and the expectations for their involvement in their children's initiatory process;
- Information about adolescent development and how to parent adolescents;
- Information that increases their understanding of and sensitivity toward developmental milestones of midlife and the potential collision of transitions, i.e., adolescence and midlife;
- A variety of strategies to interact with children around rites of passage themes during and following the proposed project.

Community Functioning Opportunities

- Identification and community linkage of resources to support the youth and parent component and mobilize the community to develop and coordinate such resources

- Administrative structure that is inclusive of a diverse representation of the community, to provide a process for program
  development, implementation, modification, and adaptation
- Promotion of an authentic sense of community by fostering a
  sense of mutual connectedness, dependency, and responsibility
- Establishment of strong and clear community standards for
  youth to learn and accept while providing positive and healthy
  elders as role models to guide youth on their rite of passage

Although the Rite Of Passage Experience, ROPE has prescribed
elements that could be considered a program, the programmatic
elements work together, not as a prescription, but as a structure for
fostering a collaborative evolutionary process within a community.
Thus, the program's utility is not in its programming, but in its ability
to mobilize a community, using a common language and shared
emotional experience to create and sustain a community-focused
initiative. Programmatic strategies and community collaboration
and coordination help promote important developmental assets in
children and youth.

Initiating Youth into the Healthy World of Fun

I shall return to play for a moment to contextualize the answer to the
question raised earlier in the chapter: "How can we provide structured activities to learn how to play?" "Let's play" could arguably be
one of the most common solicitations across species [Brown, 1994].
Has a dog or cat ever played with you? Birds do it, dolphins do it, bears
do it. Play is one of the most constant behaviors across many species
and is one of the only forms of communications between species
[Brown, 1994]. As I have discussed previously, it helps a species
develop skills necessary for survival, helping them integrate into a
social order. Play is so important that the Rite Of Passage Experience
creates a structure to help youth focus (re-search) on the elements of
play.

"I'm bored," "There's nothing to do around here," "I just want
to have fun," are frequent refrains heard loud and clear from adolescents. Anyone who has teenagers or has worked with teenagers
knows this to be true. A contemporary rite of passage utilizes play as

a vehicle to create a community context that connects the developmental and social needs of adolescents and their desire for competency with their tendency to engage in activities they perceive to be "fun." Adolescents, especially early adolescents, pursue activities where experimentation, risk-taking [Lewis, & Lewis, 1984] and "having fun" are the rule rather than the exception. The widely acknowledged pursuit of "fun" by children and youth is not frequently considered to be a vehicle to meaning-fully intervene with youth. Adults don't take fun seriously. Youth may perceive adult lives as being devoid of fun and playfulness, which in many cases they are, and adults are also seen as mediating youths' attempts to have fun.

One could consider that youth engage in inadequate attempts to have fun through behaviors that are considered to be antithetical to healthy development, i.e. sex, drugs, alcohol. For almost 20 years the Rite Of Passage Experience, ROPE has helped communities initiate their children into and through adolescence and provide a community context that initiates them into the world of healthy fun.

What Did You Do Yesterday to Have Fun?

The Rite Of Passage Experience approach helps communities construct a foundation for coordinating their resources within the context of their community, systematically guiding youth into after-school and positive leisure time activities. It also serves as a foundation for psychotherapy with youth and their families [Gavazzi & Blumenkrantz, 1993]. Phase I sets a community context for youth to learn important life skills during "teachable moments" [Blumenkrantz, 1981].

Teachable moments are used to fulfill the essential purpose of education, inherent in the Latin origin of the word *educoare*—to lead out or bring forth knowledge. The experiences are designed to facilitate a teachable moment, where a place and time for dialogue occurs between adults and students. It presents opportunities for students to observe and judge their own behaviors, beliefs, attitudes, and values. The experiences help students investigate complex elements of individual and group behaviors. Students are guided to examine their participation in the experience. The experience is like a mirror, reflecting the self-image of the individual and the individual in relation to the group.

Physical activities and cognitive challenges are used as vehicles to lead out and bring forth knowledge that youth incorporate as new learning. A teachable moment occurs when a learning experience (books, lecture, experience, etc.) intersects with a student's receptivity (interest and availability emotionally, cognitively, and physically) in a positive relationship that ignites the students capacity to receive new learning. A student must be available to learn. A teachable moment can occur when students are actively engaged in experiences at physical, cognitive, and emotional levels. They are immersed in and consumed by the experience. Experiences are examined from the inside out. Following experiential challenges and throughout each session it is essential that the group examines what they did. The examination of experience is what we call processing.

Phase I experiences in the ROPE sessions could be classified within Mihaly Csikszentmihalyi's [Csikszentmihalyi & Larson, 1984] consideration of "transitional" activities. These activities combine "challenge, concentration, intrinsic motivation, and positive affect" [Danish et al. 1990] in ways that are rewarding and enjoyable for the participants and contribute to their optimal development. Csikszentmihalyi [1975] considers enjoyment within a Flow Model construct. The Flow Model proposes that enjoyment is defined through a balanced relationship of the skills of the participant and the challenges of an activity. Using Csikszentmihalyi's Flow Model, Danish and his colleagues posit [1990]: "When the individual perceives the challenges to be greater than his or her skills, anxiety results. Boredom results when an individual appraises his or her skills as being greater than the perceived challenges. When the perceived challenges are equal to an individual's sense of skills, the experience is optimal and is labeled flow. Whether in work or play, feedback from activities wherein competence is extended to meet expanding challenges contributes significantly to self-concept and the sense of well-being" [p. 181]. This is consistent with Spariosu's account of Groos's attempts to integrate all of the rival play theories of the time into his own theory of "play as practice of skills."

A contemporary meaning of play as a practice of skills is reframed within the context of after-school or positive leisure time activities. Unfortunately, as discussed earlier, the impetus for focusing on after-school activities was in response to a growing concern for the increasing numbers of "latch-key" youth and the assumption, ungrounded by any research at the time [Lipsitz, 1986], of what "the risks are of being in self-care" [p. v].

Elliot Medrich and his colleagues summarized the situation well: "Some scholars contend that adolescence was invented early in this century to account for the increased number of years during which young people were considered reproductive and in need of supervision and training. The after-school hours are a similar kind of invention. This block of time has become distinct, ironically, through its ambiguity. It is a negotiable zone that is not wholly education, work, or free play" [Medrich et al. 1982, p. 6].

Within this historical context, the thrust of after-school activities seems to be in response to unsupervised youth and, thus, programming is oriented toward the supervision of youth. This programming may be more about controlling youth than fostering the development of their social competence. This is illustrated in both state and federal statutes promulgated to fund after-school programs. The Connecticut State statute [10-266t] providing "Grants for extended school building hours for academic enrichment and support and recreation programs" reflects the focus for the federal after-school initiative. Administrative language presents opportunities for programming to promote social competency through "funds for extended school building hours for public schools in such districts for academic enrichment and support, and recreation programs for students in the districts" [Sec. 10-266t (1–6)]. Funds distributed pursuant to the statute are directed to link communication with the child's teacher and ties to the regular school curriculum, clearly structured experiences, provide for community, business, and parent involvement and coordination with community agencies [10-266t, (e), 1–9]. Utilizing the potential of play within the context of after-school activities and in the service of promoting social competency is not strategically designed, although it may happen in some locations.

The first phase of ROPE engages youth in a series of physical and cognitive challenges to lead out knowledge about skills, attitudes, and beliefs essential for health promotion and positive youth development. Students teach each other, exploring their experience together solving problems and accomplishing challenges. This phase ranges from 15 to 40 or more sessions, depending upon the community's own innovation transfer [See Martinez-Brawley 1995, Smale 1993, and Blumenkrantz 1998 for additional information on innovation transfer and the importance of community input].

The second phase of ROPE is strategically designed to build upon the first phase and systematically guide youth to engage in positive leisure time activities—play—to practice skills learned in the first phase of ROPE. It is one community approach that systematically guides all youth to engage in positive leisure time activities and contextualizes play and "having fun" within a rite of passage paradigm. ROPE lays an experiential foundation for youth to learn essential life skills and in so doing, to investigate the elements of having healthy fun. It serves as a vehicle for the community to come together and coordinate their "Play" assets, initiating youth into a culture of healthy play and encouraging youth to experiment with the community's health-promoting play assets.

The ROPE skill-building sessions are designed to be fun and employ play, in the fullest sense of the word, as a vehicle for learning. Session activities provide the experience that help youth understand the importance of play and investigate the essential ingredients of healthy fun. Phase I sets a compelling reason for them to experiment with positive leisure-time activities. The following is excerpted from the third edition of the ROPE guide [Blumenkrantz, 1998]. It is the transitional session between the first and second phase of ROPE and illustrates how a context is set and youth are guided to "experiment" with positive leisure time activities in the second phase.

> *Facilitator:* What have we been doing together for the
>   last 6 or 7 weeks?
> *Students:* We've been in ROPE together.
> *Facilitator:* What does that mean, ROPE?
> *Students:* Rite Of Passage Experience.

Facilitator: Why are we doing this Rite of Passage Experience?

Students: To help us prepare for adolescence and adulthood.

Facilitator: Let's look at our time spent together. What did we do during each session? How did that help prepare us for adulthood?

A dialogue develops around the following issues as they relate to the ROPE sessions: trust, friendship, decision-making, problem solving, coping with stress, calming down, challenges, peer pressure, feeling good about oneself, and having fun.

The facilitator guides the discussion to examine the skills learned and how students can use them in the future. The student's review of ROPE helps them recognize what they learned, how they can apply it in the future, and why they had fun. As a result, it sets a context for guiding them toward experimentation with productive, fun, leisure-time activities. Facilitators help students draw a link between what they did in ROPE to have fun and that finding fun things to do is an important part of healthy growth and happy adulthood. Students identify the following elements as contributing to having fun in ROPE: learning a new skill, practicing the skill, working with others or alone, and accomplishing something that was difficult, or accomplishing something that they thought they couldn't do. Accomplishing difficult challenges made them feel good. This is consistent with the Flow Model previously discussed.

A dialogue in a ROPE group may be guided as follows:

Facilitator: The community expects you to get an education. There are many more things you will need to learn for you to be healthy and happy. There are many challenges you will face. One of your most important challenges is to find something you enjoy doing— something that makes you happy and is fun. Having fun is an important part of a well-rounded life. We know that many young people get into serious difficulty because they do not have healthy, fun things to do. Do you know what kind of problems teenagers can have if

they don't find fun things to do? What can you do to
have fun? What can you do to feel a sense of accomplishment? Just like when you accomplished something
difficult in ROPE. This is what you must search for and
find. This is your next very important challenge.

The discussion continues and can focus on how people may
attempt to have fun in a negative or unhealthy way, i.e., drugs,
alcohol, sexual activity. This is positioned as people taking "short-
cuts" to finding fun. Students quickly identify with the dialogue and
are excited that adults, ROPE guides, are affirming the importance
of fun and play. It has been our experience that young people do not
receive consistent messages about having fun from adults. From their
experience, adults typically tell youth what they shouldn't do rather
than offer experiences that help them understand the importance of
fun and compels them to engage in healthy leisure-time activities.

Another tool that engages youth in the process is through a
"Youth Interest Survey" that is conducted to determine in what
positive leisure-time activities youth want to participate. The community identifies and creates a pamphlet containing a wide assort-
ment of positive leisure-time activities. The community must work
collaboratively to ensure that youth have access to these activities
and barriers that prevent participation are identified and broken
down. Each youth gets a "Youth Activity Pamphlet" from which they
select several activities they would like to experiment with to have
fun. The students can review the pamphlet with their parents, ROPE
guides, school counselors, and/or older student mentors. Once they
complete their "Student Activity Plan" (SAP), it is signed by their
parents, school guidance counselor, ROPE guide, high school mentor, and themselves. Copies to review are kept at their school, with
their ROPE guide, high school mentor, and at home. It serves as a
contract and vehicle for further dialogue and support. The Student
Activity Plan includes the following:

- I would like to learn to do the following three activities well and
  have fun.
- I will speak with the following resources to help me find
  something fun to do.

- I would like my ROPE Guides to do the following to help me find something fun to do.
- I would like my parents to do the following to help me find something fun to do.

The SAP creates, as one parent describes it, a "common language," with which to talk with teenagers. It meets students where their interests are—having fun—and builds upon their positive experiences in ROPE. It sets a community structure that helps to guide youth into positive leisure-time activities. Middle school guidance counselors and homeroom teachers make the link between positive leisure-time activities and the first phase of ROPE through SAP. School personnel are encouraged to ask student daily "What did you do yesterday to have fun?" "What did you do to fulfill your SAP?" ROPE guides, school personnel, high school mentors, and parents work together to help guide youth to comply with their SAP or help them identify other activities in which they wish to engage. Intervening with students who are not engaging in "fun" activities after school interrupts the potential for them to engage in health-compromising activities.

Students who do not follow through with their activity plan are not disciplined. They are guided through the decision making process that they learned in ROPE, to make changes in their Student Activity Plan. The student can then be guided to employ the decision-making process learned in ROPE. And, a number of people, including youth mentors, are available and acting within the same framework.

Summary

Recently, much attention has been given to engaging early adolescents in positive leisure-time activities. However, most communities do not establish a context, relevant to the student, for them to find and participate in these kinds of activities. At the beginning of this chapter I posed the question "How do we help children make a healthy transition through adolescence and become successful and happy adults?" I endeavored to make a compelling case for revisiting two constructs that have been viable responses to this question for thousands of years: play and rites of passage. I've offered a new paradigm that places value on how rites of passage have traditionally been used to create and maintain a sense of community as well as guide youth along a healthy path to adulthood. In a sense we need to go back to the future, through rites of passage, and help communities reinvent themselves and re-create a sense of community. ROPE offers a positive context for the community to help youth participate in positive leisure-time activities. ROPE serves as a common language for all adults in the community to talk with youth and each other. Consider the impact of this small change in the way a teacher begins a class or greets the students in morning homeroom: "What did you do yesterday to have fun?"

It has been said that one of the greatest challenges for communities entering the century is the quest for a sense of community [Nisbet 1953]. After-school and positive leisure time activities can be used to help youth experience the joy and growth producing benefits of play while increasing a sense of community. Within a framework of rites of passage and through the process of play, a community can reinvent itself. In this way it takes a whole child to raise a village.

Notes

1. The Rite of Passage Experience, ROPE are copyrighted, registered, and licensed to the Center for the Advancement of Youth, Family & Community Services, Inc., Glastonbury, Connecticut.

References

Albee, G. & Gullotta, T. (1997). *Primary prevention works*. Thousand Oaks, CA: Sage Publications.

Bates, V. (1986). *Bringing out the best in kids*. Hartford, CT: Connecticut Office of Policy & Management.

Bellah, R. (1972). *Religious evolution: Reader in comparative religion.* New York: Harper & Row.

Bloom, M. (1966). *Primary prevention practice.* Thousand Oaks, CA: Sage.

Blumenkrantz, D. & Reslock, B. (1981). *Rite of Passage Experience (ROPE).* Glastonbury, CT: Associates in Counseling and Training.

Blumenkrantz, D. (1992). *Fulfilling the promise of children's services.* San Francisco: Jossey-Bass, 1992.

Blumenkrantz, D. G. & Gavazzi, S. M. (1993). Guiding transitional events for children and adolescents through a modern day rite of passage. *Journal of Primary Prevention, 13*(3), 199–212.

Blumenkrantz, D. (1996). *The rite way: Guiding youth to adulthood and the problem of communitas.* Unpublished doctoral dissertation, University of Michigan, Ann Arbor.

Blumenkrantz, D. (1998). *The Rite Of Passage Experience, ROPE: Guide for promoting healthy youth and community development* (3rd ed.). Glastonbury, CT: The Center for the Advancement of Youth, Family & Community Services.

Blumenkrantz, D. G. & Wasserman, D. (1998). What happens to a community intervention when a community doesn't show up? Restoring rites of passage as a consideration for contemporary community intervention. *Family Science Review, 11*(3).

Borysenko, J., Moore, T., West, C. & Winter, M. (1998) The spirit in our lives: Search for personal meaning. The Connecticut Forum: Bushnell Auditorium, May 30, 1998.

Botvin, G. J. & Tortu, S. (1988). Preventing adolescent substance abuse through life skills training. In R. H. Price, E. E. Cowen, R. P. Lorion, & J. Ramos-McKay (Eds.), *14 ounces of prevention: A casebook for practitioners* (pp. 98–110). Washington, DC: American Psychological Association.

Brown, S. (1994). Animals at play. *National Geographic, 186*(6), 2–35.

Campbell, J. & Moyer, B. (1988a). The power of myth. New York: Doubleday.

Campbell, J. & Moyers, B. (1988b). *The first storytellers.* New York: Mystic Fire Video.

Caplan, F. & Caplan, T. (1973). *The power of play.* Garden City, NY: Anchor Press/Doubleday.

Carnegie Corporation. (1989). *Turning points: Preparing American youth for the 21st century*. The report of the Task Force on Education of Young Adolescents. New York: Author.

Carver, C. & Thomas, D. (1990). Religion and adolescent social competence. In Gullotta, T. Adams, G. & Montemayor R. (Eds.), *Developing social competency in adolescence* (pp. 195– 219). Newbury Park, CA: Sage Publications.

Cohen, D. (1991). *The circle of life: Rituals from the human family album*. New York: Harper Collins.

Coles, R., Elkind, D., Monroe, L., Shelton, C., & Soaries, B. (1995). *The ongoing journey: Awakening spiritual life in at-risk youth*. Boys Town, NE: Boys Town Press.

Cooper, Andrew (1998). *Playing in the zone: Exploring the spiritual dimensions of sports*. Boston: Shambhala.

Csikszentmihalyi, M. (1975). *Beyond boredom and anxiety*. San Francisco: Jossey-Bass.

Csikszentmihalyi, M. & Larson, R. (1984). *Being adolescent.* New York: Basic Books.

Danish, S., Petitpas, A., & Hale, B. (1990). Sport as a context for developing competence. In T. Gullotta, G. Adams, & R. Montemayor (Eds.), *Developing social competency in adolescence* (pp. 169-194). Newbury Park, CA: Sage Publications.

Donaldson, F. O. (1993). *Playing by heart: The vision and practice of belonging*. Deerfield Beach, FL.: Health Communications.

Eliade, M. (1958). *Rites and symbols of initiation: The mysteries of birth and rebirth* (W. R. Trask, Trans.). San Diego, CA: Harcourt Brace Jovanovich.

Erikson, E. (1973). *Toys and reason: Stages in the ritualization of experience*. New York: Norton.

Felner, R. & Adan, A. (1998). The school transitional environment project: An ecological intervention and evaluation. In R. H. Price, E. E. Cowen, R. P. Lorion, & J. Ramos-McKay (Eds.), *14 Ounces of prevention: A casebook for practitioners* (pp. 111 - 122). Washington, DC: American Psychological Association.

Fisher, A. K. (1997). *The master of the spirit: A golf fable*. New York: Harper.

Fideler, David (1996). A natural harmony. *Parabola, 21*(4), 59–63.

Flavell, L. & Flavell, R. (1993). *The dictionary of proverbs and their origins*. New York: Barnes & Nobles.

Foster, S. (1980). *The book of the vision quest: Personal transformation in the wilderness*. New York: Prentice Hall.

Franz, M. L. von. (1972) *The feminine in fairy tales*. Dallas: Spring Publications.

Gallwey, W. T. (1994). *The inner game of tennis*. New York: Random House.

Gavazzi, S. M. & Blumenkrantz, D. G. (1993). Facilitating clinical work with adolescents and their families through the rite of passage experience program. *Journal of Family Psychotherapy, 4*(2), 47–67.

Gent, P. (1996). *The last magic summer: A season with my son*. New York: William Morrow and Co.

Groos, K. (1898). The play of animals. (E.L. Baldwin, Trans.). New York: Ayer.

Grunfeld, Frederic, V. (Ed.). (1975). Games of the world: How to make them, how to play them, how they came to be. New York: Holt, Rinehart & Winston.

Hamburg, D. (1989). *Turning points: Preparing American youth for the 21st century*. New York: Carnegie Council on Adolescent Development, Carnegie Corporation.

Hawkins, J. (1986). *Preliminary report on the evaluation of the ROPE program*. Unpublished manuscript, Yale University, New Haven, CT.

Hawkins, J. (1989). *Report on the evaluation of the ROPE program combined data, cohorts, 1 through 5*. Unpublished manuscript, Yale University, New Haven, CT.

Hawkins, J. D. & Weis, J. G. (1985) The social development model: An integrated approach to delinquency prevention. *Journal of Primary Prevention, 6*(2), 73–97.

Hawkins, J. D. & Catalano, R. F. (1992). *Communities that care: Action for drug abuse prevention*. San Francisco: Jossey Bass.

Hogan, P. (1978). The play. In J. C. McMullagh (Ed.), *Recreation alternative: Ways to play* (pp. 1–30). Emmaus, PA: Rodale Press.

Human Relations Area Files. (1976). *Source Bibliography: Cumulative*. New Haven, CT: Human Relations Area Files Press.

Huizinga, J. (1996). What "play" is. *Parabola, 21*(4), 59–63.

Jackson, P. & Delehanty, H. (1995). *Sacred hoops: Spiritual lessons of a hardwood warrior*. New York: Hyperion Publisher.

Jennings, J. (Ed.). (1995). *Tennis and the meaning of life: A literary anthology of the game*. New York: Harcourt Brace & Co.

Kelting, T. (1995). The Nature of Nature. *Parabola, 20*(1), 24–30.

Lewis, C. E., Lewis, M. A. (1984). Peer pressure and risk-taking behaviors in children. American Journal of Public Health, vol. 74, No. 6, pp. 580-584.

Lincoln, B. (1981). Emerging from the chrysalis: Rituals of women's initiation. New York: Oxford University Press.

Lipsitz, J. (1986). *After school: Young adolescents on their own*. Chapel Hill: Center for Early Adolescence at the University of North Carolina at Chapel Hill.

Loftus, G. & Loftus, E. (1983). *Mind at play: The psychology of video games*. New York: Basic Books.

Mahdi, L. C. (1987). Introduction. In L. C. Mahdi, S. Foster, & M. Little (Eds.), *Betwixt & between: Patterns of masculine and feminine initiation* (pp. ix - xv). La Salle, IL: Open Court.

Mahdi, L., Christopher, M. & Meade, M. (1996). *Crossroads: The quest for contemporary rites of passage*. La Salle, IL: Open Court.

Martinez-Brawley, E. E. (1995). Knowledge diffusion and transfer of technology: Conceptual premises and concrete steps for human services innovators. *Social Work, 40*, 670–682.

McCullagh, J. C. (Ed.). (1978). *Ways to play: Recreation alternatives*. Emmaus, PA: Rodale Press.

McMillan, D. W. & Chavis, D. M. (1986). Sense of community: A definition and theory. *Journal of Community Psychology, 14*, 6–23.

Mead, M. (1993). Men and the water of life: Initiation and the tempering of men. New York: Harper Collins.

Medrich, E. A., Roizen, J. A., Rubin, V., & Buckley, S. (1982). *The serious business of growing up: A study of children' lives outside school*. Berkeley: University of California Press.

Meeker, J. (1997). *The comedy of survival: Literary ecology and a play ethic*. Tucson: University of Arizona Press.

Michener, J. (1976). *Sports in America*. New York: Random House.

Millman, D. (1980). *The way of the peaceful warrior: A book that changes lives*. Tiburon, CA: H. J. Kramer, Inc.

Murphy, M. (1972). *Golf in the kingdom*. New York: Delta Books.

Neumann, E. (1971). *The elements of play*. New York: MSS Information Corporation.

Nisbet, R. (1953). *The quest for community*. New York: Oxford University Press.

Pearce, J. C. (1977). *Magical child*. New York: E. P. Dutton.

Plato. (1950). Laws. In J. Juizinga (Ed.), *Homo Ludens* (pp.). Boston: Beacon Press.

Price, R., Cowen, E., Lorion, R., & Ramos-McKay, J. (1988). 14 ounces of prevention. Washington, DC: American Psychological Association.

Rappaport, J. (1981). In praise of paradox: A social policy of empowerment over prevention. *American Journal of Community Psychology*, 9(1), 2–21.

Sarason, S. (1990). The challenge of art to psychology. New Haven, CT: Yale University Press.

Sarason, S. (1992). American psychology, and the needs for transcendence and the sense of community. Invited centennial address, American Psychological Association, Washington, DC.

Schinke, S. P. & Gilchrist, L. D. (1984). *Life skills counseling with adolescents*. Baltimore: University Park Press.

Shure, M. & Spivack, G. (1998). Interpersonal cognitive problem solving. In R. H. Price, E. E. Cowen, R. P. Lorion, & J. Ramos-McKay (Eds.), *14 ounces of prevention* (pp. 69–82). Washington, DC: American Psychological Association.

Smale, G. (1993). The nature of innovation and community-based practice. In E. E. Martinez-Brawley & S. M. Delevan (Eds.), *Transferring technology in the personal social services* (pp. 6–12). Washington, DC: NASW Press.

Somé, M. P. (1993). *Ritual: Power and healing and community*. Portland, OR: Swan/Raven.

Spariosu, M. (1989). *Dionysus reborn: Play and the aesthetic dimension in modern philosophical and scientific discourse*. Ithaca, NY: Cornell University Press.

Stevens, A. (1993). *The two million-year-old self*. College Station: Texas A&M Press.

Strickland, Bill (Ed.). (1997). *The quotable cyclist: Great moments of bicycling wisdom: Inspiration and humor.* New York: Breakaway Books.

Turnbull, C. M. (1983). *The human cycle.* New York: Simon & Schuster.

Turner, V. (1969). *The ritual process: Structure and antistructure.* Hawthorne, NY: Aldine De Gruyter Publishing.

U.S. Department of Health and Human Services, Administration for Children and Families, Administration on Children, Youth and Families, Family and Youth Services Bureau. (1997). *Understanding youth development: Promoting positive pathways of growth.* Washington, DC: Author.

Van Gennep, A. (1960). *The rites of passage.* Chicago: University of Chicago Press.

Wallach, J. (1995). *Beyond the fairway: Zen lessons, insights and inner attitudes of golf.* New York: Bantam Books.

Weis, J. G. & Hawkins, J. D. (1981). Preventing delinquency: The social development approach. Washington, DC: U.S. Government Printing Office, National Institute for Juvenile Justice and Delinquency Prevention.

Weissberg, R., Gullotta, T., Hampton, R., Ryan, B., & Adams, G. (1997). *Enhancing children's wellness.* Thousand Oaks, CA: Sage.

Weissberg, R., Barton, H., & Shriver. T. (1997). The social-competence promotion program for youth adolescents. In Albee, G. & Gullotta, T. (Eds.), *Primary Prevention Works* (pp. 269 - 290). Thousand Oaks, CA: Sage.

White, R. (1959). Motivation reconsidered: The concept of competence. *Psychological Review, 66,* 297–323.

White, R. (1963). Ego and reality in psychoanalytic theory: A proposal regarding independent ego energies. *Psychological Issues, 3*(3), Monograph 11. Winnicott, D. W. (1971). Playing and reality. London/New York.

Woodard, A. (1996). A helpful path to the year 2000: Evaluation of community interventions using rites of passage. Unpublished report to the Connecticut State Department of Mental Health and Addiction Services, Hartford, CT.

Zoja, L. (1989). *Drugs, addiction and initiation: The modern search for ritual.* Boston: Sigo Press.

4

Sports and Social Competence

Albert J. Petitpas and Delight E. Champagne

One out of every four adolescents is extremely vulnerable to multiple high-risk behaviors and school failures [Poinsett 1996]. With drug use, violent crimes, and gang involvement among teenagers all on the rise, it is not surprising that youth development initiatives have taken center stage in the efforts of many funding organizations. Even with an estimated 20,000 national and local youth services organizations currently operating in the United States, about one-third of our young people have minimal opportunities to participate in afterschool activities [Poinsett 1996].

In response to the many challenges facing teenagers, the Carnegie Council's Great Transitions Report [1995] identified key factors that would facilitate adolescents' personal and social development. These factors are:

- Finding a valued place in a constructive group.
- Learning how to form close, durable human relationships.
- Feeling a sense of worth as a person.
- Achieving a reliable basis for making informed, deliberate decisions—especially on matters that have large consequences, such as educational futures.
- Knowing how to use available support systems.
- Find ways of being useful to others beyond the self.
- Believing in a promising future with real opportunities.
- Cultivating the inquiring and problem-solving habits of mind for lifelong learning and adaptability.
- Learning respect for democratic values and understanding responsible citizenship.
- Building a healthy lifestyle.

Although it is doubtful that any one institution could achieve all these requirements, a number of practitioners have identified sports participation as one activity that has the potential to provide a positive influence on the lives of a significant number of our adolescents [e.g., Danish et al. 1990; Smith & Smoll 1996; Weiss 1995]. Sports participation in school and community programs has traditionally been viewed as a "safe haven" where young people acquire skills and experiences that build self-esteem and prepare them for later life. Sports are important to teenagers. Twenty to 35 million 5- to 18-year-olds participate in community sports and another ten million 14- to 18-year-olds participate in school sports [Ewing et al. 1996].

Unfortunately, increases in youth gang activity rival the increases in participation in sports that youth have been experiencing in the past decade. Youth gangs are found in almost all 50 states and on the increase in medium-sized and small cities, with many new gangs forming in rural and suburban areas [Spengel 1995; Huff 1996]. Involvement in both of these subcultures may be indicative of the significant role that peer groups play in the development of youth in today's larger culture. Indeed, sports groups and the role they play in young peoples' lives may be likened to gang involvement. Organized sports satisfies a number of needs of youth and functions in similar ways to gangs. However, sports can be considered a "positive gang" and, as such, can serve to replace the negative subculture experience offered by gang involvement.

The reasons why gang members join gangs can be quite similar to those of athletes who join sports teams. Gang members join gangs for excitement, status, protection, and a sense of belonging [Huff 1996]. They may also join for material reasons, for recreation, for the opportunity to resist parental influence, or for commitment to a community group where loyalty and patriotism can be shown [Shelden et al. 1996]. Social Disorganization Theory [Shelden et al. 1996] suggests that a young person joins a gang to acquire a personality and a name for oneself and to achieve status through the role one has in the group. Gang participation defines one's position in society and becomes the basis for conceptions about one's self.

Similar needs can be met through participation on sports teams. Sports subcultures have been shown to have a number of characteristics that overlap with those of gangs. For example, sports subcultures have been observed to allow group members the opportunity to interact with members who possess common cultural characteristics, to provide for the fulfillment of the participants' psychological, social, or material rewards such as identity, status friendship, knowledge, or money, and to unite members who have distinct qualities that are different from those in the parent or dominant culture [McPherson et al. 1989].

It is widely believed that positive sports experiences can help individuals develop self-confidence and valuable life skills that enhance their abilities to handle the pressures and temptations that they face as teenagers today. Sports participation may also foster the leadership qualities that could enable athletes to be active role models to others. However, simply participating in sports does not guarantee that a person will derive all these benefits. The purpose of this chapter is to examine the role of sports participation in the social development of youth, ages 6 through 20. In particular, several questions will be explored:

- Why is sports well positioned to make a difference in the lives of young people?
- What are some of the potential disadvantages of sports participation?
- What can be done to increase the likelihood that sports participation will foster social and personal development?
- What would a sample initiative look like?

Why Sports?

Participation in sports is a highly valued activity among young people, particularly in the United States. For the most part, sports participation is a voluntary activity that attracts millions of young people each year. Therefore, it is not surprising to learn that for decades athletic achievement has been shown to be more highly valued than academic achievements among the vast majority of young people [Coleman 1961; Eitzen 1975; Weiss 1995]. Research has shown that being a successful athlete is the most desired status among junior and senior high school students, with athletes often viewed as role models for other young people in their communities [Weiss 1995]. Why is athletic performance so revered? This is a complex question and the literature provides few empirically supported answers. Developmental theory, however, offers several viable explanations.

Building on the works of Freud and Hartmann, White [1959] proposed that individuals were motivated by independent energies that allowed the ego to go beyond the confines of the instinctual drives. Using considerable experimental and physiological evidence, White argued that all living things were motivated by a need to master the environment and to move freely in the world. He labeled this drive effectance and defined personal competence as individuals' abilities to successfully interact with the environment in a manner that allows them to not only maintain themselves, but also to grow and flourish [White 1963]. Therefore, rather than simply acting in order to satisfy basic needs, individuals gain feelings of efficacy when they are able to have an effect on their environment.

According to White [1959], even the youngest of infants engage in actions such as shaking rattles and pulling on crib toys that enable them to discriminate visual patterns and begin the process of cognitive and motor learning. Therefore, by the time infants learn to walk, they have already had numerous interactions with their environment. These seemingly insignificant sensori-motor behaviors set the stage for the development of competence and establish the range of an individual's personal effectiveness. Early successes and failures in mastering one's environment shape each persons' self-confidence and ultimately generalize over time and across situations [White 1963]. Children construct their own sense of the world based on what they have learned about their abilities. Each attempt at mastery provides evidence about what they perceive as realistically possible and what they view as unattainable. Without an adequate level of personal competence, it is doubtful that young children would have the will or readiness necessary to imitate the complex behaviors exhibited by older role models.

As children begin school age, they interact with larger numbers of their peers and have increased opportunities to engage in social comparisons. Through this process, they receive feedback about their competencies and begin to make judgments about themselves that affect the range and type of activities that they will attempt [White 1963]. For young people, these social comparisons are most likely to be made around physical abilities. When a group of children come together to engage in a sports activity, they typically identify the two best players as captains, and then the captains take turns selecting their teammates from the remaining group members. This selection process provides concrete feedback about how one stacks up against his or her peers. The captains and early selections receive frequent reinforcement for their athletic involvement. Those chosen last are left to evaluate their status among their peers, based on their interpretation of the situation. Those who are several years younger may continue to participate in hope of becoming a "captain" among their age peers in the future. Some will view their selection status as a challenge to work hard and prove their competency or as motivation to participate in other sports activities that are better suited for their physical abilities. Unfortunately, an increasingly large number of young people will simply discontinue their sports involvement [Gould et al. 1982]. The youth sports dropout rate is alarmingly high and will be examined in the next section.

The feedback that children receive about their physical competencies becomes more magnified as they continue their school experiences. Young people are gradually introduced to an array of community and school sponsored sports opportunities that tend to be more formal and in many cases more competitive. Performance is often recorded and publicly reported in newspapers and other media. The intrinsic rewards inherent in mastering one's environment are supplemented by an elaborate set of external rewards and significant parental and peer-group recognition. As discussed earlier, being a successful athlete is a highly coveted status among junior and senior high school students. Unfortunately, the measure of success is often calculated within a highly structured and competitive sports system.

For better or worse, much of organized sports is based on competition and a "survival of the fittest" mentality. As individuals progress through the various levels of competition and winning takes on more importance, playing time and opportunities to prove oneself are often reserved for the more skillful performers. Athletes are required to devote more time and energy to sports in efforts to maintain their level of achievement. By the time most athletes reach high school, however, the external rewards associated with athletic success have taken on larger importance and correlate with a number of positive psychosocial traits. Typically, successful high school athletes experience strong feelings of accomplishment and gain a sense of identity due to their sports achievements [Nelson 1983].

For many teenagers, sports team membership provides a healthy gang experience that satisfies many of the requirements for enhanced psychosocial development that were identified in the Carnegie Great Transitions Report [1995] described earlier. Ironically, there are many aspects of the sports system and athletic experience that can seriously restrict the potential of sports to have a positive effect on the development of personal and social competence and several of these are outlined in the next section.

Potential Disadvantages of Sports Participation

Much of the popularity of sports can be attributed to the belief that sports builds character and enhances children's physical, social, and psychological development [Martens 1986]. Unfortunately, it is probably more accurate to say that the value of sports participation for individuals is dependent on their experiences and resources, the philosophy of the sports organization, the quality of coaching and other types of support, and the nature of parental involvement [Danish, et al. 1993; Smith & Smoll 1996; Weiss 1995].

The most critical problem affecting the potential of sports to be a vehicle to promote social competence is the high attrition rate in youth sports involvement. It is estimated that 50% of youth sports participants discontinue their involvement by the time they reach middle adolescence [Ewing et al. 1996]. Researchers suggest that children participate in sports to have fun, be with friends, belong to a team, get in shape, and learn and demonstrate their skills [e.g., Gould & Petlichkoff 1988; Weiss & Chaumeton 1992]. For the most part, these reasons for participating are intrinsically motivated, but they are likely to be incompatible with those sports systems that are based on competition, and value winning more than cooperation. If children are not having fun or getting enough playing time, dislike their coaches, or feel too much competitive pressure, they are likely to discontinue their sports involvement [LeUnes & Nation 1983; Weiss 1995].

Of concern is the increasingly competitive nature of youth sports, particularly for younger children who have not reached a level of cognitive maturity that would allow them to understand or feel comfortable with the competitive process [Ewing et al. 1996]. Children under the age of ten are likely to perform better in noncompetitive conditions [Butt 1987] and rely on coach and parental feedback to evaluate their competence [Horn & Weiss 1991]. Ironically, it is estimated that less than 10% of youth sports coaches have any formal coaching education or training in how to evaluate and give feedback about age-related sports performance [Partlow 1995]. Furthermore, inappropriate comments and feedback from coaches have been linked to a broad range of negative outcomes in youth sports participants including distorted body image, lowered self-esteem, and increased self-doubt [Weiss 1995].

As children enter their teen years, peer comparisons and evaluations replace parental feedback as the primary source of competence information [Horn & Weiss 1991]. Teenagers do not want to look bad in front of their peers, and they are likely to react quite strongly to negative comments or feedback given by coaches in front of their teammates [Smith et al. 1979]. At the same time, teenagers want to improve their skills, and they are apt to respond most favorably to a combination of positive reinforcement and corrective information [Weiss 1995]. Those individuals who excel earn the limited spots on highly desirable high school or elite amateur sports teams and derive many psychosocial benefits. Those who are not deemed skillful enough to make the team are likely to discontinue their sports participation at this time rather than "lowering" themselves by playing in intramural or recreational leagues [Ewing et al. 1996]. As a consequence, teenagers between 13 and 16 years of age display the highest sports dropout levels.

Although the literature suggests that there are many benefits to sports participation including higher school grades, increased self-esteem, and better interpersonal skills, there is danger that too much emphasis on sports may be detrimental, particularly for older teenagers [Petitpas & Champagne 1988]. As students move into late adolescence, their developmental tasks shift from gaining a sense of industry and competence to a search for a personal identity. According to developmental theorists [Erikson 1959; Marcia et al. 1993], identity development requires two activities. First, individuals must engage in exploratory behavior in order to investigate the merits of various careers, lifestyles, and other alternatives of adult life. Second, they must make a commitment to those occupational and ideological alternatives that are most consistent with their values, needs, interests, and skills. It is the first of these two tasks, exploratory behavior, that may not be compatible with a sports system that demands conformity and requires such large amounts of time and effort.

High school sports programs promote conformity and compliance to dominant community values rather than provide participants with opportunities to engage in exploratory behavior [Ewing et al. 1996; Schafer 1971]. Research has shown that a strong and exclusive focus on sports may leave some athletes vulnerable to several psychosocial problems [Brewer 1993]. There is evidence that the dream of a professional sports career, coupled with the personal, social, and even financial rewards that come from athletic successes, often result in an overemphasis on sports involvement at the expense of the exploratory behavior that is necessary for optimal educational, career, and personal development [Murphy, Petitpas, & Brewer 1996]. It is through exploratory behavior that individuals develop coping skills and resources that allow them to become self-sufficient and better able to handle life challenges [Jordaan 1963]. Ironically, high school and college sports often promote compliance and conformity rather than leadership [Ewing et al. 1996]. Therefore, instead of developing independence, many athletes relinquish their ability to make decisions and blindly adhere to team rules and coaching mandates [LeUnes & Nation 1983].

Another potential problem is that sports is built on a premise that participants will learn valuable life skills that will serve them well throughout life. If student athletes do not understand what transferable skills they are learning through sports or if they lack the knowledge or confidence necessary to use these skills in other domains (e.g., academic and career preparation), they are not likely to realize any benefits from these skills in other areas [Danish et al. 1993]. The research literature suggests that high school athletes, particularly football, basketball, and hockey players, are often underprepared to enter college or the work place [Kennedy & Dimick 1987]. They typically do not understand what skills they have acquired through sports or how to use them in academic or work settings. To make matters worse, athletes are frequently overprotected and overindulged by a sports system that values them primarily for their athletic abilities [Lanning 1982]. As a result, many athletes have developed a sense of entitlement that hinders motivation to work hard outside of their sports participation and may preclude the development of many transferable skills [Petitpas & Champagne 1988].

What Can Be Done to Assist Individuals in Getting the Most out of Their Sports Participation?

Several national organizations, including the American Counseling Association and the National Association of Student Personnel Administrators, have identified the need for school and community-based specialized support services for student-athletes. Few training resources are available, however, for teachers, coaches, or others who want to guide these talented youth to responsible adulthood. Furthermore, most programs that have tried to address various health-compromising behaviors (e.g., substance abuse) for the general school population have not been successful. According to Shakeh Kaftarian, Director of the National Center for the Advancement of Prevention, "You can't just pull any program off the shelf and hope it works. Programs need to be collaborative efforts where community leaders, school personnel, and program specialists update, tweak, and tailor existing programs to make them work [Murray 1997, p. 30]."

Therefore, even though sports participation can be a means of acquiring valuable life skills, there are no guarantees that this will happen. In fact, the media often highlights examples of athletes who are modeling unhealthy behaviors (e.g., violence, substance abuse, gambling). How can we insure that young people gain the benefits of sports participation and how can athletes return to their place as positive role models? This is a complex question, but several authors have provided information that is helpful in planning program initiatives. It has been shown that:

- Athletes tend to have an external locus of control and coaches frequently have the strongest adult influence on their behavior [LeUnes & Nation 1983].

- Athletes who engage in leadership roles outside of sports typically display the highest levels of career and personal maturity [Danish et al. 1996].

- Pre-packaged intervention programs have not had good records of success in addressing the various health-compromising behaviors that confront young people today [Murray 1997].

- Athletes who understand and experience how the skills that they have acquired through sports transfer to other domains of life (e.g., academics and career preparation) make the smoothest school to work transition [Danish et al. 1990].

- Athletes have the highest social status among their junior and senior high school peers [Weiss 1996].

- Nonacademic variables such as realistic self-appraisal, positive self-concept, and community involvement are the best predictors of college academic performance and graduation rates for student-athletes, particularly minority athletes [Sedlacek & Adams-Gaston 1992].

Extrapolating from these research findings, it appears that linking young people up with caring adult mentors, helping them identify transferable skills, giving them leadership roles outside of sports, and educating their parents about the role of sports in building social competence offers a sound foundation for intervention efforts targeting youth sports participants. In the following sections, some suggestions for the need and content of youth sports coach and parent education programs are provided and a sample intervention program that is based on these research findings is described. The primary goals of these programs are to enhance the likelihood that sports participation will have a positive effect on youth development and make membership on sports teams a healthy alternative to gang involvement.

Coach Education

Coaches have a significant amount of adult influence on sports participants and they need to understand the importance of the role they play in fostering self-esteem and feelings of personal competence among their team members. Unfortunately, even though there are several coach education programs, including the American Coaching Effectiveness Program [Martens 1987], National Youth Sport Coaches Association [Brown & Butterfield 1992], and Coach Effectiveness Training [Smith, Smoll, & Curtis 1979], available to assist volunteer coaches in learning the skills necessary to facilitate a positive learning experience for youth sports participants, it is estimated that less than 10% of volunteer coaches receive any formal training to work with this population [Ewing et al. 1996]. In many communities, particularly in inner city locations, it is difficult to get sufficient numbers of people who are willing to volunteer their time to coach. As a result, most youth sports coaches are parents of participants and have little time or interest in investing significant time and energy to go through a formal coach education program. Parents who coach often stop their involvement as soon as their children move on to higher levels or school based sports.

Communities that attempt to mandate formal coach education training as a prerequisite for a coaching position run the risk of not having enough coaches to service their youth. On the other hand, failure to provide adequate youth sports coach education can have significant consequences in terms of quality of coaching that will ultimately affect the participants' drop-out rates [Smith & Smoll 1996]. This dilemma confronts many communities, particularly those with limited financial resources. Several of the established youth sports education programs are expensive and would require a substantial financial investment on the part of individuals or community organizations. If youth do not have opportunities to participate in constructive afterschool activities, however, they are more likely to become involved in unhealthy and sometimes criminal behaviors. In either case, community leaders need to be educated about the potential advantages and disadvantages of mandated coach education programs.

In many communities, coach education consists of a single organizational meeting in which coaches are provided with schedules, rules, and information about the mission and philosophy of the sports program. These meetings are opportunities, however, to provide information to coaches that can assist them in understanding the importance of their role in the lives of the young people they instruct. Among the many topics that can be addressed are creating a positive learning environment, giving feedback, and structuring activities to promote fun.

In cases where a lack of financial resources precludes the use of established coach education programs, it is possible to tap into local resources available through high schools, colleges, or universities. For example, many colleges have established sports psychology or academic-athletic advisement programs that have professionals or advanced graduate students who could provide basic coach education or work directly with youth sports coaches to enhance their effectiveness in teaching important life skills to their participants. There are a number of professionals who are willing to donate their services pro bono and many students are able to gain academic credit through internships or service learning contracts. Although these professional and student volunteers may not be able to offer the depth of coverage found in the established youth sports coach education programs identified earlier, they can provide workshops, reading materials, and other affordable alternatives to mandated programs. Recommendations for content areas include:

- How to give constructive feedback to participants of differing ages and across genders;
- How to create an environment where cooperation and enjoyment are valued more than competition;
- How to create activities or modify sports rules (e.g., lowering height of basket for younger basketball players) that provide opportunities for youth of all ability levels to participate and gain a sense of enjoyment and competence;
- How to teach life skills and sports skills simultaneously;

- How to recognize and take advantage of teachable moments;
- How to develop individual goals for each participant that both challenge them and provide opportunities to gain success experiences;
- How to reward risk taking and effort in a manner that is not perceived as false praise;
- How to teach parents strategies that will enable them to reinforce the positive life skills that are learned through sports;
- How to use feedback and evaluations to improve one's skills; and
- How to serve as a role model and mentor for other coaches.

Communities should not only actively recruit potential youth sports coaches and consultants, but also consider strategies to retain their services. Many youth sports coaches believe that they are not sufficiently appreciated by players' parents or by others in the community. Volunteer coaches often commit large amounts of time and effort to their coaching roles, only to become the brunt of verbal abuse by fans or irate parents who believe that their son or daughter is not being treated fairly. If coaches are not having fun or do not feel valued, it is likely that they will discontinue their volunteer services. Therefore, community and youth sports organization leaders would be wise to plan strategies to reinforce positive coaching behaviors and to publicly recognize and honor effective and caring coaches.

When bringing in outside consultants, it is important to get the input and support of the more experienced coaches. If these coaches are part of the planning process, it is less likely that they will see consultants or youth sports coach educators as threats. In addition, using the expertise of the more experienced coaches allows them to feel special, and their buy-in to program goals is often a critical factor in efforts to achieve desired outcomes. Consultants must build effective working relationships with both coaches and parents.

Educating Parents

Parents have the potential to enhance social competence in their athlete children or to hinder that process because of their involvement or over-involvement in their children's athletic experiences. Booster clubs have been the traditional mechanism by which parents have organized themselves in support of youth sports. As organized bodies, booster clubs provide one of the few opportunities for gathering parents together for sessions that may provide educational programs about the developmental needs of young athletes. A scan of booster club activities on the Internet shows little in the way of educational programs for parents, however. At best, after planning fund-raisers, sports program brochures, award banquets, and drives for new uniforms and equipment, only a few booster clubs will offer informational sessions to their members. These programs are typically related to NCAA regulations or league policies.

Programs offered through organizations such as booster clubs can provide information to parents about developmental issues facing young athletes that can make a difference in how sports affect their children. Booster clubs may also attract other sports enthusiasts and spectators, such as former coaches and grandparents, who would not only benefit from this information but also add to the discussion during the program. The content and format of these programs will depend on the nature and needs of the athlete population and the availability of the parents and other participants. In planning the content of such educational programs, a number of factors should be taken into consideration. These include: the ages of the athlete population (young children or adolescents); the type of athletic involvement (recreational, intramural, or interscholastic); the type of sport (soccer, gymnastics, or basketball); and the nature of the community (rural, suburban, or urban). Each of these factors can influence the level of competition experienced by the young athletes, the quality of coaching available, and the status of athletic participation. Parents' and children's' perceptions of athletic experiences will be formed on the basis of some of these variables and will affect the educational needs of the parents who might participate in educational programs. For example, a large suburban high school may have a highly competitive sports program, from which many professional athletes have evolved. Children in this environment may be challenged to strive for goals related to professional sports at an early age. Parents may become caught up in the professional athlete dream as well, placing pressure on their young children to excel in sports over all other endeavors. On the other hand, parents of athletes who participate in less competitive programs in recreational settings or in small towns may not be as driven by the athletic dream for their children. The needs of both parent groups would be somewhat different. Program content that al-lowed for a discussion about parents' expectations for their chil-dren in sports would be important in both situations, but a greater emphasis might be placed on this type of discussion in a more competitive environment.

In determining sports parents' educational needs, their willing-ness to participate, and their availability, a simple survey can be conducted by handing out one-page questionnaires at booster meet-ings or at the entrance to sports events. Preferred meeting times and places should be included in the questionnaire as well as potential topic areas. These topics may include: "Helping your child deal with frustration in sports", "Putting sports in perspective," "Who is the coach?", "Helping your child find career goals outside of sports," or "Real world sports: The realities of college and professional athlet-ics." Topics for the parents of younger children may include: "Get-ting off on the right foot: your child and sports", "Mom and Dad on the sidelines", "Youth sports and self-esteem", or "Talking to your child about sports". Even in the briefest of formats, opportunities should exist to discuss parents' expectations for their children in sports and children's developmental needs.

Preferences about program format (workshop series, single workshop, discussion group, support group, or keynote speaker) can also be listed. Decisions about the program format will be highly dependent upon the availability of the participants. Although a series of workshops that covers a broad range of developmental topics may be highly desirable, it might be overwhelming to busy parents who are struggling to meet the demands of their own lives and their children's athletic schedules. Survey results would be particularly helpful in assessing parents' willingness to attend such programs. Marketing the program will be an important step in making the program successful and will require the cooperation of key parents who champion the cause of the program. Fliers handed out at competitive events are obvious publicity tools, while the booster club home page may be a newer advertising vehicle.

Experienced coaches, athletic counselors, consultants, and parents who have received training may be facilitators of these educational programs. Area universities or colleges may be good resources for enlisting the services of consultants who are knowledgeable about and experienced in areas related to adolescent development and sports participation.

Technology offers new opportunities to educate parents and provide information about the needs of young athletes. Sports Parents, a supplement to Sports Illustrated for Kids, is now accessible through Sports Parents On-line, an Internet version of the hard copy publication. It offers tips to parents on such topics as "The balancing act: how to help your child juggle sports, school, and life" and "When push comes to shove: encouraging your child is fine, but don't overdo it". Discussion groups for parents are also available on line and lists of books for parents concerning their athlete children are easily obtained through the Internet. Coaches, athletic directors, recreation directors, and parent groups can give out information about these resources.

A Sample Program – The National Football Foundation's Play It Smart

Play It Smart is a school-based program funded by the National Football Foundation (NFF) that seeks to use the sports experience as a vehicle to enhance the academic, athletic, career, and personal development of high school student-athletes. Participation in a sport is viewed as a cocurricula activity that provides caring adult leadership, membership in a constructive group, and opportunities to test one's abilities and to learn how to rely on others. The goal of the program is to demonstrate that the right kind of sports experiences can provide participants with opportunities to learn about themselves and to develop skills that will not only enhance their current athletic and academic performance, but also better prepare them for productive futures.

The program is based in a life developmental framework that emphasizes continual growth and change [Danish et al. 1993]. This educational approach focuses on optimization and enhancement of skills, rather than on the remediation of pathological, health compromising, or criminal behaviors. Participants are assisted in identifying their transferable skills and learning how to use these skills in academic preparation, in developing and maintaining productive relationships, and in gaining confidence in their abilities to function effectively in the world of work. Both individual and team goal setting are used to enable participants to see possible futures and to gain the social support that is often required to form healthy habits and achieve life successes.

The pilot phase of the Play It Smart project targets student-athletes who are playing football in four inner city high schools. These four schools were selected because they lacked many of the financial and support resources available in more affluent communities. The vast majority of the student-athletes are from minority and economically disadvantaged backgrounds and live in neighborhoods with high crime and school dropout rates. As a group, they have grade point averages ranging from 68 and 72, and there is a considerable attrition rate in football participation, particularly during freshman year. Those student athletes who play football for four years, however, have a significantly higher graduation rate than their nonathlete peers.

The Play It Smart program was created to take advantage of the voluntary nature of sports participation and designed in accordance with knowledge gained from previous research and intervention efforts. Therefore, the goal of the project is to strengthen the team identity as well as provide support and skill-building activities for individual participants. For example, because of the importance of providing individuals with a valued place within a constructive group, it was necessary to understand the norms and belief system of each team. It each case, the aim is to establish a team value system in which teamwork, sportsmanship, respect for rules, and community service are set as standards.

Changing group norms is difficult work. The Play It Smart program seeks to use the unique status of coaches and team leaders to meet this challenge. Each school has been provided with an academic coach who works directly with the coaches and team leaders to design team building and group activities (e.g., ropes courses and community service) to foster constructive group norms and pride in team membership. Activities are individualized for each site and take advantage of the collaborative efforts of the team leaders and the resources of the local community and NFF chapter. Academic coaches are professionals who have training and experience in providing counseling and support services to student-athletes. They assist the head coaches by facilitating communication and collaboration among school personnel, parents, community leaders, and students. For example, each site has a "Parent Night" in which the parents or guardians of the participants are given materials about the goals of the Play It Smart program, provided information about college and vocational preparation, and encouraged to get involved in Booster Clubs. During Parent Night events, individuals who have achieved academic successes, provided exemplary community service, or made significant contributions to the Play It Smart program are honored.

In addition to the group activities, academic coaches assist student-athletes by helping them identify their values, needs, interests, and skills. Once this is accomplished, specific academic, athletic, career, and community service goals are developed. The academic coach then monitors progress and provides the resources and support needed to overcome any roadblocks to goal attainment. In each case, the goal setting program is linked to an individualized incentive plan that is based on the student-athlete's particular wish list. The incentive program is a reward for hitting goal targets and not entitlement. Student-athletes are also supported in securing leadership roles outside of sports to help them gain confidence in their abilities to transfer their athletic skills to other domains.

The success of the Play It Smart program is based on the achievement of a series of outcome measures, including (a) improvements in grade point averages, Scholastic Aptitude Test scores, and graduation rates; (b) increased involvement in community service activities; and (c) reduction in the use of alcohol and other drugs. These outcome measures are typically dependent on a series of process behaviors. For example, academic improvements typically require four specific behaviors: attend all classes, take organized notes, turn in assignments on time, and take tests on time. Therefore, academic coaches provide their student athletes with ongoing feedback about the specific behaviors necessary to achieve their goals, and these behaviors are reinforced by the coach and team leaders.

Although the pilot program targets football players who come from inner-city high schools, the NFF seeks to identify strategies that can be easily transported to all student-athletes regardless of sport, gender, or community resources available. The overriding aim is to enhance the sports experience in order to make the kind of activity that promotes social and personal development. As described in the Play It Smart business plan [National Football Foundation 1998]: "To accomplish this mission, individuals must belong to teams that encourage risk taking, that value effort as much as outcomes, that appreciate what players with differing skills and styles can bring to a team effort, and that create an environment that supports each individual's personal and athletic development [p. 6]."

Conclusions

With appropriate management and guidance, sports participation appears to be well-positioned to serve as a potential vehicle for developing social competence and for deterring destructive behaviors in youth. Although there seems to be some negative outcomes associated with sports participation, these negatives appear to be outweighed by the positive impact sports can have on the personal and social development of youth in areas that the Carnegie Council has identified as being significant for today's young people. As a positive "gang" experience, sports has the potential to help children and youth find valued places in constructive groups and develop life skills that go beyond the bounds of their sports participation.

Because of the inconsistency in the outcomes of youth sports as we run them today, caution needs to be exercised and purposeful planning needs to be added in our current youth sports programs. Intervention strategies and programs can be and have been added to youth sports programs that assist athletes in getting the most out of their sports experience. These strategies provide education and support to athletes, coaches, and parents in the form of training, coaching, teaching, advising, and counseling activities. One such program is the National Football Foundation's Play It Smart program that targets individual athletes and uses academic coaches to assist young athletes with academic, career, and life-kill development. Other programs targeted at coaches and parents provide education about the dangers of an overemphasis on sports to the exclusion of other life domains and of a win-at-all-cost sport's ethic that can be detrimental to children in their development.

In conclusion, it would be naïve to suggest that by simply participating in sports, children and adolescents can acquire the skills necessary to succeed in life. Sports participation does provide, however, numerous opportunities for youth to learn about themselves, to take risks, and to be involved in a positive gang experience. It is now up to professional educators, community leaders, and funding sources to provide the educational, training, and financial resources required to ensure that all of our young people have access to the right kind of sports activities and the availability of skillful and caring adult mentors.

References

Brewer, B. W. (1993). Self-identity and specific vulnerability to depressed mood. *Journal of Personality, 61*, 343–364.

Brown, B. R., & Butterfield, S. A. (1992). Coaches: A missing link in the health care system. *American Journal of Diseases in Childhood, 146*, 211–217.

Butt, D. S. (1987). *Psychology of sport: The behavior, motivation, personality, and performance of athletes*, (2nd ed.). New York: Van Nostrand Reinhold.

Carnegie Council. (1995). *Great transitions: Preparing adolescents for a new century*. New York: Carnegie Corporation.

Coleman, J. S. (1961). *The adolescent society*. New York: The Free Press.

Danish, S. J., Nellen, V. C., & Owens, S. S. (1996). Teaching life skills through sport: Community-based programs for adolescents. In J.L. Van Raalte & B. W. Brewer (Eds.), *Exploring sport and exercise psychology* (pp. 205–225). Washington, DC: American Psychological Association.

Danish, S.J., Petitpas, A.J., & Hale, B.D. (1990). Sport as a context for developing competence. In T. Gullotta, G. Adams, & R. Montemayor (Eds.), *Developing social competency in adolescence* (Vol. 3) (pp. 169–194). Newbury Park, CA: Sage.

Danish, S., Petitpas, A., & Hale, B. (1993). Life development interventions with athletes: Life skills through sports. *The Counseling Psychologist, 21*, 352–385.

Eitzen, D.S. (1975). Athletics in the status system of male adolescents: A replication of Coleman's The Adolescent Society. *Adolescence, 10*, 267–276.

Erikson, E.H. (1959). Identity and the life cycle: Selected papers. *Psychological Issues, 1*, 1–171.

Ewing, M.E., Seefeldt, V.D., & Brown, T.P. (1996). Role of organized sport in the education and health of American children and youth. In A. Poinsett (Ed.), *The role of sports in youth development* (pp. 1–157). New York: Carnegie Corporation.

Gould, D., Feltz D. L., Horn, T., & Weiss, M. (1982). Reasons for discontinuing involvement in competitive youth swimming. *Journal of Sport Behavior, 5*, 155–165.

Gould, D. & Petlichkoff, L. M. (1988). Participation motivation and attrition in young athletes. In F. Smoll, R. Magill, & M. Ash (Eds.), *Children in sport* (3rd ed., pp. 161–178). Champaign, IL: Human Kinetics.

Horn, T. S. & Weiss, M. R. (1991). A developmental analysis of children's self-ability judgements in the physical domain. *Pediatric Exercise Science, 3*, 310–326.

Huff, C. R. (1996). *Gangs in America* (2nd ed.). Thousand Oaks, CA: Sage.

Jordaan, J. P. (1963). Exploratory behavior: The foundation of self and occupational concepts. In D. E. Super, R. Starishevsky, N. Matlin, & J. P. Jordaan (Eds.), *Career development: Self-concept theory* (pp. 46–57). New York: CEEB Research Monographs.

Kennedy, S. R. & Dimick, K. M. (1987). Career maturity and professional expectations of college football and basketball players. *Journal of College Student Personnel, 28*, 293–297.

Lanning, W. (1982). The privileged few: Special counseling needs of athletes. *Journal of Sport Psychology, 4*, 19–23.

LeUnes, A. & Nation, J. R. (1983). Saturday's heroes: A psychological portrait of college football players. *Journal of Sport Behavior, 5,* 139–149.

LeUnes, A. D. & Nation, J. R. (1989). *Sport psychology: An introduction.* Chicago: Nelson-Hall.

Marcia, J.E., Waterman, A. S., Matteson, D. R., Archer, S. L., & Orlofsky, J. L. (1993). *Ego identity: A handbook for psychological research.* New York: Springer-Verlag.

Martens, R. (1986). Youth sports in the USA. In M. R. Weiss & D. Gould (Eds.), *Sport for children and youths* (pp. 27–33). Champaign, IL: Human Kinetics.

Martens, R. (1987). *American coaching effectiveness program: Level 1 instructor guide* (2nd Ed.). Champaign, IL: Human Kinetics.

McPherson, B. D., Curtis, J. E., & Loy, J. W. (1989). *The social significance of sport: An introduction to the sociology of sport.* Champaign, IL: Human Kinetics.

Murphy, G. M., Petitpas, A. J., & Brewer, B. W. (1996). Identity foreclosure, athletic identity, and career maturity in intercollegiate athletes. *The Sport Psychologist, 10,* 239–246.

Murray, B. (1997, September). Why aren't antidrug programs working? *APA Monitor, 30.*

National Football Foundation. (1998). *Play It Smart: Business plan.* Morristown, NJ: National Football Foundation.

Nelson, E. S. (1983). How the myth of the dumb jock becomes fact: A developmental view for counselors. *Counseling and Values, 27,* 176–185.

Partlow, K. (1995). *Interscholastic coaching: From accidental occupation to profession.* Champaign, IL: American Sport Education Program.

Petitpas, A. & Champagne, D. E. (1988). Developmental programming for intercollegiate athletes. *Journal of College Student Development, 29,* 454–460.

Poinsett, A. (1996). *The role of sports in youth development.* New York: Carnegie Corporation.

Schafer, W. (1971). *Sport socialization and the school.* Paper presented at the Third International Symposium on the Sociology of Sport, Waterloo, Canada.

Sedlacek, W. E. & Adams-Gaston, J. (1992). Predicting the academic success of student-athletes using SAT and noncognitive variables. *Journal of Counseling and Development, 70,* 724–727.

Shelden, G. R., Tracy, S. K., & Brown, W. B. (1996). *Youth gangs and American society.* Belmont, CA: Wadsworth Publishing.

Smith, R. E. & Smoll, F. L. (1996). Psychosocial interventions in youth sport. In J. L. Van Raalte & B.W. Brewer (Eds.), *Exploring sport and exercise psychology* (pp. 287–315). Washington, DC: American Psychological Association.

Smith, R. E., Smoll, F. L., & Curtis, B. (1979). Coach effectiveness training: A cognitive-behavioral approach to enhancing relationship skills in youth sport coaches. *Journal of Sport Psychology, 1,* 59–75.

Spengel, I. A. (1995). *The youth gang problem: A community approach.* New York: Oxford University Press.

Weiss, M. R. (1995). Children in sport: An educational model. In S. M. Murphy (Ed.), *Sport psychology interventions* (pp. 39–69). Champaign, IL: Human Kinetics.

Weiss, M. R., & Chaumeton, N. (1992). Motivational orientations in sport. In T. S. Horn (Ed.), *Advances in sport psychology* (pp. 61–99). Champaign, IL: Human Kinetics.

White, R. W. (1959). Motivation reconsidered: The concept of competence. *Psychological Review, 66,* 297–323.

White, R. W. (1963). Ego and reality in psychoanalytic theory: A proposal regarding independent ego energies. *Psychological Issues, 3,* Monograph 11. New York: International University.

5

Girls on the Edge: Rethinking Out-Of-School Programs for Adolescent Girls

Joann Stemmermann & Janice Antonellis

"Nurturing a young girl's unique strength and spirit—while focusing her ability to see (and rise above) cultural limits—are the most powerful weapons in the struggle for self-esteem as she grows toward her adolescence" [Mackoff 1996, p. xxxv]. In many cultures, the transition from girlhood to womanhood is considered to be a difficult one—a perception that is supported by some of our oldest stories and symbols. Persephone's exile in the "Underworld" and separation from her mother, Snow White's poison apple, and Sleeping Beauty's long sleep all strike responsive chords as they evoke the struggles of adolescence. Despite the advances made by the modern women's movement, they still speak to the experiences of the young women entrusted to our care. The voice of Ann Frank, one of the most famous modern adolescents, still echoes over 50 years after she asked this question in her diary: "Which of the people here would suspect that so much is going on in the mind of a teenage girl?" [Frank 1996, p. 169]. She speaks for all adolescent girls "on the edge" of womanhood.

The 1992 publication of *How Schools Shortchange Girls*, the report of the American Association of University Women (AAUW), conducted by the Wellesley College Center for Research on Women, piqued national concern around gender bias and the inequities in public education for girls. Concurrently, a critical mass of new research on girls' development was entering into the awareness of psychologists and educators. Work conducted by Carol Gilligan and her colleagues at the Harvard Project on the Psychology of Women and Girls' Development described the transition from childhood to adolescence as a time of "heightened psychological risk" in girls' lives. They pointed out that girls at this time can "lose their vitality, their resilience, their immunity to depression, their sense of themselves and their character" [Brown & Gilligan 1992, p. 2].

The combined impact of the gender bias and developmental research launched a concern for and interest in girls' development and education that was unprecedented. Questions first raised by academics were engaged by the wider public when Mary Pipher's *Reviving Ophelia* became a New York Times #1 bestseller, and television news and talk shows provided a forum for the discussion. Even more significant, in response, parents, educators, researchers, agencies, and girls have taken up work toward improving the understanding of girls' development and the ways in which this understanding impacts their education. All of these endeavors are resulting in trained, gender-aware teachers, educational programs that prioritize girls' needs both in school and during out-of-school time, funding for girls' math and science programs, cooperative learning environments, mentoring programs, and opportunities for girls to take up leadership roles.

As educators whose own practice was profoundly affected by the implications of this exciting new research, we formed The Center for Ventures in Girls' Education. The core of this enterprise is a journey of discovery about what girls experience and how they learn best. The Center has a broad mission: to redesign, practice, and articulate models and methods of teaching and learning that prioritize girls' needs, to raise educators' awareness of the ways in which girls are different, and to contribute to the growing body of knowledge on girls' development. The girl-centered experience-based adventure program model we have created infuses the new research on girls' development and gender bias into a traditional adventure program model. This process of bringing theory to practice through trial and error is at best imprecise and, to our knowledge, because of funding and institutional constraints, few program designers and organizations have had either the time or the freedom to experiment with new ideas.

When it was published, the Ms. Foundation's report, *Programmed Neglect: Not Seen, Not Heard*, pointed out the inadequacy of programming on a national level that addressed the complex issues that girls face today. They found that the programs they investigated tended to treat the symptom rather than explore the deeper, structural problems of inequality and lack of opportunity [Ms. Foundation 1993, pp. 3-5]. A similar critique has been leveled recently at the trend to counter the gender bias rife in schools by promoting all girl schools and creating girl only classes in coed schools. These efforts "relieve pressure on the system" without necessarily making substantive change which would create a truly fair and equal environment [AAUW 1998, p. 9]. Many organizations and schools have adopted the language of this research into their marketing literature, but truly embodying these ideas in action is a challenging, gradual, and ongoing process. The head of a thriving private girls' school once remarked, "Just because we are a girls' school doesn't mean we are doing it right." In the light of all of this, we have taken up the exciting and daunting challenge of translating research into practice and of trying to deepen our understanding of how to do it effectively.

The intention of this chapter is to acquaint the reader with the field of girls' development and gender bias research, to discuss our experiences translating this theory into practice, to summarize what we have learned from our work, and to invite others to take up the work of re-thinking other educational models.

Research Overview

> Every girl is asked to give up parts of herself as the price of entrance into the adult world. [Ms. Foundation 1993, p. 13]

The Harvard Project on the Psychology of Women and Girls' Development

Although we have always known that 'something' happens to girls as they reach adolescence, researchers began their formal attempts to document and explain it only in the last twenty-five to thirty years. There are two fields of investigation which have come together to give a fuller portrait of girls' experiences: developmental psychology and gender bias.

Dr. Carol Gilligan and her colleagues at the Harvard Project on the Psychology of Women and Girls' Development, have been pioneers in the field of girls' developmental psychology. In their book, *Meeting At The Crossroads*, Lyn Mikel Brown and Carol Gilligan described the transition from childhood to adolescence as a time of crisis in girls' lives. They write that this period creates disconnections that can leave girls psychologically at risk. According to Brown and Gilligan, early adolescence is when girls get subtle messages from the culture dictating who they are supposed to be— "the perfect girl"—rather than encouraging them to be who they truly are [Brown & Gilligan 1992, pp. 4, 58-59].

This choice to be the "perfect girl" can have problematic effects, which can lead to such behaviors as depression and eating disorders [Brown & Gilligan 1992, pp. 58-59]. Girls are forced to struggle between who they are "supposed" to be and who they really are. As a result, they dissociate from their real selves and repress their true feelings [Brown & Gilligan 1992, p. 4]. They have difficulty speaking about what they know, they cover over what they know (especially knowledge that is unacceptable in our culture), and they silence themselves. They also begin to feel unheard and to have difficulty believing in their own experience. All of this leads to the well-publicized "loss of voice." A culture that does not value or listen to girls' perspectives forces them to take their voices "underground." [Brown & Gilligan 1992, p. 10] In another diary entry, Ann Frank wrote, "I've told you more about myself and my feelings than I've ever told a living soul..." [Frank 1996, p. 222] Like Ann, girls are still made to feel that their true feelings are dangerous and threatening and that they make other people uncomfortable. They would rather utter the ubiquitous "I don't know" in answer to questions than risk exposing what they really think.

Girls and the Culture

One of the most powerful messages of the research and of all the subsequent writing on the plight of adolescent girls has been the exhortation to turn a critical lens on the culture. Mary Pipher has been one of the most eloquent proponents of the importance of shifting our focus from trying to fix what's wrong with girls to looking at what's wrong with the culture that puts girls at risk. In *Reviving Ophelia: Saving The Selves of Adolescent Girls*, Pipher, drawing on her work as a therapist, describes what girls are up against:

> Something dramatic happens to girls in early adolescence. Just as planes and ships disappear mysteriously into the Bermuda Triangle, so do the selves of girls go down in droves. They crash and burn in the developmental Bermuda Triangle...They lose their resiliency and optimism and become less curious and inclined to take risks. They lose their assertive, energetic and 'tomboyish' personalities and become more deferential, self-critical and depressed. They report great unhappiness with their own bodies." [Pipher 1994, pp. 19–20]

According to Pipher, girls are vulnerable because of the physical and emotional changes they are undergoing. In addition, they are trying to understand their place in a culture that is "rife with sexism, capitalism and lookism", and that defines maturity as separation from the people whose support they most need [Pipher 1994, pp. 20-24, 81]. Increasingly, girls get the message, especially through the media, that they must conform to an impossible idealized image of womanhood.

Gender Bias in Schools

While Gilligan and her colleagues have illuminated the interior landscape of adolescence, the late Myra Sadker, and her husband, David, of The American University in Washington, D.C., have described the landscape of gender bias through which girls travel in our schools. Because the school is a microcosm of the larger society, what goes on there has a profound effect. In their book, *Failing At Fairness*, they outlined the situation:

> Today's schoolgirls face subtle and insidious gender lessons, micro-inequities that appear seemingly insignificant when looked at individually but that have a powerful cumulative impact. These inequities chip away at girls'

achievement and self-esteem. The crucial question now is, 'How do these hidden lessons shortchange girls and women as they study along with boys and men?' [Sadker 1994, p. ix]

In conducting their research, the Sadkers examined the "pervasive sexism" in textbooks, and spent thousands of hours observing classrooms. They uncovered "an even more powerful hidden curriculum" in the interactions between teachers and students and among students themselves [Sadker 1994, p. ix].

The Sadkers' research was one of the foundations of the widely publicized report from the American Association of University Women (AAUW), How Schools Shortchange Girls. This "thorough literature review on the subject of girls and education" [AAUW 1992, p. ix] revealed that on average boys receive four times the amount of teacher attention as girls, that boys tend to dominate class discussions while girls tend to be silent, that teaching methods and testing techniques tend to be biased against girls, and that the greatest drop in girls' self-esteem occurs during the middle school years [AAUW 1991, p. 4].

Both the research in gender bias and developmental psychology point to the same conclusions. Because adolescent girls experience losses in self-esteem, achievement, goals and authentic voice, they are vulnerable to a range of at-risk behaviors. These include moodiness, discord with parents, underachievement, school refusal, depression, sexual harassment and abuse, eating disorders, early parenting, and drug and alcohol abuse. In the face of such clear evidence of their vulnerability, the only appropriate response is to look for solutions that will truly support girls as they move through adolescence.

Identifying the Psychologically Healthy Girl

Egyptian Pharaohs were believed to have chosen nine-year-old girls as companions, because they were so interesting and lively, and historians of ancient Greece record that girls of nine left their mothers and were initiated into the service of the...huntress Artemis, known for her...wildness and strength." [Elium & Elium 1994, p. 274]

Although we are aware of the difficulties girls face, it is important to keep in mind a clear picture of what young girls are like before they hit the "wall" of the culture during adolescence. Who are they when they are in the fullness of their power, somewhere between the ages of eight and twelve? Emily Hancock in her book, *The Girl Within*, fills out the picture of this wild, strong, energetic and spontaneous girl with such descriptors as "purposeful, adventurous, independent, self-directed, captain of her own soul, master of her own destiny, subject of her own experience," possessing "natural radiance, unity, harmony, integrity, initiative, and creative self-ownership." [Hancock 1989, pp. 8–10]. If "Rediscovering the girl within appears to be the key to women's identity" [Hancock 1989, p. 25], then keeping young women in touch with their strong, courageous inner selves is vital in sheltering them during the storms of adolescence. This is the purpose behind the work we do.

Translating Theory into Practice: A Practitioner's Story[1]

It is the first day of the pilot phase of a new experience-based adventure program I designed for 12- and 13-year-old girls called "Connecting With Courage." The program is an unusual combination of adventure activities, expressive art activities, and mentoring relationships with women. As the director, I am a bit out of sorts—this day has not gone as I had planned. I usher off the last concerned parent and stop to observe the first group of girls as they gather in a circle around their two women instructors. The women and girls check the clothing list with the contents of their suitcases. After a few minutes, I notice that on nearly every pile of girl's clothes is a very large stuffed animal—Garfield, Doggy, Teddy Bear, Kitty. My stomach drops. I take a short breath and ask myself, "What gives me the right to take these girls away from their mothers' sanctuary to do such bold and adventurous things?" It would be no small feat for any 12-year-old to accomplish all the challenges I have planned. Reacting quickly to the obvious situation, I initiate an unexpected new policy: "Okay, girls," I call out, "one stuffed animal per student."

As an experiential educator, it is part of my journey to reinvent powerful models of teaching and learning for girls - this is my moment of "connecting" with my own courage.

The Value of Experiential Education

Early in this century, educational theorist John Dewey identified the importance of the connection between education and direct personal experience [Dewey 1938, p. 25]. Dewey's seemingly obvious insight has profound implications for how we educate all children, but has particularly significant meaning for girls in light of the revelations of gender bias research and developmental psychology. My own most powerful learning experiences as an adolescent girl were experiential: I taught myself how to build a pair of snowshoes and then guided my entire gym class of 30 as they did the same; I designed and conducted a political opinion poll by interviewing 100 adults at nearby malls; and I learned about my potential as a human being by participating in a two-week long, outdoor adventure program. The common denominator, I realized, in all of these experiences was that each situation caused me to plan, create, risk, and engage myself fully in the process of learning.

Remembering my own experiences and speaking with other women and girls, I realized that what girls need most are authentic experiences of their own through which they can reflect and learn. The director of a girls' science and math club told me, "Girls don't need another woman to talk to them about self-esteem, they need to get out there and do it." The value for girls of learning through direct experience is critical in a culture that continually serves up curricula that ask all students to learn through vicarious accounts in textbooks. The challenge for girls' education is that these textbooks tell mostly of boys' and men's experiences and are unable to fill the void in relevant learning for girls.

Knowing that adolescent girls find little of what they need in educational settings that unwittingly favor the learning styles of boys in both content and methodology led me to create experiences that are relevant to girls' growth and learning. The more experiences girls can have that are their own, the more they will be able to embrace the learning that is around them. Erika, a 13 year-old girl involved in the pilot program I directed, wrote,

> In this program I have had some great experiences and some bad ones. Like Joann said, I both laughed and cried, and I think most people did, too. I have learned things here that will help me for the rest of my life. When knowledge is informed by experience, it holds the possibility of lasting a lifetime.

Former Dean of the Harvard Graduate School of Education Paul Ylvisaker said, "There is no learning without challenge and emotion" [Ylvisaker 1988, p. 29]. Experience-based learning puts the learner at the center of the learning process. For example, the experience of preparing for a day of rock climbing, doing the actual climb, and reflecting on it can be a particularly powerful one for a 12 year-old girl. It requires that she do more than simply talk or think about the activity. In anticipation of a rock climbing day, one girl said, "My fear is that I'll fall, and if you fall you're dead." These real fears begin a myriad of emotional processes that guide and pattern the learning of each student. Instructors lead her through a sequential approach of learning the technical skills for climbing, facing her fears, and keeping herself safe on a rope. On the rock, each girl challenges herself in a way that allows her to authorize her own success. After a day filled with fear and joy, a 13-year-old girl named Emily described her experience of the day:

> No way was I stopping now. I reached further up the rock face, pulled with all my strength, and up I went. I want to go down, I thought. But a voice inside me said, push yourself a little further. I saw a foothold and stepped up. I reached the top of the cliff. I reached my goal! Back on the ground, my legs were shaking and my hands ached. I had tears in my eyes. It's just a rock, I thought, laughing at myself. But I felt so good inside. I did it! (Emily, 13 years old)

Developing a Curriculum for Girls

As an instructor and director of early adolescent programs with a nationally known adventure organization for 10 years, I first became curious about the needs of adolescent girls, not by their presence, but through their absence. Our advertised coed courses frequently were all-boy groups or groups of 10 boys with 2 or 3 girls. Later, as a Master's student at the Harvard Graduate School of Education, I was introduced to Carol Gilligan's work, and began to look critically at the traditional adventure model of experience-based education. I began to discover where it did not meet the needs of girls, and to consider how to redesign this model of learning to address girls' most pressing needs and concerns. This process required me, as a staunch believer in the adventure program methodology, to be willing to question my own ideas and previous assumptions.

Looking back at the formative ideas of the original adventure program model, I found that the program philosophy grew out of the need to develop a strategy to prepare young sailors better for survival at sea in war time. Based on these origins, the founding ideas are innately militaristic and male-oriented. With the enrollment of girls in 1965, came a challenge to the "heroic male" emphasis of the past. Initially, girls participated in separate groups with the goal of proving their ability to complete a course identical to the boy's course. However, eventually girls participated only in coeducational courses [James 1980, pp. 7, 19]. The ultimate decision to enroll girls in coed courses may have precluded the development of a more fully adapted curriculum that would reflect a deeper understanding of their different needs, ways of learning, and knowledge. While the original foundational ideas did not address the distinct needs of girls, they are, however, still relevant to girls' overall development. I believe that the lack of research available at the time did not allow for a rethinking of program concepts to meet the needs of girls.

Gilligan and her associates at the Harvard Project on Women's Psychology and Girls' Development and the then newly released report by the AAUW, How Schools Shortchange Girls, greatly inspired me to investigate this assumption. I contacted the organization's national office to inquire about the participation of

girls in their courses nation-wide. Indeed, there was one girl participating for approximately every four boys. I realized this was an
opportunity to rethink this program model and make it more developmentally appropriate for girls. Perhaps I could redesign this model
to make it fit girls' needs better and make it more appealing to both
girls and their parents. This led me to ask, "What are the needs of
adolescent girls?" and "How could I design an experience-based
adventure program to meet their needs?"

I was curious about what girls, at the edge of adolescence, could
tell me about their experiences and their needs at the age of 12 and
13, so I went directly to the experts—the girls themselves. I developed a set of questions about what was important to them in their
lives as well as some questions related to program design, and
proceeded to interview a dozen of them.

> Erin is a 13-year-old girl I have come to interview as part
> of an inquiry process to learn the truth of adolescent girls'
> experience. It is 8:30 A.M. and Erin is dressed in her
> comfortably worn nightgown. I ask Erin, "What's really
> important to you in your life?" Ready with her answer she
> says, "To be taken seriously by adults." Her response is as
> much a response to me personally, as it is a response to the
> question I have asked. I wonder if she thinks I am taking
> her seriously?

Generally, girls I interviewed said their concerns and desires
focused on having fun, being liked by peers, being taken seriously by
adults, having free time, needing to know what they want in life,
wanting to know about social issues, making friends, and having
discussion groups. Besides what I learned from talking to girls, I also
wondered if other women instructors had thoughts about addressing
the needs of girls on adventure courses. I sent out a questionnaire to
women instructors involved in leading traditional adventure programs. Questions focused on how they would design a course differently for girls. Responses confirmed that most of the goals and
activities do work for girls, but that the process used in these
activities is key. They also indicated that socialization puts girls at a

disadvantage when it comes to the technical and wilderness aspects of the courses. Specific suggestions were: emphasizing the relationship between girls and women instructors, encouraging girls' self-expression, "challenge by choice," and a curriculum that recognizes girls' differences.

Looking for Strategies

Because much of the research has come from the field of girls' psychology, the issues that face girls today are largely viewed pathologically, from the perspective of what's wrong with girls. As discussed earlier, researchers have identified eating disorders, depression, teen pregnancy, self-silencing, decrease in school performance, and a decline in self-esteem as being connected to psychological risk [Brown & Gilligan 1992; AAUW 1992]. However, while the challenges that confront girls today seem daunting, the strategies to combat them are much more difficult to identify.

Single-sex educational programs are one of the few strategies that can immediately make a difference in addressing gender bias. In a report funded by The Carnegie Council on Adolescent Development, Heather Nicholson states, "Gender stereotypes, discrimination against girls, and lack of expectation for their performance in traditionally male areas persist in today's society." She recommends "separate settings in which girls can sort out demands and better prepare for the world they live in." [Nicholson 1992, p. 72] Catherine Krupnick, Lecturer in Education at the Harvard Graduate School of Education, has done extensive research by videotaping teachers in the classroom to help make visible the gender bias problem. She says, "The only way to get girls to dominate . . . is if only girls are present." [Steinberg 1991, p. 7]

While girls-only programming is the most obvious place to start, the American Association of University Women's report, *Growing Smart: What's Working for Girls in Schools*, offers some common denominators of other strategies for working with girls. The report suggests five key themes: celebrate girls' strong identity, respect girls as central players, connect girls to caring adults, ensure girls' participation and success, and empower girls to realize their dreams [AAUW 1995, p. 1]. All of these have been integrated into the programs we have developed, along with the defining theme of "Courage."

A Prevention Strategy: Developing Courage in Girls and Women

> Her warm, intelligent glance said she knew what I was
> doing - not because she herself had been a child but
> because she herself took a few loose aerial turns around her
> apartment every night for the hell of it, and by day played
> along with the rest of the world. We passed on the sidewalk
> with a look of accomplices who share a humor just beyond
> irony. What's a heart for?" [Dillard 1987, p. 119]

With these words, Annie Dillard reminds us of the importance of play and its connection to the heart, a concept also taken up by Annie Rogers, Assistant Professor of Education at the Harvard Graduate School of Education, when she discusses developing courage in girls as a strategy for maintaining their self-esteem. In an article in The Harvard Educational Review, "Voice, Play, and a Practice of Ordinary Courage in Girls' and Women's Lives," she uses a 13th century definition of the word courage—"to speak one's mind by telling all one's heart"—as a strategy to strengthen girls' resistance to cultural stereotypes. Rogers believes that in childhood, courage is quite "ordinary." Most children are bold, forthright, and unafraid of expressing themselves. If girls could be helped to strengthen that courage, they would withstand the erosion of self-esteem through high school. Rogers further suggests four strategies for developing courage based on what girls need:

1. Relationships with women who will speak the truth about what they know;

2. Opportunities to speak about what they know;

3. Opportunities to write as a way of expressing what cannot be spoken;

4. Opportunities to use their artistic imagination - creative/ expressive activities that uncover girls' embodied knowledge. [Rogers 1993]

Rogers' four strategies point to ways girls can stay connected to their feelings and knowledge by deliberately keeping them active and alive in their daily lives. They also underscore the potential impact of mentoring relationships between adults and adolescents. An adult woman who is willing to share her knowledge and life experiences, rather than withhold valuable information or perpetuate harmful cultural myths, can be a critical ally to a girl during adolescence.

Inspired by this work, I began to think about how to include this old definition of courage, "to speak one's mind by telling all one's heart,"—a sort of expressive or moral courage—into an adventure program model that originally focused largely on the development of physical courage. It seemed that girls needed the opportunity to develop both expressive and physical courage to equip them with the internal and external courage necessary for life's challenges. I began formulating a way to add a strong arts component to the adventure curriculum that would help emphasize the development of expressive courage and address the four strategies that Rogers suggested. Creative activities such as writing, visual arts, dance, storytelling, and theater arts could be powerful tools for girls to stay connected to their feelings and knowledge during adolescence.

For example, one activity we have used to engage girls in using their "artistic imagination" is creating a group Circle Poem. This activity depends on the idea of "stream of consciousness" or "free flight of ideas" as its guiding principle. While sitting in a circle, a group will be given a word such as "purple." The first person will respond to the word "purple" with the first word that comes to her mind when she hears it. Perhaps she says "violet." The next person then responds to the word "violet" and says "flower." This continues three times around the circle without peer help or long silences - the goal of which is to not think with your head about the "right" answer, but to respond quickly and spontaneously with knowledge from the heart. The activity is fun and helps girls trust their intuitive knowledge over what they think others want to hear.

Creating Program Frameworks

With Roger's strategy of courage at the core of the curriculum, I was ready when, at the end of my Master's work, I was offered an opportunity to put all of my research and curriculum ideas into practice. In 1992, I was invited by a nationally known adventure organization to start a preadolescent program for 12- and 13-year-old girls, which I called "Connecting With Courage." This two-week long, experience-based adventure program combined the best of the traditional adventure model with the latest research on girls. For this organization, targeting this population represented the first program for this age group open to the public, and the first program created specifically with girls' developmental needs in mind. The program was designed to cultivate both physical and expressive courage in girls through the combined use of both adventure and creative arts activities. By providing a "girl only" peer group, strong women leaders, a girl-centered learning environment, and new ideas about girls' development, it also counteracts the disadvantages that exist for girls in coed settings.

I had few guides in this dynamic process of curriculum design, and often describe the experience as feeling as if I were stepping into a swamp and having to find my way out. I felt like Sylvia Ashton Warner, an experienced New Zealand teacher, whose book, *Teacher*, describes her futile attempts to address effectively the needs of her new class of Maori students. In a moment of frustration, she decides to burn all her curriculum resources, and vows to begin to "listen" to her students and let them reveal to her what they need and how they learn best [Warner 1963, p.119]. Because of the lack of data on the ways girls learn best, I, like Sylvia Ashton Warner, had to plunge into the confusing process of learning to teach girls by learning from them.

Truth/Voice/Choice.[2] Drawing on Sylvia Aston Warner's wisdom, and grappling with the challenge of translating theoretical ideas into program activities and processes, my staff and I developed a set of guiding frameworks for the program. With a few key, easy-to-remember concepts, which we referred to as Truth/Voice/Choice, staff could begin to talk about these ideas with each other and their students in an attempt to put them deliberately into action.

- *Truth—authentic relationships*. Girls get subtle messages from the culture about who they are "supposed" to be, rather than being encouraged to be who they truly are. Instructors encourage girls to form authentic relationships with themselves and others that allow them to stay in connection with their "true self" and create a safe environment where truths can be spoken. These relationships allow space for girls simply to be themselves and stay connected to the knowledge and feelings that live in their bodies [Brown & Gilligan 1992, p. 4].

- *Voice—speaking one's mind.* As girls enter adolescence, they often come to not know what previously has been known. Words like "I don't know" begin to enter their language [Gilligan & Brown 1992, p. 4]. In the program, girls are encouraged to be courageous and embrace an early definition of the word courage—"to speak one's mind by telling all one's heart" [Rogers 1993, p. 271]. They are supported in speaking about what they know as they participate in group discussion, conflict resolution, decision-making, and storytelling activities [Gilligan & Rogers 1992, p. 4].

- *Choice—freedom and choice.* The idea of "challenge by choice" is a widely used adventure education concept [Rohnke 1989, p. 5]. In the words of Victor Frankl, "The greatest of human freedoms is the freedom to choose one's own attitude in a given set of circumstances, to choose one's own way." [Frankl 1963, p. 65] Each girl learns differently, and the rate and manner in which learning takes hold is also distinct. Students are encouraged to take control of their own learning situation, set their own goals, and authorize their own success.

Staff considerations. In addition to the normal staff expertise required to work in the field of adventure education, which include outdoor skills and first-aid training as well as teaching experience with adolescent girls, I had to add a few more requirements. Beyond the technical adventure and teaching skills, it became crucial that the people I hired were female, comfortable with the creative arts, familiar with the psychology of girls and women, aware of the dominant male culture and its effects on girls and women, and personally committed to embodying the program principles and strategies. Recruiting and finding women to fulfill these requirements became challenging, and often I referred to our qualified staff as a "maverick" group of women instructors.

From research to practice. To assist the process of integrating new research into practice, I conducted a series of instructor interviews with questionnaires designed to assist staff in making meaning of the research, developing specific practices to use in the field, identifying challenges in translating theory to practice, and making suggestions for improvement. We discovered that individual responses to the Truth/Voice/Choice ideas varied greatly from instructor to instructor. When asked to explain the importance of Truth/Voice/Choice to the program, one instructor replied that these ideas are "critical to implementing an authentic intentional experience." Another instructor described the ideas as the "construct" or the "paradigm" that defines everything that is done on the program.

Instructors were asked to describe specific strategies that they implemented to encourage the practice of Truth/Voice/Choice on the program. Several instructors discussed the importance of modeling Truth by acting "as my true self". Others described conducting activities which would support girls in sharing their ideas and feelings such as journal writing, a life stories activity, and group norm setting. Strategies used to encourage Voice on the programs included using a talking stick, sharing stories of courage, and modeling personal experiences where instructors spoke up for themselves. To encourage individual Choice, instructors generally agreed that giving girls options where they could select their own way of doing something as well as their own pace was essential. Adult leaders encouraged choices involving meals, group meetings, the level of personal challenge while rock climbing, and individual expression in creative arts activities. These insights and the process of ongoing reflection have helped us to deepen our program methods and raise the skill levels of our staff.

Circles of Courage: A New Model of Adventure Programming for Girls

The program itself is not the sacred thing. What's important is the principles the program stands for, the key ideas to which adults who work with girls are committed. [Hansen 1995, p. vi]

At the heart of the Circles of Courage program is the concept of developing courage as a way to sustain girls' voices and unique knowledge in the world [Rogers 1993, p. 271]. Girls participate in challenging activities that evoke the physical and expressive courage they harbor deep within themselves. Instructors work with girls to strengthen their confidence and their ability to express ideas and feelings publicly while they learn to stay connected to the most important person they will ever know—themselves.

After six years of translating theory to practice, I believe we have learned much about strengthening the model, which can benefit practitioners involved in similar kinds of programming. Circles of Courage is a 14-day program for 12- and 13-year-old girls. It weaves adventure activities such as hiking, rock climbing, canoeing, and ropes course events with expressive arts activities such as storytelling, journal writing, self-portraits, theater arts, and body movement. These combined activities create an arena where girls can experience themselves as courageous and capable.

Circles of Courage is designed to be a base-camp style program, in which girls go on two 3-day expeditions and spend the remaining time in base camp. This allows girls to experience having a secure "home base" while going off for two short expeditions within the two-week period. In this way, the physical challenges (heavy packs, dried foods, limited shelter, etc.) are paced at a rate that 12- and 13-year-old girls can handle. When back at base camp, the girls have a few more comforts (fresh food, showers, indoor facilities, etc.) and can focus on exploring their expressive courage and Truth/Voice/Choice themes. This is in contrast to the traditional "mobile" adventure programs, in which students arrive and depart from a base camp but are "in the field" for the entire trip. Table 1 is an example of a program flow, including components, themes, and specific activities.

The overall theme of Truth/Voice/Choice runs throughout the entire program. Physical courage, expressive courage, and cooperative courage were developed as subthemes to give specific components more meaning and focus. Hence, during the backpacking expedition and rock climbing components, instructors emphasize the development of physical courage through these physically challenging activities. During the creative days and "sola" experience—where girls spend time alone reflecting—the instructors emphasize the development of expressive courage. Finally, during the canoe expedition and rappelling and ropes course components, instructors emphasize the cooperative courage necessary to work towards a common goal.

Some examples of specific activities used to promote the Truth/Voice/Choice program goals include the following:

- *Stories of Courage*—As part of the application process, girls are asked to write a story about a woman they know or have known who is courageous. Within the first two days of the program, they are asked to share these stories orally with the other members of their group. They also write their own stories of courage at the end.

- *I Am the Girl Who*—This is a journal writing exercise in which girls write in their journals the words "I Am the Girl Who. . ." They then finish the sentence and complete a story of their own in which they are the focus.

- *Self-Portraits*—Using fabric paints and a plain white T-shirt, girls are asked to create a "self-portrait" that reflects the qualities of who they are. This activity can be done using symbols, abstract painting, or any way desired.

- *Vasilisa Dolls*—After reading a Russian folk tale called Vasilisa, girls are asked to create a small doll from colorful materials such as yarn, beads, and pipe cleaners. In the story, a girl named Vasilisa carries a doll, given to her by her mother, which symbolizes the intuitive knowledge she has. Girls carry their dolls throughout the program in their backpacks, in their pocket, or on a string around their neck.

Together, the program components, themes, and activities combine to create a comprehensive strategy to ensure that program objectives are met. Reframing the traditional adventure model using the themes and custom designed activities make this a girl-centered

Table 5-1. Sample Circles of Courage Program Flow

	Components	Themes	Activities
Day 1	Arrival/ Team Building	Truth /Voice/ Choice	Group Norm Setting
Day 2	Backpacking Expedition	Physical Courage	Stories of Courage
Day 3	Backpacking Expedition	Physical Courage	Courage Bracelets
Day 4	Backpacking Expedition	Physical Courage	Life Maps
Day 5	Rock Climbing	Physical Courage	"Belay" School
Day 6	Transport/ Re-Supply	Truth /Voice/ Choice	I am the Girl Who . . .
Day 7	Creative Day	Expressive Courage	Self-portrait
Day 8	Individual "Sola" Experience	Expressive Courage	Letter to Self
Day 9	Creative Day	Expressive Courage	Mask Making
Day 10	Rappelling or Ropes Course	Truth /Voice/ Courage	The Glade Story
Day 11	Canoeing Expedition	Cooperative Courage	Canoe School
Day 12	Canoeing Expedition	Cooperative Courage	Vasilisa Dolls
Day 13	Canoeing Expedition	Cooperative Courage	Girls Closing Ritual
Day 14	Closure/ Reflection/ Departure	Truth /Voice/ Courage	Stories of Courage

program—a program where girls' needs, girls' ways of learning, and girls' knowledge is honored and prioritized.

What's Different About This Program?

Experience-based. Learning happens best when a girl is allowed to learn through direct experience because experiential learning involves challenge and emotion. All of the aspects of experiential learning are incorporated into the program: (1) planning and preparing for the activity; (2) doing the activity; and (3) reflecting on the activity.

Physical and expressive courage. Clearly, adventure and art activities are not new to girls. They have access to them through schools, community-based youth organizations, and arts councils, and so forth. Combining these two types of activities into a program deliberately for girls, however, is new. While the blending of these two activity areas is exciting and powerful, the unique qualities of this program do not come from the activities themselves, but from being embedded in the new ideas asserted by the most up-to-date research.

Prevention program attitude. Drawing upon the research, we have developed a perspective on girls that is both positive and prevention-oriented. We believe that girls entering adolescence already have most of what they need to navigate their way through these turbulent years. Our job as adults is to help prevent the loss of these qualities by not imposing our own learned limitations and fears upon them. Our most important role is to help sustain the "ordinary," "courageous" parts of adolescent girls.

Educating the whole child. Teaching or strengthening character skills such as decision-making, communicating your point of view, risk taking, compassion, and problem solving can authorize a child to take action or make changes in her life. Character skills are at the core of all learning, and are required to flourish in the adult world. This process, rooted in the ancient proverb, "If you give a (wo)man a fish, (s)he eats for a day; if you teach a (wo)man to fish, (s)he eats for a lifetime," transmits the skills that will help girls thrive in and out of school for a lifetime. These same skills are what will guide them through the decisions they will make around drugs, alcohol, sexual activity, harassment and abuse, and eating disorders.

The Primacy of Relationship

Authentic relationship. Besides being a "girls only" program, the biggest differences occur in the way the program is conducted, and most importantly, in the nature of the relationships the girls have with their peers, the adult women, and themselves. Much of what we have learned from the research speaks to the need for adolescent girls to have important relationships with adult women. Rogers writes that "girls need to have relationships with women who will speak the truth about their experiences as women." [Rogers 1993, p. 288]. Lyn Mikel Brown further indicates that for girls "to be an authority on their own experience requires another person who will acknowledge them as such, not simply an audience but a relationship in which they are taken seriously." [Brown 1991, p. 84] Table 2 is an example of some of the subtle differences in adult-girl interactions in a traditional adventure program versus a girl-centered adventure program.

Small communities of learning. Research in the mentoring field also supports the idea that the presence of a single caring adult can make all the difference to an adolescent during these complex years. In order to honor these ideas and put them into action, we must consider seriously how many girls and women can work together and maintain "authentic" relationships. Through our work with girls we have found that a small group of girls and women - 10 girls to 1 or 2 women - is optimal for supporting authentic relationships, for allowing girls to feel that they are taken seriously, and for listening to each girl's voice. With more than ten, the girls are at risk of not being known, not being heard, and of competing for the instructor's attention.

Collaborative teaching and learning. Traditional learning hierarchies with teachers-as-knowers and students-as-learners stifle the learning process. A collaborative approach to learning allows girls and women teachers to learn with and from each other. This approach allows women to model their often hidden process of learning to students, and allows girls to share their growing knowledge with peers and teachers.

Table 5-2. Comparison of Relationships and Power in a Traditional Adventure Program Versus a Girl-Centered Adventure Program		
Adult/ Child Relationship Orientation	Traditional	Girl-Centered
Instructor Orientation	This is your program.	This is our program.
Instructor Role	Teacher/ Observer	Teacher/ Participant
Goals are set by:	Instructor	Girl
Success/ Failure Defined by:	Instructor	Girl
Child Perception of Instructor	Mysterious/ god-like	Real/ Accessible
Example of Instructor Briefing on a rock Climbing Day	I want everyone to try their best. My goal is for each person to get to the top of one climb and do a rappel. Remember to have a positive attitude.	Let's go around and hear everyone's goal for today. Tell us what kind of supoport you want when you are on the rock. Remember to set step by step goals and reset them as you go.
Goal for the Day	Get to the top of the climb.	Achieve your own goal.
Problem Sloving Strategy	Get to the top and keep trying	Step by step achievable goals.

The Center for Ventures in Girls' Education

The work that began with a nationally known adventure organization has evolved over the years. Motivated by the success in implementing this model, the organizational constraints and limitations that fettered this work in a more traditional setting, and my own growing courage, I decided, along with other women researchers and practitioners, to establish The Center For Ventures in Girls' Education. The development of a small, woman-run organization that was free of the perspectives of a male-oriented national organization was a necessary step in gaining the freedom, authority and voice to pursue our work. Since 1993, The Center for Ventures in Girls' Education has been a laboratory for translating girls' theory into practice. The Center draws on the expertise of women educators and researchers from the Harvard Project on Women's Psychology and Girls' Development and Boston-area girls to create a dynamic collaborative arena for reflective design and implementation of programs and research to strengthen girls' education and development.

The Center's work continues to move forward in new directions. Since the further refinement and development of the original experience-based adventure model we call "Circles of Courage"—we have developed two additional program models:

Project Athena —A mentoring program that brings girls and women together for a variety of one-on-one and group activities which provide girls with a nurturing place to grow and learn.

Exploring the Leader Within—An out-of-school program which introduces girls to a model of leadership that builds upon their natural strengths and engages them in community leadership.

Opportunities for learning from and deepening our program models are ongoing. We are currently piloting all three programs in five very diverse communities in and around the Boston area. In this phase, we are listening for the common denominators of successful program components as well as for the differences in the needs of these diverse populations, and are beginning to distill the learning that is available to us.

Evaluation Findings

Still considered relatively new, the field of experiential education, however, actually represents one of the oldest forms of learning—learning by doing. In contrast to other disciplines, some believe that research in experiential education is still in an undeveloped stage. According to one researcher in this field, "What practical, usable advice the research community in experiential education can give the practitioner still remains an elusive mystery." Understanding behavioral, educational, and affective components based on individual events and experience is part of the complexity of what the field strives to know [Ewert 1987, pp. 6-7]. The difficulty in successfully measuring impacts on experiential programs is well known. In spite of the lack of "hard data" to support the value of experiential education, numerous practitioners, teachers, schools, and organizations across the country know that this learning method works. The truth is that it may be a long time before we are able to "prove" the worthiness of this field through traditional research methods.

In the newly emerging field of girls' experience-based adventure programming, little has been done to evaluate either the short-term or the long-term effects on girls' self-esteem, psychological health, or learning styles. Early indications from our participant questionnaires and participant program evaluations show the adventure program having a positive effect on participants' self-concept and behavior. The following are participant, parent, and staff quotes about what they hoped to gain from the program at the beginning:

- To learn about my future and other kinds of things.
- To be able to stay away from home for a long period of time.
- To be stronger.
- To learn how to be a leader.
- To learn about womanhood.
- To make memories and meet new girlfriends.
- To gain courage, have fun, and learn new things.
- To learn how to survive in the wilderness.

The following are quotes from girls at the end of the program:

They believe in you here and encourage you to go a step further each day. Without this program, I wouldn't have noticed myself to be this courageous." (Eliza, 12 years old)

One thing I did at 'Circles of Courage' that was courageous was to allow myself to cry. All the other times in my life I hid my tears because I was afraid of what people would think of me. On this trip, by allowing myself to cry, I was allowing myself to set my thoughts and emotions free." (Adiya, 13 years old)

This course helped me learn many things. The main thing was courage. It takes courage to do just about anything. I learned more about myself and that I do have a lot of courage in me. This program helped me realize that." (Elizabeth, 12 years old)

Then there are the quotes from girls six months after the program:

Circles of Courage has influenced me to speak up and share my ideas and opinions. I notice that in school I have started to take more risks and discuss my own views." (Eve, 13 years old)

I think I was greatly changed. I came back to school not wanting to be like everyone else, wanting to be me. I think that Circles of Courage gave me the strength to believe that I could break out of the stereotype. (Amelia, 13 years old)

Parents and instructors have also provided positive feedback:

She loved it. We both cry when we talk about how happy she was and how she said she only did it because all the other girls helped and encouraged her." (Carol, mother)

Participating in the courage program has cast off the shadow I clung to for many years and has enabled me to stop being the modern woman who is pressured to be all

things to all people and to take time to heal. I am transforming into a woman of courage." (Deborah, instructor)

Ongoing Evaluation

We are currently gathering data on participant impact, impact on
adult women involved in the program, implementation challenges,
and adaptation of this model to diverse populations. Some of our
most pressing questions are the following:

- Do girls regard themselves differently from the beginning of the
  program to the end? If so, how?
- Do girls see themselves as more courageous at the end of the
  program than when they started it, or having the same courage,
  or simply becoming more aware of the courage they already had?
- How much do the goals of the program transfer into the
  everyday life of each girl once she goes home?
- Does a girl feel better prepared to tackle the challenges of school
  and adolescence because of this program?
- What is the most significant aspect of the program to the girls:
  relationships, program components, or other aspects?
- Do women staff experience any personal growth from their
  participation in the program? Do they view themselves as being
  more courageous?
- What are parents' perceptions of program impact on their
  daughters? Have they learned anything from their daughters or
  from the program that helps them to better understand their
  daughters' needs?
- How many girls completed the program from the start? How
  many girls dropped out and why?
- How was the impact of the program different for girls completing the entire program versus those who completed part of the
  program?
- Is this program model effective with all the populations with
  which we are working? How can the program be adapted to meet
  the needs of diverse populations more powerfully?

The questions are numerous and broad ranging, and represent
only the tip of the iceberg. We are interested in both outcomes and
process. As a result, we are constantly adapting our own evaluation

process as we discover the right questions to ask as well as the best tools with which to answer them.

Challenges/Recommendations

Diversity

While our programs are accessible to girls and women from a range of socioeconomic, cultural, and ethnic backgrounds, we are still learning how to adapt this model to work effectively with diverse populations of girls. Both the adventure education model and the majority of research that has been conducted on girls' development focus on middle and upper class white girls. Little information exists to help guide us in our endeavor to apply this work to diverse groups, so we have built in some important processes to keep us culturally connected to each community and reflecting on our work. First, we made it a key priority to place a leader at each new program site who is from that community and who reflects the cultural background of the population of girls there. Second, the girls and adults involved participate in ongoing program evaluations. Third, the leaders have key input into adaptations of the program at their site.

On-Going Connection Through Follow-Up

Encouraging a girl to speak her mind and stay connected to her "true" self assumes a responsibility to support each girl in her effort to do so. Follow-up activities provide girls with opportunities to return to supportive all-girl settings. These opportunities reinforce and help sustain each girl's relationship with her "true" self, as she faces the challenges of her teen years. Informal studies have shown that the impact of short-term, intensive adventure programs on youth is relatively short-lived and difficult to measure. These studies suggest that within six months, the beneficial effects of the program diminish to the point of being nearly undetectable. Our current work includes experimenting with ways to maintain connections to girls who participate in our programs. These activities include group pictures, "Stories of Courage" books, reunions, alumni programs, a newsletter, school-based programs, and a continuous two-year long adventure/mentoring/leadership program.

The Funding Challenge

In the area of non-profit grant-based programming, there is a trend towards stretching funding dollars by maximizing participant numbers. The not-so-subtle message is that program providers are expected to prove that funding dollars are best utilized when they can be seen to impact the greatest number of children. Thus, funders can seemingly feel good about the impact that these programs are having on the largest number of participants possible, while program providers struggle to balance maximum program numbers with ever diminishing program dollars. While this way of thinking potentially compromises the quality of any youth program, there are some compelling indications in the girls' development research that support a need to rethink this strategy entirely [Rogers 1993, p. 288].

In addition, the 1994 report, *Worlds Apart*, conducted by the Lincoln Filene Center, Tufts University, paints a bleak picture for funding of women's and girls' programming in the Boston area. The report summarizes what most in the field of girls' programming already know: that very little philanthropic money goes to support girls' programs. It states that roughly 6% of philanthropic funds in the Boston area go to women's and girls' causes collectively, and only a portion of that goes directly to supporting girls-only programming. This percentage parallels those in other regions of the country. Reasons offered for funders' lack of support are centered around funders' wanting to meet the needs of all people and preferring to support universal programs that include girls and women, but that are not gender-focused [Mead 1994, pp. 6, 15].

There are indications, however, that foundations are beginning to take this field of work seriously. The Ms. Foundation for Women and other regional foundations have begun to give multiyear grant awards for innovations in girls' programming. While this is exciting, there remain too few dollars to go around, and the size of the giving does not allow for anything more than direct service activities. Support is greatly needed in developing successful models and for training and technical assistance functions. There is also a need to fund longitudinal research and evaluation. It is imperative that girls' program providers continue working to develop rigorous and relevant programs for girls. At the same time they must educate foundations and individual donors to the need to support girls' programs that are striving to translate new research theory on girls' development into practice.

Shifting the Role of the Adult

One of the ongoing challenges we confront in our work is in staff training. What we have learned, both from the research and our direct experience with girls, is that in order to create programs that truly meet their needs and that address the relevant developmental issues, the traditional role of the adult has to be reconsidered. It is one thing to conduct training sessions on the implications of the research for adult women and quite another to be able to measure how much has been actually internalized, implemented, and embodied by the adult women involved in the programs.

As was discussed earlier, doing this work means shifting the perspective from the hierarchical view that the adult is the only leader/authority/teacher, to one that recognizes the adult as learner and co-creator of the experience with the girls. Just as reflection is an integral part of the program process for the girls, so, too, is it for the adult leaders. It requires a real willingness on the part of the adult to engage in the ongoing process not only of formal program evaluation, but of the challenging internal work required to look critically at one's own teaching and relational styles in order to engage in truly authentic relationships with themselves and with the girls.

Potential Impact on Programming for Boys

The research on girls has been ongoing for almost 30 years. The slowly mounting evidence has begun to result in programming and practice, which can actually have an impact on their experience. Further, while a common response to the girls' research has been "What about the boys?", the truth is that what we have learned about girls has actually led to a reexamination of what we believed we knew about boys' experience, and many books are now being written to illuminate their different and distinct needs.

Terrence Real, in his book, *I Don't Want to Talk About It*, summarizes the plight of boys in this culture:

For decades, feminist scholars and social researchers have patiently built up a body of evidence showing the psychological damage done by the coercive enforcement of gender roles in girls. But what about the damage to the psychological development of boys? If traditional socialization takes aim at girls' voices, it takes aim at boys' hearts." [Real 1997, p. 123]

So, boys, like girls, also suffer from a "relational crisis" [Brown & Gilligan 1992, p. 23]. The culture forces them to disconnect from their emotional selves, from those closest to them, as they struggle to achieve "manly" independence, and to adhere to very rigid role expectations. They are further flooded with intensely competitive and militaristic images in the media and through the sports and games they play. The task of making a difference for boys then, begins, as it did for girls, with first questioning the way we've always done things, discovering the incongruities between the way things are and the way we know they should be, and then changing our practice accordingly.

Some of the more obvious challenges would be to examine the ways in which we overtly and subtly promote competition and one-upmanship over cooperation and genuine team endeavors; to discover how we can support boys in being comfortable with the feeling level of their experience' and to consider the ways in which we discourage them from exploring roles and interests beyond the traditionally acceptable masculine domains.

Final Reflections

"Adolescence is a border between childhood and adulthood. Like life on all borders, it's teeming with energy and fraught with danger. Growth requires courage and hard work on the part of the individual, and it requires the protection and nurturing of the environment." [Pipher 1994, p. 292]

Pipher reminds us of the important role of caring adults in helping adolescent girls standing on the edge of adulthood. We are well aware of the hard work facing girls living through adolescence, but we spend less time considering the hard work required by the adults accompanying them on this journey. The bottom line is that nurturing courage in the young women under our care requires an enormous amount of courage on our parts as well. As adults, the challenge is to cast a critical eye on the culture and to understand the "toxic" parts of it that we have internalized. What, of all the elements from which we are trying to protect the young women in our care, have a hold on us as well? If we are concerned about girls' body image, then we must know how we feel about our own. If we want them to stay in touch with their feelings, then we must be free to express our own. If we are concerned about girls maintaining their voices, then we must use our own. If we want them to be grounded in their own knowledge and experience, then we must be grounded in our own.

Part of the challenge of programming is the challenge presented by the primacy of relationships. The unique personalities and needs of the girls in the program constantly challenge us to be flexible and responsive, to loosen our attachment to the way we've always done things, and to our own experience and authority. Girls' primary motivation is the need for relationship, and in order to grow, they require authentic relationship. Part of that authenticity rests on being seen as equals whose opinions and perspectives are valued and who are allowed to participate in the decisions that affect them. For the adult, it requires stepping away from looking at girls' experiences through the lens of our own, so that we can really hear and respond to what they have to say. In short, our role as adults is to become fearlessly engaged in an ongoing process that is increasingly conscious, connected, and countercultural: conscious of the impact of the culture in our own lives and in the lives of the girls we serve and willing to tell the truth about our own experience; connected to our own authentic selves and able to voice what we know as we nurture that same connection and voice in the girls in our care; and committed to making countercultural choices in our programming and in our practice against all the influences and attitudes that rob young women of their voices, their confidence, and their resilience on their journey through adolescence.

Notes

1. This section reflects the experiences of the first author during the process of developing the program model. The author's work spans many years and reflects insights and knowledge from programs conducted in two separate organizations.

2. For the duration of this section, the work described reflects the further development of the original program model called "Connecting With Courage". With the founding of the Center for Ventures in Girls' Education, the program was renamed "Circles of Courage".

References

American Association of University Women Educational Foundation. (1991). *Shortchanging girls, shortchanging America*. Washington, DC: Author.

American Association of University Women Educational Foundation. (1992). *How schools shortchange girls*. Washington, DC: Author.

American Association of University Women Educational Foundation. (1995). *Growing smart: What's working for girls in schools*. Washington, DC: AAUW.

American Association of University Women Educational Foundation. (1998). *Separated by sex: A critical look at single-sex education for girls*. Washington, DC: AAUW.

Brown, L. M. & Gilligan, C. (1992). *Meeting at the crossroads*. New York: Ballantine Books.

Brown, L. M. (1991). Telling a girl's life: Self-authorization as a form of resistance. In C. Gilligan, A. Rogers & D. Tolman (Eds.), *Women, girls & psychotherapy: Reframing resistance* (pp. 71–86). New York: Haworth Press.

Dewey, J. (1938). *Experience and education*. New York: Macmillan Publishing.

Dillard, A. (1987). *An American childhood*. New York: Harper Perennial.

Elium, J. & Elium, D. (1994) *Raising a daughter: Parents and the awakening of a healthy woman*. Berkeley, CA: Celestial Arts.

Ewert, A. (1987, Summer). Research in experiential education: An overview. *Journal of Experiential Education, 10*, 4–7.

Frank, A. (1996). *The diary of a young girl: The definitive edition*. New York: Anchor Books.

Frankl, V. (1963). *Man's search for meaning*. New York: Simon & Schuster.

Hancock, E. (1989). *The girl within*. New York: Fawcett Columbine.

James, T. (1980). *Education at the edge*. Denver: Colorado Outward Bound School.

Steinberg, A. (1991, January/February). Girls talk, boys talk more. *The Harvard Education Letter, 12,* 6–8.

Mackoff, B. (1996). *Growing a girl*. New York: Dell Publishing.

Mead, M. (1994). *Worlds apart*. Boston: Women in Philanthropy/Boston Women's Fund.

Ms. Foundation for Women. (1993). *Programmed neglect: Not seen, not heard*. New York: Ms. Foundation for Women.

Nicholson, H. (1992). *Gender issues in youth development programs*. New York: The Carnegie Council on Adolescent Development.

Pipher, M. (1994). *Reviving Ophelia: Saving the selves of adolescent girls*. New York: Grosset/Putnam.

Real, T. (1997). *I don't want to talk about it: Overcoming the secret legacy of male depression*. New York: Scribner.

Rogers, A. (1993, Fall). Voice, play, and a practice of ordinary courage in girls and women's lives. *Harvard Educational Review, 63,* 265–295.

Rohnke, K. (1989). *Cowstails and Cobras II*. Dubuque, IA: Project Adventure/Kendall/Hunt.

Sadker, D. & Sadker, M. (1994). *Failing at fairness: How America's schools cheat girls*. New York: Charles Scribner Sons.

Warner, S. A. (1963). *Teacher*. New York: Simon & Schuster.

Ylvisaker, P. (1988). *The missing dimension*. Paper presented at Outward Bound's third international conference, Cooperstown, NY.

6

Promoting Social Competency Through the Arts

Christianne F. Gullotta & Robert W. Plant

Unlike other contributions in this book, this chapter shares a cornucopia of approaches and suggestions that youth workers can use to engage young people in activities that provide learning opportunities for health promoting behaviors. The focus here is on a real world application of arts-based prevention programming.

The artistic and creative programs described in this chapter are rooted in several beliefs. First, they are intended to encourage positive self-image by offering opportunities for mastery. Second, the programs contribute to the development of a sense of belonging and community connection through interactions with peers, family members, and other adults. Third, an overarching theme of all programs is the value of community service and the importance of giving back. Fourth, the activities are experiential and include opportunities for self-reflection that help children and youth to derive meaning from their experience. Fifth, these programs provide a caring staff who support the attempts of young people to try out new social roles and practice new social skills. Importantly, this staff has been involved with these young people since elementary school. The reader should not lose sight of the power that a positive relationship between an adult and a child can have over time for good.

The Program

The Creative Experiences Program is located within a municipal agency devoted to serving the needs of youth. Reflective of the program's basic values, the activities offered must meet two criteria. First, they need to offer youth opportunities to become positively involved in the community. Next, they must provide staff with the opportunity to work with young people to develop and improve their social skills. What are some of those social skills? They include behaviors like accepting responsibility for one's own actions, being able to relate to another person without resorting to controlling tactics like manipulation or threats, and striving to do the best one can while accepting that one cannot necessarily expect to be the best. Thus, opportunities for discussion and reflection on how an event might be improved or could have been handled differently are essential. Importantly, it is not the activity per se that achieves these objectives, but the process surrounding the activity that is vital. Activities are the means to achieve the process. Interesting and motivating activities increase the likelihood that meaningful results will occur.

Our objective is to help young people in their passage from childhood through adolescence to adulthood. We have found over the years that the arts offer a vehicle for this to occur. We have also found that Carl Rogers' [1965] observations about the helping relationship ring true. What were those observations? Rogers felt that four helping characteristics in caregivers were necessary in order to facilitate change. Those characteristics were honesty, trustworthiness, genuineness, and empathy on the part of the helper or caregiver. When a caregiver truly displays these behaviors and is seen doing so by a young person, change—real change—occurs. Against this backdrop of general organizing principles, the following activities have been gradually added over the past twenty-five years to comprise the current Creative Experiences Program.

Program Offerings

Creative Arts Classes

Program staff team-teach with classroom teachers in grades Pre-K through high school. Teachers invite staff into their classrooms and participate in activities like learning noncompetitive games, mask making, scene study, interpretive dance, creative writing, stage makeup, costuming, puppetry, scenic design, play writing, photography, painting, play direction and production, television production and self-awareness exploration. Activities are supportive and promote the development of mastery and positive group process.

Crossroads

Crossroads is a filmmaking group for high school students. Participants have developed videotape movies to share with their peers relating to teen suicide prevention, adolescence, and drug and alcohol abuse. The students conduct their own research into a given topic, develop a script, and videotape the movie. A staff member then helps the students to edit the movie. Once completed, movies are placed in the town and school libraries for public viewing.

Double-Take

Double-Take is an improvisational workshop for students in grades 7-12. The group meets weekly to practice problem solving, public speaking, communication skills, and improvisational performance techniques. Participants have found the experience helpful in preparing for job and college interviews, as well handling unexpected public opportunities to speak.

Enrichment Mentoring

One of the best ways to learn about leadership and responsibility is by teaching others. Many of the activities Creative Experiences offers does just this. For example, high school students offer enrichment programs in the arts to elementary school students. Six-week programs are held after school in the school setting or the children are brought to the agency. Classes are advertised and filled on a "first come, first served basis". Classes have included; Beginning Dance, Improvisational Acting, Stage Make-up, Costuming, How to Audition, Videography, and Arts and Crafts. Classes are chosen by students based on their interest in the area. High school mentors are taught to involve everyone in the class process and to praise all that try to be successful. Supervised by a staff member, the mentors are responsible for the registration of students, creating the content of the class, gathering materials, teaching the class and surveying the participants for comments and suggestions for future programs.

Odyssey of the Mind

Odyssey of the Mind is an international organization that teaches youth how to use both critical and creative thinking skills through problem solving. Teams are given a problem to solve each year. The solution is then presented at regional competitions, state competitions, and international competitions. Each team is permitted to have seven members and requires an adult coach. Problems may range from mechanical creation to theatrical performance.

Odyssey of the Mind is one of the few activities that we are involved in that has a competitive element. Since mastery can be undermined when competitors lose, it is important that coaches focus on the process of problem solving rather than the outcome of winning or losing.

Open Houses

Open Houses are offered twice a year to eighth grade students to provide feedback to program staff. We especially seek their input because the eighth grade is a year of important transition in young people's lives, and we make a special effort to be relevant to this age group. Creative Experiences staff share program ideas and seek student input. Our objective is not only to familiarize students with the program but also to encourage their ownership of activities offered.

Pass It On and Town Hall Happenings

"Pass It On" gives students an opportunity to produce and direct a quality half-hour cable television program for the community. The program has aired weekly for the last twenty years. Program content has included entertaining, informative, and educational topics. Each month a similar group tapes a program entitled "Town Hall Happenings" for the Town Manager.

To illustrate how process rather than product governs activities, let's take a closer look at "Pass It On." Young people involved with "Pass It On" meet weekly with staff to plan future program content.

The roles of camera person, sound person, video director, and hosts are decided for each show. Opportunities for each role are rotated so that everyone has the chance to learn different aspects of the production. After a show is taped, the production crew with staff debrief. Problems like the failure of a camera person to accept the direction of the video director are worked out in these group meetings. Using positive peer pressure to effect behavioral change is too often underutilized in our society. These types of activities are structured to take advantage of these learning opportunities. Laughter, anger, and often new appreciation of another person's point of view on topics that can range from the value of a vegetarian diet to the need to preserve open space are just some of discussions we have had.

Theatrical Productions

Theatrical productions provide young people with an opportunity to be actively involved with children their own age and adults other than their parents or staff. Skills that are required for successful participation, such as dancing, singing, or set construction, are taught. Each young person is required to sign a contract of behavior confirming a willingness to try. The rewards the participants receive for their participation include community approval (applause and recognition), mastery of communication skills, and a sense of belonging and being valued within the group. Creative Experiences offers several theatrical productions, each ranging from the very small to a titanic summer musical.

For example, the Peter Pan Players are junior and senior high school students who perform children's theater pieces for the elementary schools and community senior citizen centers. Incorporated within each performance is information about the services available at the agency and an invitation to young people to get involved with a Creative Experiences activity. Performances take place during the school day, so performers are required to maintain a "B" average in the classes they will miss.

For 25 years, summer musical auditions have been held in June for a production in mid-August. Residents ages eight and up, including adults, are invited to participate in every aspect of the production, whether it be in the performance, technical crew, or orchestra. No one is refused entrance to the program. Past productions have involved as many as 480 community residents.

Volunteers are an integral part of all of the programs, but this is especially true of the musical production. All of the performer's parents are asked to complete a parent's registration form that requests them to choose areas in which they would like to help in the production including: costuming, scenic design and building, fundraising, cast T-shirts, technical crew, hall monitors, special events, and a specific position entitled: Parent Producer. The Parent Producer attends weekly staff meetings and shares areas where training and support are needed for the volunteers. He or she is available to the volunteers when staff members cannot be reached.

Parents are required to attend an organizational meeting where the needs of the production, safety, and job descriptions are explained. After the presentation chairpersons are requested. Lists of the volunteers are compiled from the information found on the parent registration forms and are given to each chairperson.

The playbill lists all of the chairpersons and volunteers involved in the production. Each year, the staff chooses outstanding volunteers for public recognition, and at company meetings everyone involved is recognized for their work and applauded. Again, our intention is to promote connections with the community and a sense of belonging and contributing at every level, from child performer to adult volunteer. We realize that volunteers must be nurtured. Without them the program would fail, but more on that later.

The fall production consists of 20 students in grades 7 through 12. The smaller size of the ensemble contributes to the discussion of a theme presented in the play. Many of the students involved are considering communications as a future career. Members of the cast take responsibility for fundraising, costumes, scenery, and other production requirements. The small group size contributes to increased opportunities for self-reflection and exploration of meaning and self-identity.

In all of the theatrical productions, staff and volunteers struggle with the balance between using talented performers and those youth for whom the experience would have special importance in their lives. A casting committee chooses the youth for roles. This committee consists of staff, students, and adult volunteers with the Creative Experiences director quietly advocating and acting to insure that the balance between using talented performers and those youth for whom the experience would have special meaning in their lives is maintained.

The Youth Services Action Group

The Youth Services Action group is a service learning organization. It meets weekly to plan and undertake community service projects like helping to staff the Nayaug Canoe Race and Connecticut River Celebration held by a local land conservation group, assisting the local arts society with its annual arts show, or helping the public library with its semi-annual book sale. At each meeting, requests for help from various organizations are considered and voted on by the membership. If a request for help is accepted, an action plan is developed and chairpersons for that one activity are selected.

An annual event for the Youth Services Action Group has been a Halloween Haunted House. Intended to offer young children a safe but scary experience, over 60 live actors create the House and perform for an entire weekend. Another annual event offered by this group of young people is a Cultural Diversity Fair, where individual ethnicity is explored and celebrated through games, displays, food, music, and arts and crafts.

As noted earlier in this paper, after each event group members process the experience and evaluate the quality of the service they provided. Sometimes projects fail to reach the goals young people set for themselves. Sometimes the promises the young people made to appear at an event in the numbers promised does not happen. Sometimes the leaders of a project do not follow through with their responsibilities. Sometimes disappointment and not satisfaction is the prevalent mood of a meeting. Here again, though, is a wonderful opportunity for growth to occur. The Youth Services Action Group, like other Creative Experience groups, is a service-*learning* organization, and learning often takes place when mistakes are made.

Organizational and Staffing Isssues

Worker Characteristics

Experience has taught us that the successful youth worker possesses several qualities. Those qualities are:

- To be a patient and good listener
- To permit youth to fail and help them learn from that experience
- To be open minded; allowing youth to form their own opinion
- To be able to make youth think
- To treat everyone equally (no favoritism)
- To be an effective communicator
- To treat youth as equal, but know where and when to draw the line and keep roles clear.

Youth workers must be able to work with a diverse group of youth (ethnic, social, suburban/urban, educational, and economic differences). Drawing from our own experience, we have found that academic training does not predict whether an individual will be able to work successfully with young people. This is not to say that academic training in the social sciences is not helpful but that what really matters are the qualities that Carl Rogers [1965] observed more than thirty years ago. Again, those worker qualities discussed earlier in this chapter were being honesty, being trustworthy, being genuine, and being empathic. Also, remember that the young person must understand the worker to possess and demonstrate these qualities toward him or her.

The Importance of Volunteers

Presently, the staff of Creative Experiences consists of two full-time employees and several part-time individuals (often college students or teachers). The sheer number of activities that we are engaged in speaks to the importance of adult volunteers. Many of these wonderful and generous individuals have been a part of the program for over ten years, (long after their children have graduated). They remain involved after their children move on to other activities because they feel valued and are included in all aspects of decision-making. They, in turn, welcome new adult members and share their enthusiasm for the program. Given the value we place on community, this program could not operate without these adults who, by their actions, promote a sense of community, provide roles models for youth, and give, by their time, opportunities for youth to connect with adults outside their family and school.

When Creative Experiences staff plan to utilize community volunteers, we engage in a self- study that requires us to answer the following questions:

- What needs can the volunteer meet?
- Is there a clear job description for the volunteer?
- What skills or knowledge are required of the volunteer?
- Is there a manual developed for the volunteer to refer to? (This manual often consists of 1 to 3 typewritten pages that answers common sense questions related to the specific activity.)
- In the volunteer recruitment process are we concrete and specific in our appeal for help?
- How will the volunteers be trained and supported?
- How will we maintain volunteer enthusiasm and commitment for this activity?

Each activity generates different responses to this set of questions. Completing this exercise provides us with clear understanding of our need for volunteers and enables us to straightforwardly explain those needs to a volunteer. It helps us to avoid one of the most common and unfortunate of all complaints made by volunteers, "I showed up, as I was asked to, but there was nothing for me to do. I was not needed!"

Program Evaluation

Evaluations can range from brief process assessments focusing on utilization patterns and internal program dynamics to long-term longitudinal outcome studies with large sample sizes, random assignment, and validated instruments. Evaluation provides feedback regarding the effectiveness of services and evidence that your efforts are worthwhile. Every program should include some form of evaluation to determine if or how well the activity is meeting its self-stated goals and objectives.

In selecting an evaluation methodology, it is necessary to measure the costs and benefits of qualitative and quantitative methods. Evaluations that meet scientific standards are expensive and may not be feasible in all settings. Qualitative analysis that seeks and obtains feedback from participants can be very useful and relatively easy to conduct. Testimonials can be very effective in convincing youth to participate in programming and potential funding sources to see the value of services.

Creative Experiences conducts process assessments at the end of each program cycle and utilizes written surveys and group process to obtain feedback about the effectiveness of services. The program is continually evolving based on the feedback obtained from these process evaluations.

Conclusion

This paper has shared a set of operating principles and suggested program activities for promoting the social competency of young people. Our work over the past 25 years has focused on providing enjoyable activities that provide youth with opportunities for mastery, a sense of belonging, and an appreciation of the value of community service. These values are present in different combinations and with differing emphasis in each of the programs described. Given the feedback we have received from children, their parents over the years, and in letters from adults who once were children participating in these activities, we believe that these programs and operating principles help ease young people along the passage from childhood to adulthood.

References

Rogers, C. R. (1965). The therapeutic relationship: Recent theory and research. *Australian Journal of Psychology, 17,* 95–108.

7

Integrating Resilient Youth into Strong Communities Through Festivals, Fairs, and Feasts

Maureen K. Porter

At the hub of every mechanical watch is the main spring. Once wound tightly, it is the wellspring of energy that drives the timepiece, distributing kinetic energy as it unfurls from its center. Much like a watch, a community derives its dynamism from a focused nexus of energy that, like the center coil, must be regularly recharged. Festivals are the way we infuse life into the places we call home.

Organized, meaningful play at regular intervals provides not only the spark to keep things moving, but also serves as the regulator for the creative give and take of crafting local and personal identities. Rituals of celebration provide a different twist on daily life, a new turn that restores energy and enthusiasm for shared civic life. Whatever form they take, festivals, fairs, and feasts are more than a luxury; they are essential to the long-term viability of any human community. For just as a watch, if left unwound, inevitably grinds to a halt, a community that does not play together cannot stay together.

Becoming wound up in a celebration, letting go of other cares, and enjoying a shared moment is particularly important for those community members at the periphery of the system. Young people are often marginal members of their hometowns, dependent on the actions of bigger cogs who are positioned more centrally in government, education, and social services. Like the outermost gears on the watch's wheel train, to those on the edge, the community may seem like a lethargic, overly predictable, impersonal machine. All too often, we maintain youth in this passive role, seldom inviting them to directly contribute to the activities necessary to keep their town running. But in a festival, regular social position takes a back seat to the new role of "participant" that all share. Everyone is invited to become a stakeholder in the success of the event, and, by extension, the long-term health of the community. Celebration demonstrates that we are all linked in one human enterprise, that we are all part of an interdependent mechanism.

Many Kinds of Celebrations

When watches are wound, all components are engaged. Likewise, at fair time, communities turn their focus inward, drawing young people in as the concentric bands of society are wrapped tighter and tighter in the shared focus on having fun. During feasts, celebrants bring their individual cultural strengths to the table and, together, create a smorgasbord of ideals, myths, goals, and identities that define who they are as a group. Festivals offer communities the chance to highlight what makes them special and what connects the various subcommunities who call a particular place home.

My use of the three pivotal terms ("festival," "fair," and "feast") is meant as a heuristic, not a constraint. Throughout the chapter I will alternate use of the terms "fair," "feast," and "festival" to stand for youth-centered community celebrations of various kinds. They are by no means the only forms available. Indeed, they are but three points along a continuum of large- and small-scale celebrations. Most of the examples I use are those that strive to involve a significant portion of a community. However, the underlying structures, outcomes, and issues involved in fostering a successful gala are just as applicable to a small recreation program's final field day or a church bazaar.

Readers may start at different points when purposely (re)designing a celebration to enhance resiliency among youth. Festivals specifically geared to celebrating the lives of children, e.g., Japan's Girl's Day, Boy's Day and Korea's Children's Day, are great occasions to adapt to United States customs and sensibilities. Holidays which revolve around child-centered activities, e.g. Halloween, can be reassessed and expanded to provide safe, prosocial opportunities for family fun. Civic holidays also offer occasions for renewal. Intergenerational events on Memorial Day or Founders' Day can bolster waning support and commitment to the values embodied in these days of recognition and remembrance.

By focusing on the constructive and inclusive potential of festivals, the emphasis shifts from consumption to community. For example, activities for children and youth can be integrated into adult-centered events such as Oktoberfest or New Year's Eve. Without the sobering presence of children, these rich events might degrade into an exclusive focus on publicly-sanctioned alcohol and drug consumption. While responsible imbibing enhances an event for some, that alone is insufficient grounds for a community to come together to sponsor such an event. There is so much more to be enjoyed, so much fun to be had in a variety of ways. If the focus is primarily on personal indulgence, much of what is truly meaningful about celebrations is lost.

As I have described in depth elsewhere [see Porter 1995], specific community celebrations have their own particular formats, strengths, and set of objectives. At the same time, they share essential elements that make them powerful and long-lasting parts of community life all over the world. Celebrations are more than opportunities for recreation and passive entertainment. They offer spectators the invitation to become engaged, to come to the table and partake of a nourishing, appealing feast. Once caught up in the fun, it becomes harder to simply push away from the table.

Format

Unlike a strictly mechanical invention such as a watch, celebrations are flexible, dynamic, and evolving. They do not proceed mechanistically, nor are they ultimately limited in their final form, action, or rhythm. Thus, what I offer is not a formula for a standard, preordained ritual. Indeed, to do so would be antithetical to the very nature of (public) celebrations. I intend this chapter to be more like a toolbox full of many-notched gears, sets of springs, and levers for change. What each community development agency, recreation department, youth group leader, or concerned parent builds with these tools is left to their own imagination.

In this chapter, I will explore the mechanics of celebration as a revitalizing enterprise. In the first section, I will outline the core characteristics that make celebrations run. Second, I present the outcomes that contribute to both strong communities and resilient youth. Some of these results are tangible, e.g. financial resources to reinvest in youth programming, while others are more abstract, e.g. a sense of legacy. I then synthesize these lessons into a list of caveats and challenges for designing enduring celebrations. In summing up, I revisit this organizing metaphor and propose three sensibilities to which public celebrations contribute: sense of place, a sense of self, and a sense of community.

Core Dimensions

What makes festivals, fairs, and feasts tick? What are the underlying structures that keep people coming back to city streets, town squares, and mountain hollers time after time? In this section I introduce five essential elements through which celebrations engage passive residents and transform them into communicant revelers.

An Excuse to Gather Together

It may be obvious to begin by stating that celebrations offer community members a reason to come out of their homes and join together. However, the simplicity of this statement belies its importance as a prerequisite for any kind of community building. All too often we allow our toys and tools to isolate us - each child has a TV in their room, we call the neighbor or store rather than walk or drive over, we cook ready-made meals in tiny, dead-bolted efficiencies rather than eat in the company of others. We fear the inner urban core or the backwoods and seldom venture outside the work-grocery-home-daycare corridor. Each loosening of the linchpins that hold us securely in place further thrusts us into an unbalanced, uncoordinated, isolated existence.

Before we can restore balance to our communities, we must find compelling reasons for people of all ages to come together. Before people can become reenergized, they must become engaged. By this I mean first-hand, direct experience: being there, smelling the food, tasting the excitement, hearing the beat of the music, feeling the chill of competition, seeing others doing the same. Just as in sporting events, the communal aspect of festival is crucial to its success (Giamatti, 1989, p. 15). Watching a parade on television is a far cry from being there in person. Although media and technology can facilitate spectatorship on a grand scale, it provides the audience of the latest Macy's Parade, Olympics, or World Cup only a media-ted, second-hand experience. Further, it encourages voyeurism of *other* people's celebrations, actions, and lifeways. There is no substitute for being there at your own celebration.

Offering first-hand engagement with others is especially important to isolated youth. This applies whether they live on a remote wind-swept plain, in a cavernous honeycomb of inner urban projects, or in a dissected, fenced-in cubicle of a sprawling suburb. Young people are at a particular disadvantage if they have been raised in an environment that encourages reliance on pre-formatted media as a means of entertainment. They need direct encounters that challenge them to make their own meaning of the event, to filter the sensory smorgasbord, and to capture their own memories. Sponsoring engaging community festivals that they want to attend is a critically important way to draw youth out into the public arena.

Time to Focus Inward

During a festival, participants are called to focus on the specific activities at hand. Events highlight that which is distinctive about the local area, ethnic group, date, or achievement that prompted or sponsored the gathering. Fairs offer members, newcomers, and spectators the chance to take a close look at what a community stands for. As Giamatti (1989, p. 13) asserts, "we can learn far more about the conditions, and values, of a society by contemplating how it chooses to play, to use its free time, to take its leisure, than by examining how it goes about its work." It is the unique local synthesis that is so rich. Individual community members and personalities, regional cuisine, musical traditions, particular institutions and social clubs all are given center ring.

Turning inward during times of celebration does not mean that influences of the mass public media culture are suspended. Indeed, how could they be in a world so saturated and defined by Disney, cable programs, mall fashions, Nike, Coke, and so many others? Instead, focus turns inward, past the generic toward that which is unique and worth noting.

Promoting and constantly (re)creating their festivals does more than mark a group as present. Burke states that such "exclusive moments - coalescing around class or ethnicity - are associated with a resistance to modernization and a (re) affirmation of an oppositional identity" (1992, pp. 293-294). Festivals answer the questions of who "we" are and what we stand for. By critically reexamining which parts of an event are still relevant and which have become even more important at a particular point in time, organizers have to come to terms with their place in the larger world.

Festivals reflect the changing needs and perspectives of the sponsors. Especially for groups who feel threatened with amalgamation into the melting pot or homogenization into nothingness, standing for something is a way of standing fast in uncertain times. What does it mean to be a Chicano/a in this place at this time? Which elements of our Mississippi River heritage inform what we want to stand for in the next century? There are many ways to approach this dilemma. Sponsors may honor the past and enact replicas of traditional kinds of festivals, reinvent long-standing events, or purposely create entirely new fairs that meet emerging needs (Stern & Cicala 1991).

Organizers need to ask themselves questions about the focus, and hence the purpose, of the event. As feminist, multicultural, and/ or environmental ethics become more a part of everyday discourse and practice, how should we interpret long-standing activities? Should there be a queen or beauty pageant? Should there be vegetarian options available at some or all food stands? Should traditional,

German-speaking polka bands dominate, or should we invite the polka avante garde?

A Distinctive Space and Time

Having a place to hold an event is another essential element of festival planning. Many celebrations can lay claim to a particular location, such as the county fairgrounds or the lakefront, for the duration of the event. Knowing that a place is held sacred, that is, set apart for special ritualized activity, can reinforce its potency. Festival grounds, once decorated and brought to life, are transformed into an "elaborated place" (Abrahams, 1982, p. 161). A grand entryway lets you know that you have arrived someplace special. Icons, decorations, tents, special rides, or exhibits all display the themes of the event. Within the grounds, "kiddie rides" or "teen tents" further demarcate places reserved for special cohorts.

It takes concerted efforts to defend what has been established. Buffering fairgrounds from encroaching development, preserving park space, and rebuilding a dance hall are ways of symbolizing that the need for these spaces remains, that the community's cycle of celebrations goes on. The simple existence of "the commons" takes on new layers of meaning. Residents have a tangible place to refer to when thinking of and anticipating meaningful activities. As Fitchen [1991] notes in her study of rural life, the land itself becomes both setting and symbol of rural folklife.

Although the luxury of separate competition fields, powwow grounds, or rodeo arena is wonderful when available, festivals need not have physically distinct locations to be powerful. Indeed, sometimes it is the transformation of private spaces into public places, of the mundane into the magical that marks a successful festival. Church yards and cemeteries can become the meeting grounds for kinship celebrations, family reunions, and annual pilgrimages (Neville, 1987). Main Street is more than a major avenue when it is lined with throngs of spectators waiting anxiously for the Juneteenth parade to start. The town's seashore takes on a new sheen when it is draped with blankets and picnic paraphernalia, as visitors "ooh" and "aah" to the crackle of Fourth of July fireworks. These spaces have been reclaimed, they have become "places." And people "come home" to places.

Most festivals happen as part of an annual cycle. Once, nearly all were inspired by natural phenomenon and in many places there are still clear linkages to agricultural and climactic cycles. We have harvest fests, winter carnivals, and summertime waterplay, fish boils, and corn roasts. Through public affirmations of the cyclical nature of life, young people come to understand the importance of seasonal activities in their region. They develop finer sensibilities about the nature and qualities of their homeplace.

Official celebrations remind us of important turning points and natural processes. But just as important is what setting time aside to celebrate symbolizes—an awe for life. Baylor's [1986] evocative book about celebrating the wonder in every season reminds us how important it is to simply take time to acknowledge the majesty of life itself.

Having a special place to hold a feast, or having a special weekend set aside to hold a fair both contribute to the power of rituals of renewal. However, organizers do not need a great deal of lead time or a change of seasons to call for a celebration. Mayors and other leaders should feel free to recognize the unexpected. The girls' lacrosse team wins the state competition! The local macaroni company owner is named Small Business Entrepreneur of the Year! Selfless residents' massive sandbagging maneuver has saved downtown from river flooding! The important thing is to draw attention to the kinds of events, people, and ideals that make this a place to be proud to call home.

Whether specific times to celebrate are planned or arise spontaneously, they are all good. The important thing is that we take time to do so. Just as children search for meaning with an open, questioning mind, so too must we nurture a sense of "reenchantment in everyday life." Celebrations make sure that we pause long enough to reflect at least once in a while. Seeking out personal places to recharge is important in creating meaningful spaces. These need not be grand venues, in fact, as Moore [1996, p. 237] notes: "Spectacle and festival are part of athletics, but if our stadiums become too big and too sensational, then the power of the game to satisfy the soul may falter . . . The simple, the ordinary, and the intimate always give more to the heart than the extraordinary and the grand, which enhance the spirit but not necessarily the soul." Communities need places for spontaneous, informal celebrations to nurture the best in young people. Parks, playgrounds, halls, pick-up ball fields, and community centers all can be sites for celebration.

Freedom to Play

We cannot overlook the importance of simply playing. Festivals offer participants the chance to relax from the pressures of the school, workplace, and home. Many fairs feature rides, games, storytelling, musical entertainment, competitions, races, animal rides and other activities that are not otherwise available. Families come out for fairs because they want to have fun together.

Young people need safe and inviting venues in which to develop personal and interpersonal skills. Athletic field days offer opportunities for competition as well as cooperation. If they are well monitored, the games are fair, the rules known, and the bounds of sporting behavior are maintained, they provide an exciting climax to a season of preparation and practice. Within these relatively safe boundaries, the challenge of personal accomplishment comes to the fore.

Play is liberating, and through playful expression, creative. At play, we see, model, and reward certain values—stealth, speed, cunning, wordplay, athletic prowess. Winning is not always the primary goal, but rather it may simply be participation and striving toward worthwhile, valued ends. Young people see that adults value the development of these skills enough to put in the time in organizing a public forum. By playing with and under the watchful eye of their mentors, play is a particularly engaging form of moral education [Kridel 1980].

Opportunities to gather and play may be increasingly rare, but they have never been more important. Gallagher [1993, p. 180] notes that, especially in large urban settings, playing and eating offer two of the few reasons that large numbers of people voluntarily come together. When such gatherings bring together thousands of residents, or even tens of thousands, the elements of frivolity and feasting help to diffuse the tensions of being crowded together, both during the festival as well as in urban life in general. She adds that participants generally do respect a truce of civility and try to get along with other partygoers. However, she wonders whether the politeness may only be superficial and thus perhaps insincere, like using a new acquaintance's first name too easily without actually getting to know the person underneath.

Likewise, civic festivals may provide a pressure valve for pent up ethnic, racial, or neighborhood animosities. By using shared spaces and enjoying barbecues or spaghetti suppers, people who might not otherwise have—or seek out—opportunities to be together can congregate. Opportunities to play together give residents something external to either group on which to focus. Shared interests and enjoyments can emerge.

Although festival organizers can offer refreshing waters of reconciliation, whether this confluence leads to any fundamental shift in the flow of social discourse remains a highly personal and idiosyncratic thing. However, if subcommunities remained completely segregated, the likelihood of even civil exchange developing is slight. And, given the decidedly uncivil ways of claiming and marking territory that are rampant from many inner urban zones to small towns, perhaps simply raising our expectations of friendly interaction is a necessary precondition to successful community building.

Lastly, the playful, or ludic, aspects of festival gain momentum when they offer participants the opportunity to re-create themselves. Masked balls, costume contests, and cross-dressing revues are obvious forms of trying on and satirizing different personas. They offer little risk for behaviors that otherwise might be deemed unseemly. In fact, in a parade an exhibitor can be excused for his or her flamboyance or wackiness by spectators with "he's just pretending," or "she'd make a good Annie Oakley, wouldn't she?" Many parades offer children the chance to see and be seen, to strut their stuff. When else would they - and their parents- be publicly praised for the child's wearing a favorite Superman outfit out on the sidewalk and then at the grocery store? Costumes offer both refuge and plumage. Marching band members can hide behind uniforms and blend into the troupe or can use the same uniforms to attract paramours' and peers' attention as members of an esteemed cadre of young performers.

Networks and Teamwork

Feasts are a lot of work. They also offer many rewards, some of which are personal and intangible while others are communal and tangible. Fair time offers the opportunity for groups—from Boy Scouts to B'hai B'rinth youth groups—to gain visibility, income, and experience. Simply seeing and being seen is an important part of coming out for a celebration. Young people see others working hard for the common benefit. Residents of all ages get the chance to see beyond media caricatures and stereotypes. Instead of the predominant picture of young people as lazy, rude, uncontrollable, apathetic, and worse, fairgoers see young people staffing food booths, taking an order or providing change cheerfully, involved and responsible. Conversely, young participants see adults giving volunteer time and labor rather than simply complaining about others' leadership (or lack of leadership).

Personal rewards can be significant. The more youth groups are highlighted and young leaders' work recognized, the better young people feel about themselves and their place in the community. Tangible recognition for the roles that they have played and are playing further reinforce young contributors' sense that they have a personal stake in the success or failure of an event. Staff T-shirts, ribbons, or a post-event recognition banquets all prolong the sense of being important and needed beyond the duration of the event itself. These elements are essential to building solid support for future events.

Other elements contribute to strong communities. Civic groups and service clubs can earn a large portion of their annual revenue at a good-sized event. Hopefully, the clubs will reinvest in the community by spending profits on town decorations, services, a youth center, service-learning projects, recreation programs, intergenerational activities, and other local projects, as well as the next feast or fair. This is so important that in some communities, local clubs' reinvestment in the local recreational and social infrastructure is a prerequisite for being offered a chance to earn funds. By taking the funds and reinvesting them in the next event, they contribute to an interdependent clockwork of celebrations. Within the cycle of annual festivals, there is thus a linked chain—one profitable, successful event provides energy and enthusiasm for another.

Taken on a larger scale, working together to design and carry out a festival provides valuable experience in working together and mobilizing regional resources. This may start as a youth group sponsoring a highway cleanup weekend, which down the road spurs an ongoing recycling program. Connections, friendships, exchanges, and physical property all can be accumulated and put to effective use. Aronoff notes that this helps more than just the local town: "celebrations offer residents a low-risk arena in which to develop a region-wide identity, social relationships, and organizational linkages that subsequently become available as resources for direct economic planning" (1993, p. 3). Interested and motivated young people really can get older residents moving in positive directions if it is in the guise of having fun.

Together, these essential qualities of good festivals are what bring communities together around pivotal points of agreement. By drawing in young people as integral, meaningful partners, celebrations offer them venues for becoming participants rather than peripheral spectators. Like the gears of a watch's wheel train, the energy that youth bring to these fairs is tremendous, but unless channeled and focused it remains only potential energy. Once turned on by a festival, they are transformed into enthusiastic, kinetic movers and shakers, ready to contribute to the growing momentum of civic renewal.

Outcomes

Both watches and communities are tools that humans have created and constantly tinker with. Both are particular responses to deeply-felt human desires to bring order, continuity, and aesthetic sensibilities to an otherwise abstract and chaotic lifeworld. In addition to being a tool to use time well, a watch also reifies a particular concept of time itself. Thus, it is not enough to know "how" a watch works or celebrations do their thing; rather, we need to know "what" they do for the participants.

When a watch works well, it provides its human creators with the means of conceptualizing, understanding, and marking time. Our thinking is fundamentally metaphorical. For example, common American phrases about time reflect our conceptualization of "time as commodity" [Lakoff &Johnson, 1980, p. 7]. In our Western, capitalist mind frame, we thus can "clock," "allocate," "spend," "give away," and—heaven forbid—"waste" time. We also watch the progress of the clock hands in circles and conceptualize time as discrete units, strung together in a never-ending, never reclaimable chain of events. This in turn provides that basis for thinking that the "past" is gone and irretrievable, provides a sense of orderliness to the "present," and provides a sense of continuity with which we can anticipate and respond to a "future." Certainly these time-as-commodity metaphors are neither universal nor the only ones we could invent; the fact is that they dominate our current level of thinking about the world.

In a similar way, when a celebration functions well, it provides its human creators with both the tools for marking off when we have accomplished something, as well as for reinforcing underlying concepts about what it means to belong and strive as one entity. They give participants a sense of being part of a continuing cycle of celebration that their forebears started and that they perpetuate for the benefit of the generations to come. Well-planned and executed feasts, fairs, and festivals reinvigorate their host communities and engage young people in meaningful play. What are the resulting lessons when things go well? The following section highlights some of the principle outcomes of good community celebrations.

Provides a Focus and Highlights That Which is Noteworthy

Every chamber of commerce leader designing public relations materials and every child trying to define his or her place in the world searches to identify those features that make their homeplace special. Public celebrations make the symbols of a community explicit, i.e. the ideals, logos, slogans, and mascots that mark a place as being distinctive [Grimes 1976; Hinsdale et al. 1995; Lavenda, 1997]. In public forums and parades, both participants and organizers have the chance to see these unique elements on display. The more often the symbols are displayed in conjunction with the celebration, the stronger they become. Thus it is the repetition of these core symbols on floats, T-shirts, trophies, displays, uniforms, entryways, and more that make it clear to any passerby that something exciting and meaningful is underway. Golbeck (1985) notes that such markers, boundaries, and landmarks are particularly important for children who are trying to make sense out of complex environments. By making these guides as explicit as possible, we can help novices develop confidence in their ability to fit in and join in the fun.

When organizing a complex community-wide celebration, it is often preferable to search for a core icon or identity around which to organize the festival theme. Organizers may choose an ethnic, geographic, or historical basis for this theme. A monocultural focus, such as Cajun Days or Rodeo Revival, need not imply that the focus is narrow, just that a specific core exists. Internal diversity will still be present, but the focus is on commonalties, kinship, a (mythical) ethnic past, and honorary membership á la "Irish for the Day."

Whatever theme is chosen, the challenge is to highlight that which is special. Who wants to attend an exhibition where there is nothing new, creative, or vaguely stimulating? If the wares, entertainment, and displays are those that could be seen anyplace, why come? Kids need to know that there will be something curious, something exciting waiting there for them.

Fairs are not the time to hide residents' prowess and local pride. What is this community/club/school about? What do we do particularly well? Celebrations are about highlighting what is unique, and, if not singular, that which is highly valued and noteworthy in a place. Residents need to know that they live in a homeplace that inspires pride rather than embarrassment. Teenagers, who are quick to be candid about adult failures and foibles, are in particular need of something that they can point to with pride. Festivals provide that canvas upon which a positive picture of local life can be painted and then displayed to the greater public.

In a lively community, celebrations happen on a regular basis, but no two are exactly alike. Part of making a forum unique is to use props to set the stage. The first impression created by an event's physical structures is key to making it distinguishable from other feasts that may take place on the same school grounds or at other times of the year. Decorations, tents, ribbons, and trophies can usually be bought or rented locally (and should be whenever possible). Use of stock items need not lead to a generic Everyfest. While stores may stock only a very limited supply of party goods (or seemingly endless variations on what amounts to an equally small number of themes), the key to their successful use is in adapting them to fit particular needs and competitions.

Give participants a momento to take home. And it need not cost anything extra—a collectable, well-designed entry ticket, wristband, or pin can be included in the cost of admission. Label them with where, why, and/or how they were acquired. Personalized souvenirs and awards are much more meaningful than carnival kitsch that could be purchased anywhere. The result is that participants have something tangible that they can collect, display, and show off.

Food booths featuring regional cuisine are a key component of almost any public gathering (Humphrey &Humphrey 1988). They provide prime venues to showcase the skills of local chefs and connoisseurs. Chili cookoffs or other appropriate contests highlight the regional tastes and specialties. Most groups, including youth groups, welcome the opportunity to raise money and gain recognition by staffing their own booths. The service that they provide is more than repaid by the pride, recognition, reputation, and exposure that they derive from being in the public eye. Furthermore, the quality of their work nearly always surpasses the kinds of perfunctory service provided by underpaid, nonlocal vendors for whom this is just another place to earn a buck.

Creates a Sense of Perspective

A festival can only be understood in context. Who started this annual event? How has it changed? Why has attendance dropped off or increased? How does this festival compare to others during the year or in other parts of the state? Participants come to see that they are part of an ongoing chain. Only by developing a sense of perspective, of history, can they begin to imagine a future for the event.

Just as the hands of a watch make the passage of time visible, so too do the elements of a feast make the work behind the scenes tangible. Youth who are involved understand that the success of festivals depends on the "ordinary courage" shown by leaders. Persistence, e.g. despite adverse weather conditions, are all lessons in resilience that young people can see modeled by adult organizers.

If they are part of the planning process, youth enter into critical discussions about the purpose and future of civic events. Which holidays do we deem worthy of recognizing? Which beliefs, ideals, and structures are to be given center stage? In their landmark collaborative study of the role of community festivals in transforming a community, Hinsdale, Lewis, and Waller [1995, p. 104] found that "the parades and rituals anticipated the changes and new themes that the community was creating. Blending old meanings and new forms, combining a re-union and a new union, calling forth relationships from an earlier era, community rituals are an important part of the community development process." If this process is civil and constructive, young people gain a poignant illustration of how communities negotiate what they stand for. By helping to choose the symbols and characters in the town's parade and oral history program, they become partners in creating a living legacy. By being involved firsthand in the work behind the scenes, they further gain a sense of perspective about the amount of time and variety of skills that are necessary to pull off even a small event. By working with their leaders and community officials, young people can see a more human, personal side to these adults that can further strengthen respect and admiration for them.

Conservation of achievements over time can also be enhanced by utilizing technology and multiple media. These can be great assets in documenting, assessing, prompting, and archiving your own celebrations. However, they should be complements to, even vehicles for, direct participation rather than substitutes for direct involvement. Young people may be particularly adept at creating an interactive or real-time documentary of a festival if provided skilled instruction and sufficient tools.

Dramatizes Valued Traits and Skills

When people gather to celebrate, they hopefully bring their best with them. They tell old family stories, retell community histories, recount ways of understanding relationships between the sexes, different classes, or school teams. The public nature of such celebrations is critical. For they offer a "common ground," where shared values and standards come to the fore. Kemmis [1990, p. 75] notes, "What barn building and violin playing, softball and steer raising all have fundamentally in common is this: all of them deal with questions of value, with what is good or excellent (a well-built barn, a well-executed double play), but they all do so in an explicitly social setting, wherein purely subjective or individualistic inclinations are flatly irrelevant, if not counterproductive." Through pageants, contests and judging events they recognize those who have achieved in valued categories. Who has the fastest toddler? The best jam? The most stylish fashions inspired by traditional ethnic fabrics? Who has the strongest street rod? Who has the best home remodeling project or urban redevelopment plan?

Whether a school science fair or a county fair, most of the space is reserved for displaying (youth) achievements. When projects are coupled with a live interpreter or written explanation, the teaching value of the event is greatly increased. For example, visitors learn that a doghouse was made out of recycled siding. The young exhibitor choosing to highlight this on his tag is reinforced in his knowledge that recycling would be valued by those who see the doghouse. Visitors who can praise the creator or question the apprentice about some aspect of the project get more out of the experience. Both learn from the encounter when more experienced exhibitors recount a story of their own participation, as in "When I was your age I did this too . . ."

While many core values endure, others change. Humor is essential to any intensive project. However, this too is subjective and shifts markedly over time and location. Nothing kills enthusiasm for a festival more than the sense that it is stale and unseemly.

Like an old joke that has outlived its welcome, humor changes with the times to reflect the sensibilities, concerns, and lingo of the age. Ethnic and stereotype jokes that once may have been considered part of the culture may no longer be acceptable parts of public discourse. Organizers need to offer opportunities for exchange that are con-structive and inviting, not alienating or marginalizing. Young people search for a welcoming face need to know that they will not be publicly singled out or attacked because of their race, sexual preference, or neighborhood. We cannot publicly sanction these kinds of divisive behaviors.

Stars Local People

Most of the things that need to be done to make a festival a success can be done with local people and resources, although external consultants, managers, supplementary vendors, and sponsored art-ists could all have a role. Once a festival is established, however, organizers need to cultivate regional leaders. Then, the key is to rotate powerful positions, not letting the festival be run by a small cadre or an exclusive club (Lavenda 1997). With mentorship and experience, most people can become quite adept when they feel that they are leaving a personal legacy. The important thing is that local people work with local people for local people. In other words, in order to have a great parade, one does not need to hire the best marching band, the important thing is that it is "our" marching band. Quality is often in the eye (or ear) of the beholder.

Successful festivals cultivate a sense of responsibility. Which generation of festival organizers would not be motivated by being responsible for the 14th or 100th celebration? Why go through all the work if it is never to be repeated? I love the audacity of festival organizers who declare their event to be the "First Annual." What better inspiration for success than to assume that they are starting something worthy of continuing?

Feasts enhance the capacity for local leadership when there is a wide enough base of people involved to ensure that they do not become too narrow in their appeal, focus, or contacts. A party in which the only guests invited are those who all work together every day or who are all committed to a singular political or religious viewpoint makes for polite banter but little dynamic exchange. Whether the elite cadre is one leader-demagogue or a clique of forty, if leadership positions are exclusive and require strict adherence to an orthodox way of hosting that festival, the celebration will surely disappear as soon as the so-called leader(s) are removed from power.

Hosts who overtly press an agenda or promote one side of an issue alienate those who might make substantial contributions to an open civic discourse. While it may take some urging and even go against the personal preferences of a particular organizer, leaders should make sure that multiple sides are represented. If a pro-life organization buys a booth in the Merchant's Hall, a pro-choice group should also be strongly and sincerely invited. Democrats, Republicans, and any other viable, peaceable political group should be encouraged to send representatives. In situations where space is very limited, alternate or opposing groups should not be placed too close together or set up in flagrant competition with one another. In order to ensure balance over the course of a year or years, they may have to rotate prime spots or even timeslots. This kind of equity may go against traditional practice, but it is necessary if the festival is to be truly representative of the range of views, lifestyles, and affiliations that already exist in even a small community.

Invests in Community Members and Infrastructure

Feasts and potlatches have long been means of building bartering networks and solidifying relationships of reciprocity. In complex, heterogeneous communities, they are no less important for bringing people together (Humphrey &Humphrey 1988). Each guest at a potluck brings something to the table. They go away having sampled fare that they might not otherwise know how to prepare for themselves. Participants leave with more than they arrived carrying, because at a feast the banquet experience is greater than the sum of its parts. Dinner guests, be they field hockey players or finishing school students, can come to the same table and partake of something that each would find nourishing. In the process, they have created, at least for the moment, a new kind of corporate identity in which they both are equally welcome. The shared feast offers one of the few cooperative ventures where both are invited to contribute to something greater than themselves, the well-being of their community (Kemmis, 1990).

Most communities have a wealth of civic, religious, social, and school organizations who can form ready teams for festivals. In addition to providing the needed labor, they provide organized, ongoing ways of involving youth over the long-term. Young people who might not otherwise find a way in could participate through such an organization, e.g., the high school marching band, the Boys and Girls' Club float in the parade, the Slovakian dancers' demonstration, the 4-H Dairy Bar, or a youth center drumming group. And, as emphasized previously, many service clubs or religious congregations will reinvest their profits into local community programs, quite unlike itinerant vendors, crafters, or outside food service companies.

Formal organizations are not the only, perhaps not even the most, influential groups in most young residents' lives. Teenagers, who often hang out in cliques, can be worked in as subcultures, by respecting their clique's peaceful, athletic, and/or intellectual pursuits. What holiday parade or fair would not be richer for a demonstration by in-line skating dervishes, chess club champions, local library read-a-thon challengers, or garbage can percussionists? Certainly a wider array of subcultures could be effectively integrated into celebrations that purport to represent the entire community than is currently the case in most municipalities. Involving them in a formal way legitimizes their interests and tells them they too are a valuable part of the community. I need to note, however, that strategies for working effectively with gangs would be the subject of another entire article.

What if you gave a dance and nobody took to the floor? Whatever the entertainment, make sure that it is accessible and inviting. Maybe few teens know how to do smooth ballroom moves, square-dancing, or schottisches. Those who have been taught may be shy about getting up alone and actually showing that they know these dances in front of their peers. Invite local capoeria or Armenian folk dancing groups, sponsor dance school performances, bring in young poets as school classes. Offer organizations a public forum in which to hold their final recitals. Make it a tradition to showcase their best students at an annual event. Let them run free workshops to recruit more young people into their fun. Public fair-time performances are great advertising for both the activity itself and for the organization. Further, as many kinds of dances are multigenerational activities, spectators see that these are athletic, artistic activities appropriate across the life span.

Be sure to plan for a variety of appealing entertainers. Rotate the stages and invited performers. Offer the types of music and dance environments that are welcoming and will get people up and moving. Try new (and reinvented) traditions; group line dancing has made a remarkable comeback in many communities and is surprisingly applied to a wide variety of musical styles. The beginning moves can be learned by even the least coordinated, with a reasonable degree of practice.   More sophisticated footwork and rhythmic movement are a delight to see done well, especially in a town square by several hundred people.

Involves Youth in Meaningful Roles

Festivals require a great deal of people power. They offer opportunities to do everything from parking cars to building stages and floats, roasting food, staffing dunk tanks, running errands, cleaning display barns, judging, organizing races and derbies, collecting tickets, and much more. Young people may be brought into service roles to gain money, experience, and/or approval. They come away from a major undertaking with a sense of having been a part of something worth remembering. Learning means engaging in a social exchange. Even if their initial roles seem supplementary to more experienced members' contributions, young people learn by watching and being "legitimate peripheral participants." As their expertise grows, they slowly earn the right to become more central members in "communities of practice" (Lave & Wenger, 1991).

One of the essential elements of any successful service encounter is that the work must be meaningful to both the giver and the receiver. Parking cars may not seem intrinsically meaningful, but if it earns a Girl Scout troop money for a kayaking trip and provides visibility for them as an active, positive community organization, it has purpose. The service rendered must be an actual rather than a contrived need, and it must provide a service that is important to the overall effective and enjoyable functioning of the event.

Young people who feel that their labor is not only welcome, but actually needed, gain a sense of themselves as capable members of vibrant communities. We all need to be needed. If they are actively involved rather than simply entertained, more of the next genera-tion will see their towns as places where they belong and have something to contribute. Even if they do grow up and leave that particular community, the sense of having been a part of something larger than themselves stays with the festival worker. In turn, they are more likely to seek out leadership roles in their new hometowns.

In addition to feeling appreciated, young workers who give to others come to anticipate the time when they will come of age and be the beneficiaries of future cohorts' work. An example is useful: Many towns have turned to alcohol-free lock-in style Graduation Night parties for graduating seniors. Most of the work in elaborately transforming the high school into a jungle, Las Vegas scene, beach party, etc. is done by the junior students and their parents. Door prizes are solicited from local merchants and can be quite expensive and are usually highly coveted. By setting up the often elaborate games, dances, lounges, food courts, and more awaiting the seniors, the juniors gain a sense of what awaits them if they make it to graduation. They see that the lock-in is not a substitute for a "real" party, but a celebration that they could not duplicate on their own. Only by coming together can a town make such a strong statement about how much it values the very lives and accomplishments of each new set of graduates.

Caveats and Challenges for Successful Celebrations

We can all recognize a bad party when we get trapped at one. Nobody is dancing. The jokes are old and grating. Stale and unappetizing food is served perfunctorily by surly, underpaid staff. The games are sophomoric and the decor generic, if not garish. The host is preachy and we try to duck the alienating and rude company. We regress into the corner with the person or group we arrived with and talk of work, taxes, enemas, *anything*. It is a ritual that could take place anywhere, and all too often does. Rather than finding ourselves someplace special, we wish that we could be anyplace else at all. Without care, community festivals can become these sort of dreary, superficial rituals, something to dutifully endure rather than to enjoy.

What makes some community feasts, fairs, and festivals success-ful year after year? Why do some generate a level of energy and enthusiasm that diffuses well past the actual fairgrounds or festival weekend? What are some caveats and challenges that the savvy host must consider? From a decade of working at, with, and on community festivals, I propose the following set of issues. This list builds on the elements and outcomes from the previous sections, and extends them by highlighting those issues that are central to integrating resilient youth into sustainable, strong communities.

- **Foster local governance.** Whenever possible, cultivate local leadership and decision-making bodies that include a spectrum of relevant community members. Stakeholders from key youth organizations, educational institutions, and social services should be consulted and brought into the management team. Make it clear to the next generation of leaders how, when, and why current directors are chosen so that they can aspire and prepare to take over the helm.
- **Display that which is unique.** Does your town have a moniker, mascot, or cause for renown? If so, elaborate on it. If not, earn one. Make it clear to the next generation what you stand for.
- **Provide a variety of accessible venues and events.** While you cannot be everything to everyone, there should be a sufficient number and variety of events and entertainment to attract a wide spectrum of visitors. Events catering to children, youth, and their families need to be clearly advertised and welcoming. These activities need to be scheduled at appropriate places and times so that they are accessible, both physically and psycho-logically. Preempt chaos by giving attention to maps, time-tables, and programs of events. These guides provide not only needed structure, but demonstrate a concern for making new-comers and novices feel welcome and capable of participating.
- **Design multiple outlets for creative expression.** Why rely on a prepackaged McFestival when you can design your own? Run

public competitions for kids to design the logo, slogan, or
featured event.   Let creativity run the gamut by inviting
community organizations and individuals to contribute at all
phases: beforehand, by building floats and preparing performances; during, by staffing children's science or nature areas;
and afterward, by creating multimedia documentation. Respecting and rewarding achievements in these areas will spur on
interest and build a base of recognized expertise on which to
draw for other community functions.

- **Invest in community members.** Recruit, respect, rely on and
then rotate community leaders. Make sure that leadership
positions are, in actuality and in perception, to be, open to all
regardless of gender, race, ethnicity, neighborhood, etc. Previously underrepresented cohorts (e.g., young men, ethnic mi-
norities, professionals, "bad kids," religious leaders) may need
special, sensitive, and sustained encouragement. Any efforts in
these directions will more than pay off by the renewed energy
brought by these new cadres of leaders.

- **Provide meaningful roles for youth.** Whether providing paid
or volunteer service, exhibiting or staffing booths or events,
young people need to know that their labors are truly needed.
Have specific suggestions ready for ways that they can contribute. Work should be meaningful and purposeful. In this way,
it will also be fun.

- **Highlight accomplishments and talents.** One of the most
important roles of local media is to cultivate ownership of local
events, issues, and trends. Make sure that leaders and exemplary
participants receive sufficient coverage and profuse, public
thanks. Spotlight younger or newer achievers wherever possible, as well as those who have reached milestones of service.
Offer constructively critical reviews that have at heart the well-
being of the festival and its organizers. Provide guest editorial
space for critique and suggestions so that the media's role is not
that of a Pollyannaish cheerleader, but coach.

- **Feature events that mark coming of age .** One of the key ways
to showcase the achievements of the next generation is to have
formal rituals of maturation. Whether pageants, parades, or

performances, make sure rites of passage are open to as diverse a pool as possible. Awards and public recognition should clearly convey to everyone who participates the sense that the effort has been worthwhile. Provide "queens," or other selected honorees with meaningful, respectable roles rather than just decorative functions.

- **Accentuate the playful.** Play is its own reward, so make sure there is space and time to just let loose and enjoy oneself and the company of others. Reward silliness, good-natured fun, and jokes that are productive rather than derogatory. Provide venues for satires and skits, songs, community theater, and other forms of creative expression that are not always recognized as recreational pursuits.

- **Enforce a zone of safety and sanctuary.** Participants will not come out year after year if they feel that it is simply too dangerous or oppressive. While allowing for free speech and freedom of assembly, organizers need to monitor participants and spectators for criminal or abusive behavior. Much more important and influential than a police presence however, is a culture of civility. This expectation of cooperation can only be fostered by successful festivals in the past and the clear expectation of success each and every year.

- **Reinvest outcomes into community infrastructure.** The significance of rituals of renewal lies not so much in their singularity, but in their integration into the annual cycle of celebration. Reinvest funds, continue to train leaders, reuse the fairgrounds, renovate public parks. All of these resources will, when coupled with ongoing educational and recreational programs, increase the base of interest and readiness for next year's festivals.

- **Use media to enhance direct experience rather than substitute for it.** Offer youth or intergenerational groups the chance to create live web coverage of the event. Let school classes cover the festivities and perhaps do a spot on the radio or television. Help young people be producers of multimedia documentaries rather than passive, uncritical consumers. Find ways of bringing people as close as possible. Offer the final products to libraries and other archives, and use them in community development and promotion programs.

- **Honor community organizations.** Involve as wide a spectrum of groups as possible. Strive to offer balance when scheduling preferred venues or lucrative opportunities. Recognize and reward those who are essential to the success of the event. Thank them profusely.

- **Be inclusive and have dialogue.** Having a core concept, set of goals, or organizing theme is often critical for making a complex community festival manageable and cohesive. But even though organizers may decide to hone a particular focus for an event, it cannot be at the expense of silencing all others. Whether there is debate about a different interpretation of the community's history or a less offensive icon or mascot, festivals are a fluid, social performance. Each year they are reinvented and performed in ways that reflect the ever-changing host organization or setting. Those who adapt and respond are those who will survive.

- **Multiple uses of facilities.** A community that commits resources to creating permanent spaces can reap benefits all year. Spaces can go beyond physical structures such as bandstands and storage facilities. Public art in the form of murals or beautification projects enhance any community. Encourage many groups to see the spaces as their own. In this way, the spaces are less likely to be vandalized or torn down. If festival spaces are those that already exist, such as Main Street, make sure that they are appropriately transformed when they become temporary sacred ritual space. Banners, hangings, flags, paint, entranceways, and detoured traffic all signal that something grand is about to take place here.

Summary

In winding up this metaphorical analysis of festivals as timekeepers of their host communities, let me restate the major benefits of cyclical renewal through celebration. All the commotion is not just about Ferris wheels and fudge. These are simply outer signs that something significant is going on under the surface. To start, fairs, festivals, and feasts are essential to the long-term viability and vitality of communities of all sizes. Second, by engaging young people in positive and creative ways, they offer hands-on ways of fostering resiliency and competence. In summing up, public celebrations achieve these dual goals by developing three sets of sensibilities: a sense of place, of self, and of community.

Sense of Place

Celebrations are vivid expressions of civic commitment and creativity. Whatever form they take, festivals reinforce particular locations as desirable places to call "home." As young people think about their future and where they want to live, it is essential that they gain a sense of perspective about the place(s) that they come from. They need to feel grounded in a place, to have a tangible sense of what makes places special and appealing. What do people care about here? Do we have something particular to call our own? What kinds of skills are publicly lauded? Do adults want to see youth strutting their stuff? Assuming that the answers are positive, the reassurance will serve them well. For whether they decide to stay or leave, an enhanced understanding about the role that places play in shaping who we are provides the firm foundation that they can build upon throughout their lives. Because they mark moments of coalescence, celebrations offer youth rare opportunities to experience shared sensibilities about place. Feasts offer young people the chance to define, critique, and enjoy where they come from.

Festivals offer young people critical opportunities to see the skills, relationships, and ideals that other residents care about explicitly displayed. Fairs highlight the unique path that a community and/ or region has taken through history along with its folkways of talking, cooking, dancing, harvesting, and recreating. Celebrations legitimize setting aside a day, weekend, or period to simply celebrate the deep, personal pleasures of "dwelling" in a place compared to temporarily occupying a space (Sale, 1991). By becoming personally involved in a place, in having a stake in the success of events there, young people feel that they are part of the "heart" of a place.

Whether spectators, participants, or creative agents, being part of a celebration strengthens young people's ties to and affinities for the underlying values and lifeways that are celebrated.

Fairs link the past, present, and future in tangible ways. Youth can see that just as a particular feast has endured, albeit in changed form throughout the years, so to their homeplace and traditional ways of doing things can also survive even if they are modified. In this way they see resilience and adaptability modeled by adults. Planning for and being part of the public drama of parades, skits, and sporting competitions offers young festivalgoers the challenge of critiquing what has gone before and assessing what they wish to display anew each year. Celebrations offer participants an annual opportunity to reinvent their homeplace, to create an amalgam of preindustrial and postmodern, core and peripheral, traditional and avante garde.

Last but certainly not least, feasts are excuses for shared fun. If a hometown is not somewhere that can be remembered fondly, a place that was home to "the good old days," new generations of young adults are likely to establish and raise their families elsewhere. Fun means being inclusive and open to good-natured exchange. Festivals offer young people from different neighborhoods perhaps an all-too-rare opportunity to socialize with others from across their home city. Fairs offer fairgoers the chance to see diversity displayed and to see how much more their town has to offer than might have been previously appreciated. Well-run feasts offer kids and their parents low-risk, fun-filled forums in which to partake of their own and others' cultural heritages. All of these contribute to a more inclusive and proud sense of "home," a sentiment that is an absolute prerequisite for any future "Homecoming" celebrations.

Throughout the planning and performance, good celebrations remain focused on one of their most important and perceptive audiences: young people. Organizers evaluate the relative importance of different activities and the lessons they teach. Family-centered fun means that events designed for children and youth are given center stage. Such celebrations say loud and clear that this is a good place for kids. .

Sense of Self

Resilient young community members know that they belong. They know that they possess the personal traits and skills that will help them contribute to their homeplaces, both now and in the future. They recognize that they are capable of doing needed, meaningful work. They can locate themselves in relation to the community's mainstream definitions of a model member. They aspire to achieve respected adult status and can identify means of reaching that goal.

Festivals showcase excellence. Young people need well-attended forums in which they can publicly demonstrate crafting and showmanship abilities, cooking and serving skills, organizing capacities, float designing skills, and other abilities and orientations that are valued—and needed—locally. Without something to work for, a final deadline and forum, there would be considerably less incentive to perform as well as possible. Fairs that have diverse exhibit or competition categories provide opportunities for youth to test a range of skills. The more creative outlets that are planned, the better. If others arise spontaneously, even better.

Feasts provide "something to do," and through that doing, provide a means of "being somebody." Having a festival to care about, anticipate, participate in, lead, and sponsor gives young adults something they can see as their role in the community now and in the future. There are plenty of places to structure in meaningful work and service roles for individual youth and youth organizations. The key is that young people recognize the valued roles that they play and realize that the festival could not be the same—perhaps could not even exist—without them. Whatever their occupational or social status otherwise, when they have the opportunity to be leaders, they recognize that they have a stake in building a better place. They know that they are worthy of being partners. This sense of responsibility to others is further buoyed by a growing sense of responsibility to their best selves.

Another aspect of this refined sense of membership is a growing awareness of their possible places within the community. When there is public play with the town's mascot or symbolic ethnicity,

participants have the opportunity to reassess and (re)define themselves in terms of the community mainstream. For those in the
mainstream, festivals can be wonderfully affirming of public support
for their accepted role. And if they find themselves on the periphery,
they can then more clearly see the distinguishing characteristics of
their subculture as well. This growing sense of self in relation to
others provides the basis for serving and giving of oneself.

Festivals often revolve around one or more pivotal end ceremonies which are the culmination of the activities at that fest and
perhaps an entire year's preparation [Porter 1995]. These rites of
passage mark successful participants' entrance into higher status
positions. These new identities indicate expert, adult, or experienced status. At the same time, successful transition to these new
stages means incorporation into the community on a higher, more
responsible, more mature level (Van Gennep, 1960). Ceremonies
showcasing a coming of age can take the form of a medals ceremony,
the crowning of royalty, the final sale of an animal at the Junior
Livestock Auction, a confirmation rite, and more. Whatever the
forum, youth gain a more mature, complex sense of themselves as
capable young adults. Just as importantly, the audience that they are
granted at the festival recognizes and rewards this transition.

Sense of Community

The prerequisite for any community celebration is the existence of
a fellowship of people. A community need not be large or widely
dispersed to need a festival. Indeed, a community may be a small
town, a league of semi-professional soccer players, an association of
horse racers, a neighborhood youth center, a gathering of Central
American refugees, or a city's hip hop scene. Whether well-
established or fledgling, highly diverse or selective, numerous or
small, groups seeking "intentional communitas" (Turner, 1969)
come together to celebrate. By successfully convening, they assert to
themselves and to others that they exist and, further, that they are
viable and meaningful. In our often fractured municipalities, simply
pulling off a community-wide feast is a triumph in itself.

Festivals are one of the few reasons we have to come together for
shared pleasure and profit. Cycles of public celebration offer people

regular excuses to gather together. Whether simply stepping out on the front porch to see the distant fireworks or serving a seventh term as a rally officer, participants engage one another in merry-making. Fun fests are inclusive and welcoming. Thus one of the core elements of community gatherings is the suspension of artificial boundaries. People meet who might not otherwise cross over the boundaries of their home territory to the other side of the tracks.

Rituals of renewal bring neighborhoods, cities, or regions together. Celebrations such as Take Back the Night or Neighborhood Night Out are ways of asserting solidarity and shared concerns that this become/remain a safe place for all. Young people are keen observers of their homeplaces; they know if adults are willing to act assertively on their behalf. Young people are also often painfully aware of where they are told they belong and do not belong. Public, youth-centered celebrations are a sure sign that adults care about the welfare of young people.

Festivals are also an important means of generating resources to reinvest. This is not just limited to the financial rewards that accrue to those who work at and sell goods. When communities commit financial and human resources to maintain aesthetically pleasing spaces for future celebrations, the whole community benefits from this infrastructure. When civic groups cooperate to organize a complex ceremony, there are long-lasting benefits from their experiences of working together in a positive way for something worthwhile.

In youth-centered festival planning, the cycle of renewal begins and ends with kids in mind. Feasts, fairs, and festivals are all about celebrating youth and celebrating *with* youth. When things go well, festivals offer compelling reasons for community members to see themselves as sharing something in common. When those who have given of themselves and their talents are lauded publicly, it generates feelings of civic pride. When young people are drawn in, they gain the sense that their community is a tangible, dynamic entity that can function smoothly, almost like clockwork.

Once they have found a meaningful place in the wheel train of their particular community, young people realize that they are important components in the larger human community. By having successful, enjoyable experiences in local festivals, young people recognize that they are capable and creative members of a team. In turn, the energy that they bring to the larger public sphere reinvigorates the community, keeping it moving and marking off a growing chain of accomplishments. Fairs, feasts, and festivals give full play to these two interlocking processes of individual and group movement toward shared goals. All of this is lubricated with a healthy dose of food, music, competition, displays, and even a Ferris wheel or two. Without regular moments to pause and to celebrate together, communities would quickly fall into disrepair. But, by periodically recharging through festivals, organizers can be certain of an energized atmosphere that expects and celebrates the very best.

Acknowledgment

I would like to thank the members of the Gimbel Learning Community for many provocative and encouraging discussions that led to the final version of this text. I wish to acknowledge the assistance of Rich Stalter of Southside Jewelers of Pittsburgh, Pennsylvania while tinkering with the watch metaphor that gives structure and rhythm to this piece. I also wish to thank Steven Porter, the Community Services Coordinator of the White Bear Lake (Minnesota) public schools for sophisticated and insightful editing of an earlier draft of this manuscript. His practitioner's eye and keen sense of when I drifted away from my major points made this a stronger, more cohesive chapter.

References

Abrahams, R. (1982). The language of festivals: Celebrating the economy. In V. Turner (Ed.), *Celebration: Studies in festivity and ritual* (pp. 161–177). Washington DC: Smithsonian Institution Press.

Aronoff, M. (1993, Winter). "Collective celebration as a vehicle for local economic development: A Michigan case." *Human Organization*, 368–379.

Baylor, B. (1986). *I'm in charge of celebrations*. New York: Charles Scribner & Sons.

Burke, P. (1992). *History and Social Theory*. Cambridge, UK: Polity Press.

Fitchen, J. (1991). *Endangered spaces, enduring places: Change, identity and survival in rural America*. Boulder, CO: Westview Press.

Gallagher, W. (1993). *The power of place: How our surroundings shape our thoughts, emotions, and actions*. New York: Poseidon.

Giamatti, A. B. (1989). *Take time for paradise: Americans and their games*. New York: Summit Books.

Golbeck, S. (1985). Spatial cognition as a function of environmental characteristics. In R. Cohen (Ed.), *The development of spatial cognition* (pp. 225-256). Hillsdale, NJ: Lawrence Erlbaum.

Grimes, R. (1976). *Symbol and conquest: Public ritual and drama in Sante Fe*. Albuquerque: University of New Mexico Press.

Hinsdale, M. A., Lewis, H. M., & Waller, S. M. (1995). *It comes from the people: Community development and local theology*. Philadelphia, PA: Temple University Press.

Humphrey, T. & Humphrey, L. (Eds.). (1988). *"We gather together": Food and festival in American life*. Ann Arbor: UMI Research Press.

Kemmis, D. (1990). *Community and the politics of place*. Norman, OK: University of Oklahoma Press.

Kridel, C. (1980). "The play element in culture and the use of festivals in the general education curriculum." *The Journal of General Education*, 32(3), 229–238.

Lakoff, G. & Johnson, M. (1980). *Metaphors we live by*. Chicago: The University of Chicago Press.

Lave, J. & Wenger, E. (1991). *Situated learning: Legitimate peripheral participation*. Cambridge, UK: Cambridge University Press.

Lavenda, R. (1997). *Corn fests and water carnivals: Celebrating community in Minnesota*. Washington, DC: Smithsonian Institution Press.

Moore, T. (1996). *The re-enchantment of everyday life*. New York: HarperCollins Publishers.

Neville, G. K. (1987). *Kinship and pilgrimage: Rituals of reunion in American Protestant culture*. New York: Oxford University Press.

Porter, M. K. (1995). "The Bauer County fair: Community celebration as context for youth experiences of learning and belonging." *Journal of Research in Rural Education*, 11(3), 139–156.

Sale, K. (1991). *Dwellers in the land: The bioregional vision*. Philadelphia: New Society Publishers.

Stern, S. & Cicala, J. A. (Eds.). (1991). *Creative ethnicity: Symbols and strategies of contemporary ethnic life*. Logan: Utah State University Press.

Turner, V. (1969). *The ritual process*. Chicago: Aldine Publishing Company.

Van Gennep, A. (1960). *The Rites of Passage*. Chicago: University of Chicago Press.

8

Issues in After-School Youth Development Programming

Kathryn Edmondson

To develop socially competent and resilient children and youth through sports and after-school structured activities, we need to build, extend, and/or reinforce competent, resilient, accessible, and flexible structures and systems, which we as a society commit to sustain over time. These structures and systems must provide sufficient and diverse opportunities for participation and operate at scale. In this chapter, I describe the status of some of three of these structures: private, nonprofit organizations; parks and recreation programs; and school-based, after-school programs. The descriptions are based on interviews in the field, observations, and personal review of the programs rather than a formal review of the literature. Some of the key elements, challenges, and opportunities are considered, especially as they relate to positive youth development programming. The special circumstances of organized sport programs conducted by these systems is also examined.

Profile of Key Nonprofit Youth Serving Organizations: A View from the Field

A key theme of this chapter is that programming for youth development is implemented by a loose connection of organizations and individuals serving young people, with unevenly distributed and inadequate funding, advocacy, research, policy, and technical assistance supports. Although there is a better understanding of this problem now than there was 10 years ago, there are still no regular funding streams, common standards for operation, performance, or

217

success, and few training programs that offer professional degrees for the individuals serving the youth.

Some 17,000 national and local youth organizations in the United States serve children and youth. Some are big, national direct service institutions such as Boys and Girls Clubs of America, 4-H Clubs, YMCAs and Big Brothers/Big Sisters that provide programs largely through local affiliates or chapters. Most, however, are programs run by a multitude of local and independent youth organizations and through sporting organizations, museums, libraries, and parks and recreation departments. In general, the evolution of such programs has been in decentralized fashion, in part because there are few predictable centralized and systematic funding streams. Competition for funding is fierce. System incentives for collaboration and cooperation have been minimal. Many organizations have risen in response to a need in the community and are small, neighborhood-based, after-school and weekend programs. Such community programs tend to suffer from a lack of sufficient, predictable funding, the uncertainties caused by volunteer staff, and a lack of capacity to easily increase delivery to scale.

Types of key youth service organizations include: *mentoring organizations* such as Big Brothers/Big Sisters; *service organizations* focused on urban children and youth such as Boys and Girls Clubs of America and Girls Incorporated; and *membership and youth membership organizations* such as YMCA and YWCA, Boy Scouts of America, Girl Scouts of the USA, Camp Fire Girls and Boys, and 4-H Clubs. *Youth sport organizations* will be considered separately later in the chapter.

Mentoring Organizations

Big Brothers/Big Sisters of America is a national organization with local affiliates. The national organization provides programming, implementation guidelines, and training. The local organization matches adult volunteers with children ages 5-18, in a one-on-one relationship. BB/BSA focuses on children in single parent households and provides mentoring training for adults, as well as ongoing support. Big Brothers and Sisters are asked to commit for at least a year and to meet with their Little Brother or Sister two to four times per month for periods of three to four hours.

Estimates for the entire field are that up to 350,000 kids are enrolled in all kinds of mentoring programs and that Big Brothers/Big Sisters serves about one-third of these children, with 30,000 additional children on their waiting list. BB/BSA plans to increase their relationships to 200,000 by the end of 2000 according to interviews with the national staff.

One of the most significant evaluations in the entire youth development field is a national study by Public/Private Ventures (P/PV) of Big Brothers/Big Sisters, which showed that the BB/BSA program reduced the incidences of school violence and drug use and improved school performance. [Diluilio &Grossman, 1997, pp. 48-50]. Even though the program addresses young people's positive aspirations and not their negative potential, it was still found to reduce participating youth's chances of ending up in trouble. It is important to note that P/PV did not suggest that all mentoring programs are effective. The BB/BS program provides for a high level of contact; and the mentor role is that of a friend and supporter, not of a teacher or preacher. P/PV found that 70% of the adults who think they will be reforming the children they are mentoring drop out within nine months, while 90% of the adults who thought they were to be friends with their Little Sister or Brother remained.

Overall, P/PV identified cost as a critical problem for mentoring programs. They estimated the cost at $1000 per relationship, with much of the cost being subsumed under staff support and screening of potential mentors. Some agencies are forced to ask volunteers to pay for their own background checks. The screening may take a year and include a criminal background check, interviews, and an application that runs to 22 pages. As a result, less than half who call to find out about the program apply, and of those, only 37% complete the process of being matched.

Among the difficulties that must be resolved in the mentoring field are: streamlining the matching process and ensuring appropriate expectations on the part of the adults; collaborating with other service providers; and finding and retaining volunteers of color, particularly men, in cities. One frequently expressed need is for a national, funded data base with the capability to perform background checks wherever there is a volunteer program.

Service Organizations

Boys and Girls Clubs of America (B&GCA) is a national organization with some 2,000 service locations for 791 affiliate local clubs. B&GCA serve 2.6 million girls and boys aged 6–18 on a daily basis. B&GCA provide training, consulting, management, and resource development for local clubs and local communities trying to establish clubs through a five-region structure. B&GCA sites offer drop-in recreational, sporting, and life skills activities. Some 320 clubs are located in public housing serving 100,000 youth. B&GCA projects the number of clubs will continue to grow 25% per year to 2000. Research conducted on the program [B&GCA 1997] suggests that when compared to other public housing sites, those with Clubs experienced: 25% reduction in the presence of crack cocaine; 22% reduction in overall drug activity; 13% reduction in juvenile crime; a lower percentage of academic failure; and fewer behavioral problems. One question that has remained unanswered is whether the total mix of activities, supports, and structures, including those that extend into the communities in which the children and youth live, is responsible for the success rather than only the work of B&GCA.

B&GCA has specialized in addressing the needs of disadvantaged youth. A frequently B&GCA-cited study by Portland State University/University of Wisconsin-Madison looked at 30 Clubs designated as gang prevention sites and three as gang intervention sites. The researchers found that the clubs had recruited 1,900 youth at risk or on the fringe of gang involvement. At the end of one year, 48% of youth demonstrated improved school behavior, more than one-third showed improved grades, and juvenile justice system involvement and gang activity declined for youth participating in the program. [B&GCA, 1997]

Other youth-serving organizations of size and significant in this field include: Advocates for Youth, formerly called Center for Population Options. Child Welfare League of America (CWLA),

Congress of National Black Churches (CNBC), Girls Incorporated, Jewish Community Centers Association of North America (JCC), and Junior Achievement Inc.

It is important to note that big youth-serving organizations have taken advantage of the movement toward more positive models of youth development to secure more funding to serve additional children and youth. Nevertheless, serving all the children and youth that need voluntary programs and services with quality opportunities and choices is a dream far from reality.

Membership and Youth Membership Organizations

YMCA, YWCA, Boy and Girl Scouts, Camp Fire Girls and Boys, and 4-H are the major membership organizations.

The YMCA serves some 14-plus million people a year, almost half of whom are under 17 years old. Nationally, they have focused on developing capacity to deliver programs to children and youth. Some local YMCAs are particularly effective. The YMCA of Greater New York, for example, is partnering with the New York City Board of Education to pioneer an extended school day initiative by putting "virtual" Ys in schools. The YWCA is the nation's oldest and largest women's membership organization, representing 1 million women and girls in the US and 25 million women worldwide in 95 countries. They are one of the largest providers of youth services and the oldest and one of the largest nonprofit providers of sports/physical fitness programs.

The Boy Scouts is a national membership organization serving 4.4 million members through 407 local affiliates, organized into troops led by volunteers that take children through various stages from Cub Scouts to Explorer Scouts. They teach personal fitness, citizenship training, and character development. The Girl Scouts has 333 regional councils and is organized into troops led by volunteers, serving approximately 2.6 million girls ages 5-17. Girl Scouts offers recreational activities and camping, and other structured programs to teach girls social, moral, and intellectual skills.

The National 4-H Council helps 5.4 million school-age participants through 169,000 clubs based in schools, camps, community centers, and neighborhoods. 4-H works with the U.S. Department of Agriculture and the network of land grant universities and colleges and county and state government partners that make up the Cooperative Extension Service. 4-H is in the middle of an aggressive effort to reinvent the organization to serve the evolving needs of children and youth in a changing economy.

Challenges Faced by These Organizations

Review of the key national delivery systems highlights a consistent cluster of challenges facing current and expansion of delivery of services. Some of these issues are not discussed publicly and for attribution, perhaps understandably given the intense competition for funds. Nevertheless, they are obstacles to providing quality opportunities for children and youth.

Data Gathering: What Do We Know?

The great desire to serve children and youth and the need to have numbers for fundraising purposes makes national data gathering in this area problematic. For example, a child who attends every day may be counted the same as a child who attends occasionally. It is not likely that these two children are having the same experience. Thus participation rates and other numbers related to the services provided by programs may paint a rosier picture than actually exists.

There is incentive for organizations to inflate their numbers in an era of scarce resources. Even the largest organizations feel pressure to justify cost-effectiveness, reach, access, and scale because funding sources are increasingly using attendance as a criterion for funding decisions in the absence of data about program effectiveness. Data about program effectiveness are hard to collect because programming varies within organizations from affiliate to affiliate and among organizations.

Serving Disadvantaged, Urban, and Youth of Color

Informal reports suggest that up to one-third of all children and youth are unserved, most of whom are disadvantaged, urban, or of color. Moreover, as youth age, the opportunities for maximal impact diminish. It is likely that this number will continue to grow unless there are significant leadership and funding initiatives undertaken.

Lack of participation of inner city disadvantaged youth is related to fees, equipment and/or uniforms. Fees are variable by organization and affiliate. Lack of ability to pay fees forces organizations to raise funds from elsewhere to serve youth who cannot pay. If there are multiple children in a family, the problem is compounded. Families are reluctant to trade off one child for another. One preferred solution is for none of the children to attend programs, but to stay home after school together. Lack of available or affordable transportation to and from programs and issues of safety can also compound the problem.

Programming for Girls

Girls are underserved for a variety of reasons, particularly girls of color. There is less funding for girls; males are seen more "at risk" or at least a greater threat to the community. Whether one is worried about at risk girls or all girls, girls are underserved in existing programs, particularly in the cities. Boys and Girls Clubs do not serve as many girls as boys, and in some organizations serving girls, the percentage of girls of color is small.

There is new concern about girls and teen girls involved in negative behaviors, heretofore considered more likely to be the domain of boys and young men. This concern has highlighted the disparity in services to girls. It has also called into question the assumption that whatever program works for at-risk boys will work for girls. One example is the need to have programs focusing on girls who have been the victims of physical and sexual abuse.

Limited Expansion

Although there is apparent willingness to serve more children and youth in their programs, the mission and capacity of these organizations to expand is limited. At present there is no consensus, will, or mission to serve every child or youth. Coordination, collaboration, funding, and capacity building are all required but may be insufficient. What is required are more resources for such items as increased staffing, staff training, upgraded facilities, insurance, and technical assistance. Alternatively, collaboration across programs and agencies might facilitate serving more youth. However, no one should underestimate how difficult and complex a local organizing effort would be. The commitment to collaborate is not strong.

Most national youth serving organizations also do not systematically reach out to immigrant children and youth, to those who have special needs because of disabilities, or to troubled children and youth. Accommodating and integrating diversity of culture and experience into after-school activities is yet another challenge, in part, because of problems related to the differences in language. As with the challenges of language and culture, the problems faced by youth with disabilities generally are issues surfacing at the local level. Advocates for people with disabilities report that two significant barriers are accessibility to facilities, and staff or volunteers trained and comfortable working with youth with disabilities.

Volunteers

Volunteers are viewed in a mixed way by youth organizations. They are necessary, but require recruitment, training and support, which in turn strains the capacity and resources of the organization and staff. For some organizations, especially those in big cities, they are essential to expand their service base; for others, the ability to professionalize current paid staff is much more important. Even when the number of volunteers is sufficient, their training is often inadequate. Training to date is largely the result of national organizations seeking outside funding to make it available to as many local affiliates as see the need for it or are paid to take it. At present, there is more training than certification, more voluntary certification than mandatory. The need for increased, ongoing training will also continue as organizations work with children and youth who have heretofore not been served and who need more intensive attention.

Parental Involvement

Parents stand in multiple relationships to these programs. Sometimes programs serve as substitutes for parents. In some families, parents need some of the supports being provided for their children. Because parents are working, unavailable or unreliable, many youth service programs do not automatically have programs for the caring parent or relative. Given the vast number of challenges facing the field, involving parents, caregivers, and "gatekeepers," where possible and appropriate, is an important way to serve children and youth and, at the same time, increase parenting and caregiving skills. Unfortunately, few programs have the resources to develop and sustain such programming.

Educational Components

One of the major challenges that exist is how to link the matrix of current and evolving after-school initiatives to educational enrichment and workforce and career development issues without making "it feel like more school." Helping youth make the transition from school to work is a large concern in most cities, especially for the business community. Positive youth development programs represent the first stage of the transition. In Detroit and Los Angeles, for example, federal summer jobs money has been a significant source of funds for local youth service organizations, although amounts vary annually. As urban school systems struggle, and as cities move to develop an array of after-school supports, youth service organizations will increasingly be asked to add programs and services to their existing offerings.

In this section, I have tried to identify some critical challenges faced by organizations serving children and youth. Two issues serve as a backdrop to the challenges and continue to require attention as we try to face the challenges. The first is the issue of how much theory and proof we need before we practice. The practitioners say we do not need more research to document what "we already know"—that children and youth need caring people in their lives and access to healthy, safe, developmental activities in which to participate, and they need them now. Those who finance the building, rebuilding, or extension of these structures and systems desire workable programs for children and youth. They demand justification, bases for making their investments, as well as evaluation and modeling that gives proof of (comparative) performance prior to additional, expanded or to scale investment. As might be expected, the theoretical basis to justify the effort is probably stronger in many eyes than the empirical data. The attention to "translation" between research and practice [see Danish, this volume] is needed. As the field emerges, it is important to develop elements and programs of "best practice," but also capture and disseminate how to translate and transfer what we know and are learning that can help youth, and those that care about them, learn.

The second issue is the debate over the relative financial weight to place on positive development approaches as opposed to negative approaches. This debate is especially difficult where organizations serve only one aspect of a child or youth. Even though the 1990s have seen a movement toward increased attention and resources devoted to positive, comprehensive approaches, there is still confusion and uncertainty with different actors and segments in the field "rowing in different directions."

Those who work in this field—whether funders, researchers, technical and organizational assistance providers, or service providers—need to figure out how to blend their various expertise to serve the range of needs that children and youth have. There is great expertise and experience among those who work with children and youth. Some of these youth are at risk; some have already become involved with the justice system. How can we work at preventing or diminishing risk factors and develop protective factors as well?

Those who argue that we as a society should pay more attention and put more resources toward children and youth who have already had a brush or worse with the justice system also insure that less will be available for those who have avoided involvement but are at risk. Moreover, there may be few resources for providing for the reconnection and reintegration of children and youth into our communities. We all know the arguments about the benefits of preventive activities. Similarly, those who want positive approaches to children and youth and who try to realize that vision in the way they organize and operate their programs find it sometimes difficult to justify or manage additional resources to support children and youth in more troubled circumstances.

This is no mere academic argument since public, private, and nonprofit funding sources often have different values and orientations and ultimately influence what happens in our communities. Organizations are often unsure how to carve out a distinctive place for themselves with the audience to whom they are talking and secure resources and support. Terms like "prevention" and "positive youth development" have become the fieldspeak currency of the realm, yet the meaning of these terms and others like them lack a definitional quality. There is a need to develop a common language with commonly understood definitions. One consequence of such clarity might be a willingness among organizations to learn from each other and work together and with funding sources to try to create a continuum of a variety of services and activities for children and youth.

Structured Activities for Children and Youth in Public Settings

Public parks departments have too often been forgotten as a medium for providing structured activities to all children and youth. Lessons in some of big cities suggest that public parks and recreation departments have been underperforming, and in some ways, conceded serving youth in the after-school hours to private, nonprofit organizations. These parks departments have had to confront a number of difficult problems. They have underfunded operating budgets; they have greater needs for maintenance, capital improvements, and construction than there are funds available. Their leadership varies in quality. Union, fee, and contract rules make community use and community partnerships more difficult and expensive. Finally, the public and political systems send mixed messages about value. They endorse the need for parks and recreation but are willing to trade support off for police, fire, and sanitation services.

It is difficult to generalize what constitutes parks and recreation departments across the country. Nationwide, they are responsible for different clusters of functions, which may include, or be included under, economic or community development, tourism, operation of both parks and recreation centers/facilities, and art and cultural institutions. Therefore, comparing intercity revenues and expenditures is meaningless.

However, if opportunities are to be available for more children and youth to participate in developmentally-friendly structured activities, municipal parks and recreation departments will have to be involved, available, developed and funded. Municipal public funding for parks and recreation departments has been declining nationally, sometimes dramatically. Declining municipal funding is being reinforced by lack of support from the federal government. Instead of increasingly scarce federal funds going to support parks and recreation centers nationwide, resources are going into land and water conservation or to such nonprofit organizations as Boys and Girls Clubs. The funding of nonprofit organizations highlights a significant development: municipal parks departments are increasingly competing for both public and private funds with private, nonprofit child and youth service providers. This has upped the ante in the funding and turf wars that have been so destructive in the field of child and youth development services. As a result, parks departments are being forced to reinvent their organizations if they are to be a significant player in providing services and facilities for use by children and youth in non-school hours. To better understand the problem, it is important to consider the historical evolution of parks and recreation and its interrelationship with sports.

Taylor [1996], using Detroit as a case study, notes that by the end of the 19th century, parks and recreation programs emerged as social movements supported by private agencies, parks serving as escapes from city life, and programs for youth as character development and diversion. Local governments assumed a larger funding and programming role in the 1920s, and parks and recreation grew increasingly popular into the 1940s with special levies for parks and recreation funding common, and volunteers serving as a major resource for recreation programs. However, by the 1950s, parks and recreation programs were perceived as a service. Recreation was no longer seen as a vehicle for positive development; rather, it was regarded as an end in itself, and the departments became more professionalized.

As a result, urban parks grew slowly, and as the suburbs became self-sustaining, suburbs developed their own parks and recreation programs, facilities, and municipal departments. The middle-class exodus to the suburbs weakened the city's tax base, and maintenance became the largest expense for parks and recreation departments. The oil crises of the 1970s and the taxpayer revolts of the early 1980s increased the difficulties for parks and recreation departments nationwide.

During the late 1970s and early 1980s, there were pressures for the departments to "be more like businesses" by becoming more self-sufficient, including generating revenue for operations via usage and entry fees. The results were a shifting bases of income and the loss of key constituencies for which the parks and recreations departments had been programming—those who could not afford entry fees and those who could not reach the suburban locations. These changes were exacerbated by cuts in federal aid to cities during the first term of the Reagan administration in the early 1980s.

Organizations began to rent facilities for their programs. Eventually, the cost of using the facilities limited access to children and youth who could not afford to pay. The fee-for-service trend hurt the ability of these departments to offer high quality programming. If a city doesn't need "parks" people to run programs because people are paying money to use facilities for their own programs, one does not need as many staff. If one doesn't need these staff, one has fewer programs, and these programs are less well distributed throughout the city, and less is offered. As a department has fewer programs, there are fewer options for children and youth in public facilities except sports. Although sports may be played without the proper training and supervision, they may be played incorrectly, without the necessary safety precautions and without the processes designed to teach sports and life skills through the activity.

If park departments are going to regain their role as a provider of quality after-school structured programming, they need to become competitive for funding and return to their original mission of being a primary service system for children and youth. Mission alone gives parks departments the opportunity to be, with the school systems, one of two publicly funded entities that is charged in all neighborhoods with serving children and youth in a positive way.

Municipal policy advocacy efforts must encourage cities to look at parks and recreation departments as community assets that any self-reliant community must have. Cities must adequately fund baseline operating and maintenance budgets. The fee-based system has distorted the parks departments by reducing support for programming as opposed to rental of facilities. Park program budgets need to be reconnected to city goals and reintroduced to city operating budgets.

The Opportunity for School Involvement in After-School Programming

One recurring theme in this book is the difficulty that is anticipated and already experienced by cities in trying to find sufficient safe and accessible sites for after-school activities. As Fukusawa [this volume] notes, schools have many potential roles to play, in addition to serving as a facility for programs. They have trained staff with developmental expertise.

The most interesting recent trend in this area is a recent program of federally-funded after-school grants given to schools. Additionally, private foundations have also begun to fund schools to develop after-school programs. An important question becomes what should be the role of schools in the after-school hours?

Using schools as "after school" facilities can be problematic. Some of these are: categorical funding constraints, jurisdictional issues, union rules for custodians, and concerns from school administrators about whether programs are sufficiently educational, whether security of facilities and participants can be maintained, and whether additional use of schools will make them inhabitable on the next school day. Despite these reasonable concerns, there are opportunities for schools to contribute.

We should be concerned not to lose the contribution that education can make to the process of helping children grow up healthy. The schools organize instruction by age, with some sense of developmental levels. School is at its core about learning and *practicing* what is being learned. It is an *iterative* process. The daily schooling process can and should give children the chance to be taught the value and content of physical fitness and health, the requisite skills, and the chance to practice them. It is important to note that school districts must continue or return to offering physical education.

It is virtually certain that we cannot make up for that lack of educational content in the structured activity after-school environment, particularly in urban areas, if only the school building and not the philosophy of education, is involved. The schools have human resources in teachers, workers, and coaches that can help creatively develop after-school activities. They have expertise in child and youth development and in teaching and coaching techniques, which volunteers and undertrained youth workers may not have.

The new focus on a publicly financed locus for after-school activities may contribute to partnerships between parks departments and school districts. There is general consensus that school facilities must be available for after-school community needs because parks and recreation department facilities are not sufficient or, perhaps, locally situated.

At present, parks will be more interested in collaborations than schools. We see signs, however, that schools may soon be where parks are now. They seem unable to secure the political support needed to address severe overcrowding in some elementary schools. There is a system-wide deferred-maintenance bill and a need to build additional schools for the projected enrollment increases. These expenses may cause school systems to look with new interest at collaborations with parks departments. Alternatively, parks departments may fare poorly as school systems argue for priority public support.

Organized Sports for Children and Youth: A Case Example

Because children and youth choose to be involved in sports more often than any other activity, I've chosen to consider this activity separately. Additionally, given the potential impact that sports plays in the lives of our children, youth and culture, addressing issues presented by organized sports also provides an opportunity to ensure healthier outcomes for children and youth.

Ewing et. al. [1996] identify six types of organizations that have youth sport programs. The first are community-based sport programs with national affiliations such as the Lions and Kiwanis Clubs, the Police Athletic Leagues, Little League Baseball, and Pop Warner Football. The second set of organizations are national youth service and membership organizations that offer sports programs within the broader context of youth development, such as Boys and Girls Clubs, YMCA, and YWCA. Some of these organizations may affiliate or coordinate with the national programs such as the Boys and Girls Club's affiliation with Major League Baseball's RBI (Reviving Baseball in the Inner-city). The third type of organization is fee-based sports programs. These programs are usually connected with national sports organizations like the American Athletic Union (AAU) or national governing boards of the United States Olympic Committee such as U.S.A. Swimming. Club sports conduct year-round practices and competitive opportunities, require a participation fee, and employ salaried coaches. Recreational programs offered by parks departments is a fourth organizational type. These programs emphasize fun, participation for all, social interaction, and physical skill development. The philosophy of maximizing participation places some recreation programs in a second-class position when representatives of competitive agency-sponsored programs recruit the most skillful athletes from the recreation programs. There are two types of school-based programs: intramural programs (competition between teams within a school) and interscholastic programs (competition between teams from different schools). Often intramural programs are short-changed, primarily because both programs compete for the same facilities, clients, administrators, finances, and prestige within the school population. As a result, many intramural programs have been eliminated, and the participants in these programs have been forced to become nonparticipants or must choose to participate through another organization.

The elimination of intramural programs, along with the fact that physical education is no longer a mandated activity in any of the

50 states, means that some children and youth may have no opportunity to learn to play sports through school. Moreover, they may lack even a basic knowledge of movement and fitness. Given the estimates that children are heavier and more sedentary than a decade ago, the elimination of these programs has serious consequences.

Ewing et al. [1996] estimate the number of sport participants at 48,374,000 children and youth in the 5–17 age range. Twenty-two (22) million, or 45%, of the children and youth are participating through community-based sport organizations such as Little League Baseball and Pop Warner Football. Almost 2.5 million, or 5%, are paying to participate in sport activities such as ice skating and swimming; 14.5 million, or 30%, participate in recreational sports programs; 451,000 participate in intramural sports in middle, junior and senior high school; and 12% of all children play interscholastic sports.

By far the largest number of youth participants are involved in non-school-based programs. In the past five years, there has been a particularly significant increase in participation in youth sports leagues. This increase, in part, is a function of shift from recreational programs to youth sports league programs that are more competitive, plus the recruitment by youth sports leagues of younger participants. Accompanying this trend toward participation in youth sport leagues is a movement toward specialization in a specific sport at a younger and younger age. With this specialization has been a decline in the opportunities for participation by at-risk youth. Also, new sport facilities are often built in the suburbs, making them inaccessible to youth from urban areas. As a result, estimates of participation rates in the suburbs approach between 80% and 90%, while in the city they are approximately 10%–20%.

There are several critical challenges to those designing and implementing after-school sport programs. The first is the need to develop a strong coaching base. Volunteer coaches must be recruited, trained, and retained. They are the "caring adult" that many of our under- and unserved children and youth need. If the coaches are untrained, however,. there are serious risks for the participants, not the least of which are physical injuries. The second is that, because of the elimination of physical fitness and intramural programs in schools, the burden has been placed on non-school-based youth sports to provide education-based physical training.

A second challenge is how to ensure youth sports programs contributions to youth development. As both school-based and after-school sports have become more specialized, the emphasis on fun and play has become less important. Furthermore, perhaps because of our society's ambivalence about the value of "fun and play" in children's lives and its relationship to positive youth development, youth sport remains out of the mainstream when researchers and practitioners focus on how to enhance youth development. Danish [this volume] argues that sports should, in thought and practice, be included in what we consider the critical elements in helping children and youth build the skills they need to become healthy and productive adults. This is particularly salient when we note that more children and youth choose to participate in sports than any other structured activity.

Because so many children choose sport as their primary after-school activity, we need to work to prove that the skills learned in sports can be transferred to other domains. Sports will then be seen as an activity that fits under a healthy, developmental umbrella.

The Present and the Future

In the late afternoon and evening after school, and on weekends, children and youth have discretionary time. Some have places to go where they are connected with adults, see friends, pursue hobbies, play sports and engage in other structured activities that challenge them and help them grow. But for some children and youth, especially those home alone, the situation is different. They lack accessible safe places, involvement with a caring and responsible adult, and opportunities to be engaged in interesting, developmentally appropriate activities. Consequently, they can create situations in which they put themselves and their communities at risk.

How has this happened? There are fundamental changes in the way families are organized and a deficit in national and local "field building" leadership. The local public institution traditionally responsible for providing activities for children and youth after school, the parks and recreation department, has been under-financed, under-performing and under-supported. Facilities are often under or inappropriately staffed, under maintained and inappropriately set for current needs. Parks are now competing for private *and* public dollars and with private youth serving programs. The other public institution, the school, has been under siege, under-performing, and under-prepared to fulfill its own mission to educate; while increasingly under pressure to develop into a community service institution that "extends" operating hours into the evenings and welcomes the community and its various activities.

There are a large number of youth-serving organizations but they are fragmented, decentralized, intensely competitive, and given the number of under and unserved children and youth, especially in large urban areas, eager to provide *additional* services rather than focus on quality or organizational capacity building. The quality of staff is uneven and pay rates are substantially below those for workers in school-based systems.

The youth development field is in its infancy, where the child development field was 20 years ago. Principles and best practice have yet to be translated into programs and replicated in a significant way. Evaluations of promising programs have been sparse. There is even some lack of acceptance of the legitimacy of "youth development" as a credible field into which to put resources.

Researchers and key organizations are trending away from a deficit-based model. This model emphasizes all that children and communities are not. Instead, there is an increasing realization of the value of an asset-based model. In this model, the basic needs and competencies for all children and youth, and the opportunities cities have to provide these supports, are examined. The focus is on all children and youth, not just ones "at-risk," on "whole" children, not just facets of their behavior. As a result of this expanding asset-based focus, efforts should concentrate on comprehensive services and supports that recognize the full range of needs and competencies.

There is increased interest in and attention to providing safe, accessible, and diverse structured activities for children and youth where they can come into contact with a caring, trained adult in after-school hours. Additionally, communities have come to understand that they have a new role in this process. They are beginning to recognize, even if other levels of government do not, that punitive justice programs will not be enough. Instinctively, in and around the get-tough rhetoric, there is a local awareness that more than just police, jail, and control measures must be available if children and youth are to grow up healthy. Additionally, there appears to be an emerging sense that in all communities, large and small, there *must* be more available for children and youth, even if community resources are disorganized or inadequate at present.

Emerging community-level awareness and activity will continue and grow with or without outside or additional support. The pressure to act is based on an awareness of the enormity and complexity of what needs to be done for children and youth, given how little infrastructure exists and the significant numbers of children beginning to show up in elementary schools. If a community is to be the level where change takes place, it must increase its own capacity. It must have sufficiently-developed strengths and skills, or have access to resources to acquire and institutionalize what is needed.

National leadership is needed in areas of agenda-setting, funding, convening, program structuring, partnership development, technical assistance, and communications innovations. The capacity to serve and grow nonprofit organizations, public systems and field supports are also in need of attention. The goal is to increase opportunities for youth to experience healthy, developmentally appropriate, accessible, consistently available, diverse, fun, and enriching activities where they can come into contact with a caring adult.

Author's Notes

1. Research assistance was provided by Beryl B. Dithmer.

2. Most of this work is based on original research and interviews. A number of confidential phone and in-person

interviews were conducted with practitioners, academics, policymakers, researchers, and funders.

References

Dilulio, J. & Grossman, J. (1997). *Youth Crime and Substance Abuse—Act-Now Strategies for Saving At-Risk Children*. Philadelphia: Public/Private Ventures.

Ewing, Martha, Seefeldt, V., Brown T. (1996). The role of organized sport in the education and health of American children and youth. Unpublished paper commissioned by the Carnegie Corporation, New York.

Taylor, C. (1996). Sports and recreation: Community anchor and counterweight to conflict. *Peace and Conflict Journal of Peace Psychology, 2*(4), 339–350.

9

Re-Creating Recreation in the Inner City: A Youth Development Initiative in Detroit

David Fukuzawa

The nonschool hours, and after-school programs in particular, have moved from the margins to the center of public policy discussions about how to address problems of teen violence and crime. The Carnegie Council on Adolescent Development report, *A Matter of Time: Risk and Opportunity in the Out-Of-School Hours* [1992], has been singularly instrumental in creating broader public awareness about how critical the nonschool hours are for youth development. The report brought attention to the fact that 40% of young adolescents' time is discretionary. It is during this discretionary time, most of it concentrated in the hours after the end of the school day, that young people engage in health compromising activities and crime.

More recently, Fight Crime-Invest in Kids, a national crime prevention group, issued a report [Fox & Newman 1998] based on FBI data that the peak hours for violent juvenile crime are from 3 to 8 p.m. The report also goes on to cite numerous studies that show that quality after-school programs can help prevent crime and delinquency [Sickmund 1997; Fox & Newman 1997; Jones & Offord 1989; Tierney et al. 1995].

Nowhere is the need for quality after-school programs more evident than in America's inner cities. At the same time urban areas face serious social barriers to increasing such programs. The *City Kids Count* report [O'Hare 1997] reported that for the largest American cities every indicator of child well-being was on average worse than for children in the nation as a whole. City kids are twice as likely as suburban kids to grow up in single parent family homes. They are more likely to live in poor families in neighborhoods with high concentrations of poverty. City kids are also twice as likely to drop out of school. African American youth are disproportionately reflected in these figures. To make matters worse safe havens and good programs, which can often spell the difference for a young person between a productive life or a life mired in crime or addiction, are few are far between [McLaughlin et al. 1994]. Although the needs for more quality after-school and organized recreational programs are profound in urban areas, the task of increasing these programs to sufficient scale faces daunting odds. Strained city budgets make it difficult to maintain recreation budgets, much less increase them [Seefeldt 1995; Lupher 1996; Rauner et al. 1994]. One consequence of this is that the recreational infrastructure—parks and playgrounds—has deteriorated [Coleman Children & Youth Services 1995; Seefeldt 1995]. Even successful community-based youth-serving agencies find it difficult to secure the resources to keep up with the demands for more services [McLaughlin et al. 1994; Seefeldt 1995].

Despite the renewed public spotlight on after-school programs, the bulk of public dollars spent on youth are still for "specialized" services rather than "primary" services [Wynn et al. 1994]. Specialized services are narrowly targeted at youth considered at risk, or in need of treatment or residential care. Such services are aimed at dealing with problems, instead of fostering youth resiliency and positive youth development. Primary services, those "activities, facilities and events provided by organizations that are part of families' familiar social world" [Wynn et al. 1994, p. 7], such as recreation, sports, public parks, museums, libraries, culture, arts, and music, still get short shrift in tight city budgets. These primary services, however, contribute to an overall quality of life in communities and provide an infrastructure that supports a wide array of positive influences in a child's life.

The new interest by policymakers on after-school programs is often still focused on the problem-preventing aspects of these programs, despite the much stronger and robust research that shows that quality recreational, sports, and other organized leisure activities can enhance a host of positive attributes, such as social skills, resiliency, academic achievement, self-esteem, career maturity, and career efficacy, as well as improve overall health and fitness [Gambone & Arbreton 1997; Eccles et al. 1993; Csikszentmihalyi 1982].

Since the mid-1980s, a growing body of research has focused on the "protective" factors in a child's environment that engender "*resiliency*"—an ability to resist the negative factors and influences that lead to delinquency, teen pregnancy, and drug abuse [Benard 1987, 1992; Brewer et al. 1994; Smith et al. 1995]. This research has investigated specific factors within a child's family, school, peers and community, as well as within the child him or herself [Hawkins et al. 1989; Werner & Smith 1989] that contribute to resiliency. Communities where strong norms discouraging alcohol and drug abuse and establishing clear rules and boundaries about public behavior are promoted and reinforced have lower incidence of delinquency and drug abuse. Another critical factor is the density of social networks within a community [Gabarino 1989; Miller & Ohlin 1985]. These are the interpersonal, intergroup and interorganizational relationships that bind a community together and build social cohesion. Such socially cohesive communities can tap into these networks—their social capital—and solve the problems and meet the challenges that occur in all communities [Coleman 1987; Benard 1989]. Within such communities, youth find the opportunities for prosocial involvement with other youth and adults. Recreation and leisure programs serve as a prime venue for these activities [Brewer et al. 1994].

Several other policy-related issues, however, stand in the way of improving the social and physical environments for youth. These include lack of commitment to recreation and sports, lack of leadership, poorly managed public systems and low program quality [Rauner et al. 1994]. Further, until sports, recreation, and other organized programs in the out-of-school hours can be brought to sufficient scale, their effect will continue to be marginal [Schorr 1988; Karoly et al. 1998].

This revived interest in the out-of-school hours has brought new attention to such local initiatives, such as L.A.'s BEST and the Virtual Y in New York City. Well-established, comprehensive programs such as the Beacons' Schools in New York are being replicated in communities such as Savannah, Oakland, Minneapolis, and Denver. The Clinton Administration raised the issue to the level of federal policy with its 21st Century Community Learning Centers initiative, which provided $40 million in 1998 to local school districts to enhance and expand quality after-school programs. Congress has also approved $200 million—the full amount requested by the Administration—for the second year of the initiative. The C.S. Mott Foundation, based in Flint, Michigan, has formed a collaborative partnership with the federal government in this effort, with a pledge of up to $55 million to provide technical assistance, training, and support to the program and its grantees.

Another local initiative to address this issue has been the Youth Sports and Recreation Initiative in Detroit, supported by The Skillman Foundation. The initiative, launched in 1992, is a long-term, comprehensive effort to increase the participation of urban youth in quality sports and recreational programs and also to increase the numbers of adults and parents involved directly with youth in these programs.

The initiative represents an attempt to address the key barriers—policy, program, infrastructure, financial, and social—to improving after-school opportunities for youth in a major American city. Based on an extensive two-year needs assessment, the initiative also calls for a new model for providing youth development and recreation services in an urban area.

This chapter will not only attempt to describe what happened specifically in Detroit, but also why Detroit's experience might be instructive for other urban areas, which struggle to foster positive youth development in the face of daunting odds. Although we have certainly not yet achieved all of our aims, the progress—as well as the continuing challenges—have provided us with some broad, general lessons about developing urban youth programs and bringing them to scale.

As the Skillman program officer responsible for this initiative, I have been directly involved in helping shape and guide the initiative through its planning and early implementation phases. Although this chapter draws on my experience of this process, most of the chapter is based upon the research and analysis of several independent investigators. The Foundation supported these separate studies in order to assemble detailed information about the status of recreational opportunities for youth.

The first and most important of these investigators was the Institute for the Study of Youth Sports at Michigan State University (MSU), led by Vern Seefeldt, who was also one of the principal consultants for the Carnegie Corporation's report, *A Matter of Time*. The MSU team conducted an initial needs assessment of youth development and sports activities in Detroit, Hamtramck and Highland Park, which was then followed up by an in-depth needs assessment [Seefeldt 1994, 1995]. The Citizens Research Council of Michigan, a tax policy analysis organization in Michigan, assessed the current financial and funding status of the recreation departments of the three cities [Lupher 1996]. Finally, Moore & Associates, Inc., a metro-Detroit area survey and research firm, conducted a sample assessment of community use of schools policies and practices in the Detroit Public Schools [Moore & Brown 1998].

Clearly this and other initiatives to improve positive opportunities for youth in the nonschool hours are essential to youth development. Community-based after-school youth programs provide opportunities for youth to learn critical life skills, such as goal-setting, communication, decision-making and problem-solving [Carnegie Council 1992].

Initiative Background

The Skillman Foundation is a private, independent foundation, which makes grants mostly in the metropolitan Detroit area, with a focus primarily on children and youth. As noted earlier, it launched the Youth Sports and Recreation Initiative[1] in 1992 to significantly involve more youth, parents, and mentors in sports, recreation, and

leisure activities in Detroit, Highland Park, and Hamtramck
(Hamtramck and Highland Park are two encapsulated municipalities within the city boundaries of Detroit). That initiative was
announced by the Skillman Foundation via a concept paper in 1993
[Skillman Foundation 1993]. The paper stated that the goal of
initiative would "be accomplished by improving, reorganizing and
expanding a wide variety of sports, recreation and youth development activities and opportunities for youth ages 6 to 16. It is
important that the goal of the initiative be viewed in the context of
developing children and youth to their maximum human potential."
[Skillman Foundation 1993, p. 3]. The goal was to be achieved
through a three-phase process, beginning with a Phase I planning
and needs assessment process, followed by implementation and
operational phases. The needs assessment was deemed critical, since
data on sports and recreation in the cities of Detroit, Highland Park,
or Hamtramck was scant and unreliable, especially regarding existing programs, facilities, and playing fields. Little was known about
the effectiveness of the known programs. Unlike specialized programs for troubled and at-risk youth in Detroit, many of which have
been extensively evaluated, primary programs—those which serve
the general youth population—had few thorough or reliable evaluations.

The need for such an initiative was articulated not only by such
documents as the Carnegie Council's watershed report, *A Matter of
Time*, but also by many local reports and experts, which cited the
drastic loss of recreational and other leisure time activities [Univer-
sity Cultural Center and Zachary & Associates 1991; United Community Services 1987].

Several specific objectives were set forth in the concept paper:
• Improve access to services and activities and availability of
quality programs.
• Increase diversity of recreational offerings.
• Support existing providers and develop new providers
• Provide training and technical assistance to improve pro-
gram quality.
• Increase numbers of youth in a wide variety of activities.

- Increase numbers of parents and adults in youth sports and recreation.
- Increase awareness of recreation and youth development as critical public issues.

From the outset, Skillman envisioned a long-term, comprehensive effort to improve opportunities for positive leisure, recreational, and other youth development activities. The initiative was not to be narrowly focused on individual programs, but simultaneously moving on several fronts, from improving infrastructure to building grassroots and nonprofit capacity. This was not merely an effort to support a number of model or demonstration programs. The vision was to bring these programs to scale and lay the ground for their long-term sustainability.

The initiative was seen by Skillman as part of a trio of major initiatives, which dovetailed with each other to improve the overall environment for children. The other two initiatives were major school reform initiatives—Comer Schools and Families, and Schools of the 21st Century—and the Parenting Matters Initiative.[2] Each of the three initiatives were directed at improving a major environment affecting the development of children and youth: family, school and community. The Parenting Matters Initiative seeks to improve parenting skills of families in Detroit and increase the overall awareness of how good parenting affects child development. The Foundation's education initiatives are comprehensive, whole-school reform efforts, aimed at improving the learning environment for children in the Detroit Public Schools.

Needs Assessment

Phase I of the Initiative was devoted to gathering detailed information about youth and youth participation in sports, recreation, and other youth development activities. This was a task that clearly required some expert help, since there was little research to help Skillman determine methodologically how to proceed [Carnegie Corporation 1992]. Through a request for proposal process, Skillman selected the Institute for the Study of Youth Sports at Michigan State

University (MSU), to conduct the assessment. The MSU team was charged to:

- Assess the demography of youth 6-16 and their families in the target area;
- Identify and assess needs, including facilities, access, providers, youth and adult involvement, and outreach;
- Assess the environment for improving, reorganizing and expanding programs and activities, including barriers to improvements;
- Make recommendations for meeting needs, including structure, programs and activities;
- Present an action plan for implementing the recommendations.

Skillman staff also thought it critical that the needs assessment process be guided by local government, civic, community and church leaders, as well as by both professionals and volunteers involved in youth and recreational services.

A Recreation Advisory Committee was formed, which included 58 individuals representing public recreation departments, public and private schools, youth-serving agencies, major civic organizations, youth sports associations, as well as professional sports teams, a commercial provider of recreation, faith-based organizations, community groups, health and social service agencies, universities and foundations. There were several reasons why convening such a large, representative group was crucial for the initiative. The group included the key providers of recreational and leisure services, who understood the challenges and needs in the city. Ultimately, if the initiative was to have legitimacy within the community, then the community needed to be genuinely involved in the process of developing and shaping the initiative. Looking beyond the needs assessment itself, Skillman realized that its resources alone could neither sustain the initiative over time nor bring the effort to sufficient scale to make a city-wide impact. The future of such an initiative would depend upon marshalling untapped citizen and parent volunteers, influencing public policy and allocation of funds for recreation and youth services, enlisting community leadership to advocate for youth development, and bringing other partners and resources to the table.

For three months, the MSU project team interviewed the 58 RAC members. Members were questioned specifically on various aspects of nonschool youth sports and recreation programs, including the roles programs play in the lives of youth, what makes particular programs successful, ideas for new programs, and the barriers to provision of quality programs.

The MSU team also gathered information from other sectors of the community. The team conducted a series of sample written surveys of public and private schools in the target communities, commercial and non-profit providers of recreational programs, community recreation centers, churches and businesses. The process included conducting 15 focus groups with children and youth, program providers and community leaders on how community residents viewed nonschool hours programming. The focus groups were conducted between November 1993 and April 1994. The MSU team also made twelve site visits at neighborhood, community, volunteer, social service, and private programs. The agencies visited represented a broad cross-section of the diverse array of youth serving organizations in the tri-city area.

Findings

Demographics

The changes in the population of the city over the past several decades have been profound. Detroit is a city of roughly one million people (1,028,000 according to the 1990 U.S. Census 1990). This is about 44% fewer people than resided in the city in 1950. Although many cities of the industrialized "rust belt" regions of the country have lost population, the decline in Detroit has been steeper [Neithercut 1993].

The number of youth in the city has also declined dramatically. In the last 20 years alone, the number of youth has dropped from 494,000 in 1970 to 302,000 in 1990 [U.S. Census 1990]. Of the 302,000 children and youth, an estimated 184,000 are between the ages of 6 and 16. These youth represent about 17.3% of the population of Detroit, 14.2% of the population of Hamtramck, and 16.3% of the population of Highland Park.

Youth by Race/Ethnicity. Much of the population loss, although not all, is due to exodus of whites from the city. The result is that Detroit is now a city that is over 77% African American. The percentages are even higher for youth. In Detroit, over 81% of youth ages 6–16 are African American, while Highland Park is 97.8% African American. Hamtramck—from its origins a destination for immigrants from Poland and eastern Europe—still is predominantly Caucasian, at 77.7% of the population.

Youth by Gender. The percentage of males ages 6–16 in the tri-city area is slightly over half the population (average of 50.97% for Detroit, Hamtramck, and Highland Park). These percentages roughly mirror statistics for the rest of the country. But to be a young African American male carries a particular risk. Nationally, homicide is the leading cause of death among 15- to 30-year-old African American males. In Michigan in 1991, 66% of all deaths for 15- to 24-year-old males occurred in Detroit [Michigan Department of Public Health 1992].

Families and Poverty

In Detroit, 56.4% of households with children are headed by single females. The percentage of female-headed households is even higher in Highland Park (71%). In Hamtramck, the majority of households with children (52.8%) are married couples, but the percentage of single-female-headed households is still high (41%).

Of the nation's ten largest cities, Detroit has the worst rate of childhood poverty (46.6%). Most of Detroit's poorest children live in households headed by a single female (82.6%). The rates for Highland Park and Hamtramck are comparable (54.7% and 44% respectively) [Seefeldt 1995].

For those familiar with data on the urban poor and underclass, these statistics are not surprising. It is just that in Detroit the statistics are generally much worse in many categories. The implications for recreation and positive after-school programming are profound. Youth are not only walking into recreation centers and onto playgrounds with more needs, there are fewer adults, especially adult men, to provide supervision, guidance, and coaching. The majority of youth come from homes without the constant presence of a father. In many communities, fathers and other adult men traditionally provide the bulk of the volunteer leadership for organized sports. In Detroit, it is difficult even to find adequate professional help. During the course of the initiative, Skillman staff frequently heard complaints from Detroit Recreation Department officials about the difficulties of finding enough competent play-leaders who did not test positively for drugs.

The Role of Public Recreation

Finding enough play-leaders, however, was not the most serious problem confronting the Detroit Recreation Department. Although recently rejuvenated with new leadership following the election of a new mayor, the department had already suffered years of steep budget cuts. The study conducted by the Citizens Research Council of Michigan, funded by the Skillman, estimated that the expenditures for recreation within the department had decreased by over $1 million from 1990 to 1994 [Lupher 1996]. But the Council's investigators could not determine the exact amounts spent for recreation, and for youth recreation in particular, because of inadequate record keeping and cost accounting methods by the department.

The MSU survey of public recreation centers also revealed that most centers required immediate and extensive attention regarding their general maintenance [Seefeldt 1995]. Only one of the 33 centers reported that conditions were good. Most of the centers reported leaking roofs, loosening plaster, or missing windows. Equipment was in generally poor condition.

Many of the 800 parks, playing fields, and play lots in Detroit, Hamtramck, and Highland were also poorly maintained and in need of major refurbishment. Much of the playground equipment, for example, was built for an earlier time, and rarely met current safety standards. Uncut grass left baseball and football fields unplayable. Not only unplayable, but unsightly too, due to copious litter.

The MSU team compared the current distribution of the youth population in the tri-city area with the availability of recreation centers, using GIS (geographic information systems) technology.

The geocoded mapping showed that there was serious mismatch in the placement of the centers and areas of the cities with the highest concentrations of youth (see Figure 1). Geocoding was not only useful in this particular instance, but was an extremely important tool in visually displaying such key information as placement of community based programs, school facilities, churches, and many other important community assets.

Interviews with community residents, leaders, and youth also brought a key issue to the surface: the loss of confidence in the Detroit Recreation Department to deliver services that the community itself desires. This issue manifested itself in two ways: first, the Department was simply unable to perform roles expected by the community—such as cutting grass on playing fields or fixing faulty equipment in centers—and secondly, by offering programs without input and feedback from community residents. The MSU needs assessment report was critical of this "top-down" approach, and proposed a more community-based approach to recreational services. Such an approach would involve more community participation, both at the planning and also programmatic stages, and also greater collaboration with neighborhood groups and organizations that may be already providing some form of recreation.

Schools

Schools may be perhaps the most important community asset as far as children and youth go. They are the places not only where children go to get educated, they also serve as sites for latchkey programs and other after-school activities . The model after-school programs cited earlier in this chapter—Beacons, L.A.'s BEST—are all school-based. Schools potentially can play a critical role in providing safe havens for children in a city such as Detroit, where recreation centers are not located in the areas of highest concentrations of youth.

With this in mind, the MSU team developed an extensive survey instrument, which was distributed to every public and private school in the target area. The instrument asked each school to answer questions regarding facilities, types of programs offered, participation rates of youth, program leadership, and community

Figure 9-1. Public Recreational Centers Detroit, Hamtramck, and Highland Park, Michigan

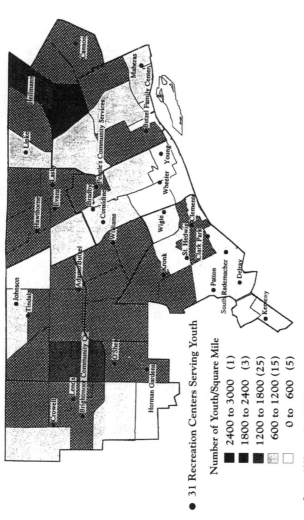

● 31 Recreation Centers Serving Youth

Number of Youth/Square Mile

■ 2400 to 3000 (1)
■ 1800 to 2400 (3)
■ 1200 to 1800 (25)
▦ 600 to 1200 (15)
□ 0 to 600 (5)

Source: 1990 census (ages 3-13)

resources in the vicinity of the school. With the help of a retired high school principal who served as a consultant, the team was able to garner a 93% rate of return of the surveys from the Detroit Public Schools and 100% return from both Hamtramck and Highland Park Schools. Private school retrieval was the lowest at 47%. {Seefeldt 1995].

The primary finding of the survey was that a relatively small number of youth participated in after-school programs. A little more than one-third (about 77,500) of children ages 6–16 were involved in these programs. But this number does not represent an unduplicated count, hence the actual participation was probably much lower. The survey also revealed wide variances in the number of programs offered in different regions of city. One region offered 256 activities, involving 26,649 participants, while another region, with a similar sized youth population, had only 115 activities, involving 2,998 participants—almost a ten-fold difference.

Through focus groups of school and community representatives, the MSU team uncovered reasons why school facilities were not more frequently used. The key issue here was community use of schools. One hypothesis considered by MSU was that schools would more likely be open for programming in the after-school hours, if they were more accessible to community groups for use. From the focus groups, MSU heard that the inability to pay the cost of supportive services, including custodial care, utilities, and engineering, was the primary reason (27.4%) schools were not used more. School principals, on the other hand, stated that a primary reason was the incompatibility of the building with the intended purpose (20%). Other reasons given by principals were inability to provide supervision (14.9%) and concerns involving the safety of the potential users (11.8%). A little over 10% of the principals also stated that no one requested to use the building.

Nonprofit Organizations

Neighborhood organizations, usually small nonprofit and church-related agencies, often serve not only as safe havens for children in poor, inner-city communities, but also places where they find the support and guidance to develop their best selves [McLaughlin et al. 1994; Cahill et al. 1993; Gambone & Arbreton 1997]. These organizations offer programs that teach life skills, such as goal setting and negotiation; they provide opportunities for community service and to develop special interests and nurture talents; and they give children an opportunity to engage in constructive, organized activities, such as sports [Carnegie Council on Adolescent Development 1994].

An MSU scan of community agencies revealed that approximately 465 organizations in the tri-city area were providing some form of youth programming. MSU sent an initial survey to randomly selected organizations in 1993 during the first phase needs assessment, with 54 responses. This was followed by the in-depth survey in 1995, which had 61 responses.

The survey responses showed that these groups offer a comprehensive array of programs, including organized sports and recreation, educational, life skills, culture and arts, aquatics, special events (e.g. field trips), and informal recreation. One of the issues raised by the MSU team, however, was the lack of coordination among the agencies. The team found duplication of services in some areas or gaps in service, "turf protection," lack of focus on areas of greatest need, and an ineffective utilization of scarce resources. The Detroit Recreation Department, weakened by budget cuts and loss of staff, was unable to provide coordination or even to ensure that baseball diamonds or football fields would be ready for play by community groups.

These agencies, often competing for these scarce resources, frequently struggle to keep afloat. Securing adequate funding is an ongoing effort and none reported that they received adequate funding for their programs. Community groups also must rely more heavily on volunteers. Although volunteers are a valuable asset for youth, they are a "mixed blessing" (to borrow a quote from McLaughlin et al. [1994]). They must be recruited, screened, trained, managed, and motivated.

Common complaints raised by the community, not only about private agency programs but also about public sector ones, were centered around the main issue of access: program times, transportation, and safety. The MSU team found that there were few programs offered on weekends. The most frequently mentioned barrier was the absence of safe and reliable transportation. Children often reported feeling unsafe traveling to and from recreation programs and mentioned that their parents often had to accompany them. Children and parents described parks as being particularly dangerous because of shootings.

Faith-Based Organizations

In addition to the 465 community-based agencies operating in Detroit, Hamtramck, and Highland Park, the researchers counted 871 religious organizations. Their original conjecture was that these organizations—which have historically played a powerful role in African American communities—would also be playing an important role in youth development activities. But of the 871 surveys sent in the first phase of the needs assessment to churches and other faith based organizations, only 27 were returned. The second phase needs assessment of churches was only slightly more successful: 44 organizations responded to the questionnaire.

MSU researchers were able, however, to gather information from third party sources, principally members of the local school community organizations ("LSCOs" are affiliated with most schools in the Detroit Public Schools system and operate somewhat like Parent Teacher Associations do in other districts). Through the input of LSCO members and school principals, 358 programs in sports, recreation and other youth development offered by faith-based organizations were identified.

Although it was possible that there were more programs being offered by religious organizations, the researchers concluded that this was not likely and that churches were probably providing much less youth programming than originally estimated. At the same time, the MSU report highlighted churches as an area of opportunity for expanding the number and distribution of youth programs.

Organized Sports

The needs assessment also included surveys of organized sports programs, including for-profit commercial providers. The first phase needs assessment yielded a broad picture of organized sports. Agencies reported that funding, facilities, and equipment were the major barriers to greater youth participation. The second in-depth needs assessment provided more detail about organized sports programs.

A survey of 44 nonprofit providers showed that programs were available in baseball, basketball, bowling, boxing, cheerleading, figure skating, floor hockey, football, golf, gymnastics, ice hockey, martial arts, skiing, soccer, softball, swimming, track and field, and volleyball. In total, agencies reported that 20,669 youth were involved in 18 sports, with basketball (N=5394) and baseball (N=5219) boasting the highest participation. Male participation was 7,750, and female participation was 4,182.

Recreation departments in Detroit, Hamtramck, and Highland Park reported much lower participation numbers. The total number of participants in public recreation programs was 6,257. The number of males participating in these programs was almost three times as much as females (although departments' records frequently did not record gender).

Based on its findings, the MSU team concluded that:

- private, not-for-profit program providers support programs in most sports and reach more athletes than programs sponsored by public and private schools and public recreation departments;
- recreation departments sponsor the most programs but reach relatively fewer youth;
- school-based programs reach the highest average number of athletes;
- team sports are most common—with traditional sports of baseball, basketball, football, and softball dominating;
- life-long sports (such as swimming, tennis, or martial arts) involved barely 16% of the youth.
  [Seefeldt 1994].

Youth Participation

Overall, the results of the needs assessment indicated that the participation of children and youth in organized and supervised out-of-school hours programs was relatively low. Exact numbers were hard to come by, given the inconsistent or inadequate record keeping of both public and private agencies. The MSU team estimated that about a third of youth in the tri-city area are involved in sports, recreation, and other youth development activities offered by public recreation, private nonprofits, community groups, and religious organizations.

The unresolved challenge of the overall needs assessment was gathering actual participation data. The largest public provider of services, the Detroit Recreation Department, frequently was unable to provide participation data for its programs and recreation center usage. The survey responses from nonprofits and from faith-based organizations, in particular, were disappointing. In retrospect, had the MSU researchers been able to recruit one or more individuals with entrée to the city's churches—as they did with the Detroit Public Schools—they might have had better success. However, the researchers' conjecture that churches were not providing as many youth recreational programs as originally estimated has so far not been proven incorrect. Since the release of the needs assessment in 1995, the overwhelming majority of programs seeking funding from Skillman or from intermediary organizations which re-grant its dollars have come from public recreation, non-profit youth serving agencies, and emerging, grassroots organizations.

Recommendations and Action Plans for the Initiative

The recommendations and action plans for the Skillman initiative were finalized together by the MSU team and Skillman staff (cf. Table 1]. These, together with a summary of the MSU needs assessment, were published by Skillman [Seefeldt 1995] in a report entitled, *Re-creating Recreation in Detroit, Hamtramck and Highland Park*. The recommendations and action plans of the report provide the framework and foundation of the Skillman Youth Sports and Recreation Initiative. The underlying premise upon which the recommendations themselves rest is that the out-of-school hours represent a time of risk and opportunity for children and youth. Increasing opportunities for positive, supervised, and constructive activities during this period can foster positive youth development

Table 9-1. Recommendations of *Re-Creating Recreation in Detroit, Hamtramck and Highland Park* to Improve Youth Sports and Recreation Services

Programs, Services, and Facilities

1. Design programs to meet the needs of all children in the community, increase diversity of programming, and emphasize the comprehensive development of youth and the need to target those who have been underserved.
2. Improve safety at neighborhood and program facilities and sites.
3. Increase accessibility to programming through increasing availability of transportation and convenient program times.
4. Increase opportunities for children and youth to participate in organized sports and recreation activities.
5. Locate programs and services in neighborhoods with high concentration of youth and expand the number of facilities and sites in areas that are not currently served by increasing the use of school and religious facilities for after-school activities. Promote establishment of multiservice centers and programs.
6. Improve the condition and maintenance of public recreation facilities and sites.

Funding and Resources

7. Increase fiscal resources for public and private youth sports and recreation programs and facilities.

Implementation, Cooperation, and Coordination

8. Establish a broad-based public/private organization as the mechanism to provide leadership in implementing the Skillman Youth Sports & Recreation Initiative recommendations and oversee the planning, development, coordination, maintenance, and evaluation of youth sports and recreation programs.

Community Involvement

9. Shift from a "top-down" model to a model involving community-based planning, implementation, and evaluation of programs, and redefine the roles and responsibility of public and private providers and professionals and volunteers in the delivery of programs and services.
10. Increase the involvement of families and citizens as volunteers and mentors in the planning, management and delivery of programs and services. Support

Table 9-1. (Cont'd)

and encourage volunteers through professional assistance and training to improve program quality.

Planning, Evaluation, and Professionalism

11. Develop a future plan for sports and recreation utilizing standards for national accreditation as a guide, where appropriate.
12. Assess and evaluate sports and recreation programs on an ongoing basis.
13. Establish a computer-based Management information system for public recreation departments to facilitate communication among recreation departments, center, and private youth-serving agencies that may wish to be linked to the information system.
14. Assist professional staff to adapt to new roles and responsibilities and program models.
15. Educate policymakers and the general public about the importance of youth sports and recreation in the positive development of youth and the prevention of delinquency, crime, educational underachievement, substance abuse, and teenage pregnancy.

and reduce incidence of health compromising behaviors. The report also calls for the establishment of a coordinating mechanism—the Youth Sports and Recreation Commission—as the key to increasing these opportunities.

The Commission was viewed as an integral component of the entire Skillman initiative. It would be the entity that would drive the implementation of the recommendations of *Re-creating Recreation*. The needs assessment revealed that the whole arena of youth development and recreation lacked the kind of broad public/private leadership demanded to foster greater cooperation and coordination among the public recreation departments and 465 community groups in the tri-city area. The services provided by tri-city organizations were fragmented, sometimes overlapping, and weak in reaching certain groups, such as girls and children with special needs. Smaller, grassroots organizations lacked organizational capacity to sustain programs and were in need of much technical assistance and training. A strong, unified voice was also clearly needed to advocate for greater citizen involvement in and increased public and private resources for youth development. Although the MSU report emphasized the importance of the potential leadership role of public recreation, it recommended that a commission be established to bridge the gaps between public and private providers, and also to bring local community groups into the process of community planning.

During late 1994 and early 1995, the Foundation set in motion the process to create such a body from the ground up. Through a consultative process that included the Detroit Mayor's office, it was determined that the commissioners of the new body would be appointees of the mayors of Detroit, Hamtramck, and Highland Park. The Commission itself, however, legally would be a 501(c)(3) nonprofit organization.

In the fall of 1995, the Commission was officially established with 15 members. An executive with many years experience at the YMCA was hired as executive director. The Commission and its staff quickly found that their plate was already filled to the brim. There were already several important projects underway that would require the Commission's leadership and involvement. These are briefly summarized below.

Community Use of Schools Task Force (CUSTF)

The CUSTF, convened by Skillman in 1995, was a 16-member body, representing the Detroit Public Schools, the City of Detroit, and several community youth-serving agencies. The Task Force's charge was to:

- determine the current status of the community use of schools, based on the MSU survey data;
- identify issues involved in community use of schools that inhibit such use; and
- explore and recommend ways to increase and improve community use of schools; and develop a realistic plan for implementing the recommendations.

The CUSTF is seeking to improve access to schools for community and non-profit organizations that serve youth. The Task Force has unearthed several major obstacles to community use of schools and sent its recommendations to the Detroit Board of Education (cf. Table 2). The Commission helps to staff this continuing effort.

Pistons-Palace Foundation's Partnership Program to Adopt and Renovate Parks for Kids or P.A.R.K. Program

The Pistons-Palace Foundation, which is the corporate giving arm of the Detroit Pistons professional basketball team, developed the program in collaboration with the Detroit mayor's office. The program, originally an $8 million, now an $11 million, effort to refurbish and renovate 33 public playgrounds and parks in the city. Foundations, corporations, and other businesses were approached for contributions.

In the early stages of the initiative, the Pistons-Palace Foundation and its partners determined that the program would not only focus on capital improvements, but also on community building. No park would be selected unless there was a strong local base of community support. Community residents, grass-roots community organizations, and churches would have to commit to helping maintain the parks and also help plan and operate programs at the parks. The Commission has partnered with the Pistons-Palace Foundation in the community building component of the P.A.R.K. program.

The Re-Capitalization of Recreation Centers Project

This is a joint funder collaborative involving the City of Detroit, and the W.K. Kellogg, Kresge, and Skillman foundations. This initiative is applying $11 million toward the renovation of four recreation centers in Detroit. The Youth Sports & Recreation Commission was handed the responsibility of both fiscal and construction management of the recapitalization project to the Commission.

The Tri-Cities Sports Coalition

The Commission organized this coalition to improve coordination among teams and leagues involved in diamond sports (baseball, softball, and T-ball) and soccer. The coalition has been instrumental in improving scheduling of playing fields with the Detroit Recreation Department and coordinating activities between different leagues. It has also helped create and organize annual, city-wide baseball and soccer tournaments.

Each of these four efforts addresses one or more of the recommendations of the *Re-Creating Recreation* report. The report recom-

Table 9-2. Community Use of Schools Task Force Recommendations

Public Policy

1. The school community partners should adopt a policy statement emphasizing the importance of positive youth development, recreation, family support, and similar preventive programs as well as the important roles the schools and community play in meeting these program needs.
2. DPS and its stakeholders should adopt a policy statement that the community's use of schools during nonschool hours is important to the entire community and is a component of "school day."

Access, Operation, and Management

3. Develop systemwide "guiding principles" for schools and groups to use schools based on successful afterschool programs.
4. Develop model compacts or user agreements.
5. Develop a comprehensive model community use of schools program in one or more schools.
6. Develop additional latch-key programs involving parent/adult volunteers from community.
7. Explore use of insurance pool which might be available to nonprofits and community groups to reduce liability concerns.
8. Explore and revise current DPS policies and procedures and make process for community use more "user friendly."

Funding and Costs

9. "Piggy-back" concurrent use of schools.
10. Assess and make public current funding sources for community use of schools and seek additional resources.
11. Assess cost components of community use of schools and seek ways to reduce costs.

Training and Public Awareness

12. Inform public through media and forums about importance of afterschool programs, extension of school day, guiding principles, and community use of schools procedures.
13. Train principals, administrators, and teachers about community use of schools.
14. Involve LSCOs and parents in public information, advocacy, and coordination of community use of schools.
15. Explore use of ombudsman to assist community.

mend improving access to programs and increasing the number of after-school programs, goals of the Community Use of Schools Task Force. The reports recommendations of improving recreational infrastructure and increasing citizen involvement in recreation are aims of the P.A.R.K. program and Re-Capitalization of Recreation Centers project. The Tri-Cities Sports Coalition seeks to increase voluntarism and opportunities for organized sports, which were also recommendations of the report. What is common in all these efforts is that they involve collaborative planning and intensive community involvement. The Commission has been instrumental in helping to organize and staff these activities. But what has given each of these efforts momentum and energy has been the enthusiasm and responsiveness of the other partners.

Other Commission Projects

Grants and Funding. Besides acting as a coordinator, the Commission also acts as a funding resource, both directly and indirectly. As a direct funding source, it provides small grants to community organizations for youth programming in the out-of-school hours. The grants are flexible and are intended to cover a wide range of needs, from equipment and minor capital needs to helping defray program staff expenses. As an indirect source, the Commission acts as an advocate and liaison with corporate and professional sports funders seeking opportunities to invest in youth programming. The Commission, for example, has worked with Major League Baseball's RBI or Reviving Baseball in Inner Cities program and with the World Cup Host Committee in diverting funds for youth sports.

Technical Assistance. In 1997 the Commission joined with New Detroit, Inc.—one of the city's major civic organizations—and Skillman to establish the Community Grants and Assistance Partnership. New Detroit was invited as a partner, due to its long history of providing technical assistance to grassroots organizations. The Partnership seeks to coordinate technical assistance and training opportunities for these organizations, through workshops, consultants, and linking to other technical assistance providers. The need for such a partnership became apparent as the Commission began to fund these small community-based groups, which frequently needed help with grant writing, program development, evaluation, and financial reporting.

Summer Youth Employment. The Commission provides grants to local public and private, non-profit groups grants to provide employment, job-preparation and leadership training for youth during the summer months. This program was initially developed in response to cutbacks in the federal summer jobs funds under the Job Training and Partnership Act (JTPA). But its scope has broadened to support more comprehensive work-readiness, community-service programs that seek to prepare youth for future careers and work.

Meeting the Challenges of Replication and Sustainability

In the fourth year of implementation, the Youth Sports and Recreation Initiative and the Commission have clearly begun to make noticeable changes in Detroit, Hamtramck, and Highland Park. Without an objective evaluation of these changes, however, one cannot yet make any broad, unbiased assertions about whether these changes have been significant. An evaluation is currently in progress. It is possible, on the other hand, to assess what challenges still loom. The challenges can tell us a great deal about not only how far we have yet to go, but also what kind of environment we ultimately hope for our children.

The two principal challenges for the initiative, which were mentioned at the beginning of the chapter, are replication—and by this I also include the issues of scaling up—and sustainability. There are no clear, single-shot answers to either of these. These are fundamental challenges that must be confronted across the entire range of programming for children and youth. These have become more prominent largely, although not solely, because of the shrinking portion of tax-payer dollars devoted to the support and care of children. The dollars have shrunk for many reasons—changes in public policy, a general tax-averse climate, and continuing hemorrhaging of the tax base in inner cities. Convincing lawmakers, civic leaders, and the public that recreation and after-school programs should be considered primary public sector responsibilities, instead of marginal, is one of main objectives of the Skillman initiative. Developing a comprehensive plan to move public will in this direction is a step that at the moment lies in the future. The publication of *Re-creating Recreation* itself was a communication event, intended to build a case among community leaders and policymakers for after-school and other recreational programs. Research and evaluation studies such as this will continue to play an important part in the overall communication strategy.

Skillman also is seeking to play a larger role as a public advocate and champion for children and youth in general. Collaboration with other funders, public and private, is also a means to moving an agenda for children. Skillman's role, for example, in a funders collaboration on community development is helping to increase community development organizations' roles in providing after-school programs. Similarly, its involvement in a major school reform collaboration is helping to ensure that after-school programs are included in school improvement plans.

Bringing after-school and organized sports programs to scale will not only depend on additional funding. They will also depend heavily on the capacity and commitment of three other segments of the community: the schools, public recreation, and community and faith-based organizations.

Central to Skillman's future strategy is a partnership with the Detroit Public Schools to replicate quality, comprehensive after-school programs throughout the district. The work of the Community Use of Schools Task Force has revealed numerous barriers to this effort. What has become clear through the process of investigating these barriers is that they are system-wide, embedded in the culture and practice of the district, intertwined with contract issues and often determined by the priorities of the local school principal. Currently, Skillman is involved with members of the district and with leaders from local civic, governmental and community organizations to develop a plan that will not only keep schools open, but leverage both public and private funds and also facilitate the involvement of community groups in the operations of after-school programs.

The MSU report [Seefeldt 1994] underlined the important role that public recreation departments can and must make to restore recreation in the city. With fewer resources, however, public recreation is faced with the challenge of trying to maintain a crumbling infrastructure, provide programs to low-income children and families at little or no cost, and coordinate its programming with the needs and wishes of community residents and youth-serving organizations. The Detroit Recreation Department, for example, has historically not coordinated its efforts with community groups. Both the PARK program and Re-Capitalization of Recreation Centers project mentioned earlier are both experiments in a new form of public/ private cooperation in recreation. Both programs are seeking to develop a model for future infrastructure improvements to be carried out by the department. A major challenge for the Detroit Recreation Department in the future will be simply to maintain and improve its infrastructure. Deferred maintenance on many recreational sites means that it has a lot of catching up to do. The PARK program will affect only 33 of the approximately 800 parks and playgrounds in the tri-city area. The Re-Capitalization of Recreation Centers project will renovate four of over 30 centers in Detroit.

The good news here is that many of these problems are fixable. These problems—from leaky roofs to uncut grass—in many cases were the result of years of budget erosion. The challenge for the Recreation Department will be to regain a larger share of the city's general operating budget and to forge more successful partnerships with the corporate and business community. What Skillman hopes to generate through the work of the Youth Sports and Recreation Commission is greater public support for recreation and youth services.

Another serious challenge for the initiative is the capacity of neighborhood nonprofit organizations to carry out and sustain programs for youth. These organizations are not only constantly in need of more funding, but frequently need considerable technical assistance in areas such as board and staff development, fiscal and program management, volunteer recruitment and training, proposal writing, and evaluation and computer technology. Furthermore, there are few sources or providers of technical assistance available for

these organizations. The Community Grants and Assistance Partnership, which was mentioned earlier as a Commission project, was
created to address these needs.

Ultimately, much of the success of the initiative will depend on
the response of the community. As the *Re-creating Recreation* report
states in its recommendation number ten: "Significantly greater
numbers of volunteers must be involved in planning, conducting,
and evaluating programs and services if community-based programming is to have credibility, especially since significantly reduced
budgets for public recreation has resulted in reduced services, programs, and maintenance of sites." Recruiting and training more
volunteers, however, faces considerable obstacles. The MSU needs
assessment pointed out that the changes in family composition, the
high mortality rate of young African American men, and the
concentration of poverty in many neighborhoods present daunting
challenges to raising the number of volunteers for youth. As a recent
edition of the Search Institute periodical, *Assets* [Kimball-Baker,
Roehlkepartain 1998], observed, finding good and willing volunteers is often difficult even in less distressed communities. One of the
promising signs in Detroit, as well as in many other cities, is that there
is a newfound zeal among faith-based organizations to rouse their
congregations to work with youth. Community service initiatives,
such as AmeriCorps, are also helping to generate grass-roots
voluntarism. Further community organizing will be a key component
of the initiative in the coming years.

Other Lessons Learned

In addition to the above challenges, here are some other lessons that
both Foundation and Commission staff have gleaned from their
experiences thus far with the initiative.

- Providing positive leisure time activities for children and youth
  in sufficient enough scale will require much greater collaboration, cooperation and coordination among public, private nonprofit and community groups than ever before. A corollary to
  this is that public and private sector agencies will have to learn

how to operate differently than they have in the past. This will mean, for example, cooperative planning efforts and willingness to sacrifice turf. It will also mean jettisoning old ways of doing business, especially for institutions such as schools and public recreation, and a much higher level of flexibility.

- Bringing in programs will not be enough just to increase the numbers of programs and opportunities for children in the nonschool hours. Improving quality must also be a fundamental goal. The success of programs depends upon quality of the staff or volunteers. These are staff who are not only properly trained, but who come with the requisite attributes of working with youth, especially at-risk youth [McLaughlin et al. 1994]. Poorly implemented programs and unwelcoming staff are prime causes for underutilization of programs [Rauner et al. 1994]. Programs must be responsive to the needs and wants of young adolescents if they are to attract them [Carnegie Corporation 1992]. Programs must also be of sufficient intensity to affect necessary changes in adolescents. Programs too frequently do not offer youth the opportunity to contribute and be of service, a critical component of healthy youth development [Carnegie Corporation 1992]. Training and technical assistance will clearly have to play a major role for the initiative as it seeks to build the capacity of local groups and organizations to deliver services for youth.

- The growing consensus about the need for positive after-school programs is apparently both widespread and deep. This represents a significant opportunity for advocates of youth development to build public will for increased support for after-school programs. The C.S. Mott Foundation recently conducted a nationwide poll (August 17–20, 1998), which found overwhelming public support for expansion of after-school programs. This support crossed party lines and included both parents and nonparents. Ninety-three percent of the 800-person survey sample said they would favor more programs offering safe and enriching activities for children and youth. Perhaps even more heartening is that over 70% said that they would be willing to pay $10 more in taxes every year to support such programs.

In Detroit as well, a survey conducted by the United Way for Southeastern Michigan found that lack of recreation ranked among the top four needs of the city [United Way for Southeastern Michigan 1993].

Such public support, of course, does not automatically translate into increased funding for recreation and after-school programs. A major task for the initiative in Detroit will be to continue building support among all segments of the community and making the case that recreation can be more than "fun and games," a point that I am making in this chapter.

- After-school programs and youth sports are a critical component of building caring communities for children and youth, but they are only a part. Resiliency research presents increasingly convincing evidence that children develop best when they are enveloped in protective factors in all domains of their lives, especially home, school, peers, and community. The best after-school programs cannot by themselves overcome drug-abusing parents and dysfunctional schools. But these after-school programs can be even more effective if they can be linked to school reform and family support initiatives.

- Two of the most serious obstacles to increased participation in after-school activities remain the lack of transportation and fears about safety. The quality of public transportation, of course, is different from city to city. Detroit, the motor capital of the world, has long relied on the automobile as the dominant mode of transportation. As a result, public transportation has suffered. This situation is unlikely to change. Creating recreational opportunities in nearby schools, parks, and other sites will help alleviate some of the travel problems. This will address some of the safety issues as well. But the issue of safety will also need to be squarely addressed. Recreation providers, youth serving agencies and neighborhood groups must forge stronger partnerships with law enforcement to increase safety around recreational sites and programs. Law enforcement must also increase its efforts to reduce firearm violence. The prevalence of guns on city streets has radically changed the nature of urban violence [Canada 1995; Marshall & Wheeler 1996].

Epilogue

One of the things I have frequently heard throughout the entire process of helping to get this initiative on track are the stories from people from every walk of life about how important nonschool hour activities were to their development as children and adolescents. More significantly, each person reminisced how much of these programs were simply taken for granted. They were deeply woven into the fabric of the community. The Foundation's own trustees had their own stories to share. Indeed, from the beginning, this initiative seems to have been one that proceeded from the heart. Although the release of A Matter of Time virtually coincided with the inauguration of the Skillman initiative, this was simply fortuitous. The empty playing fields and broken playground equipment in the city of Detroit had been evidence enough that something needed to be done.

One of the very hopeful signs for the future of the initiative is that better recreational opportunities is an issue that residents of Detroit—from young to old—have embraced. Policymakers and community and civic leaders have also become increasingly persuaded that improving the environment for children during the nonschool hours is critical, and probably cost effective.

This is not a matter of bringing back the "good old days." This is a matter of concern to us all, because it is about creating the kinds of environment in which children can grow and develop. It is creating the space for children to play and to experience what childhood should be about.

Notes

1. The title for the initiative suggests a sports-oriented effort, but the initiative actually has a much broader scope. The initiative

seeks to increase the quantity and quality of positive *youth development* activities for youth during the nonschool hours. These activities include not only sports and recreation, but cultural and arts, academic enrichment, social skills programs, community service, job training, and preparation and other activities that contribute to youth development. There was considerable discussion about what to call the initiative, given all that it was meant to address. The decision to use "youth sports and recreation" was based on a sense that the broader public could relate to and easily understand this language and also on the original inspiration for initiative—that the empty playing fields of the city were the sign of something terribly wrong.

2. The Comer Schools and Family Initiative is a ten-year school reform initiative in the Detroit Public Schools, based upon the successful School Development Model of James Comer of Yale University. The Schools of the 21st Century is a $60 million school reform effort aimed at improving the Detroit Public Schools at three separate levels: student-teacher interaction, local school – central administration interaction, and community involvement. It has received one of several national Annenberg Challenge grants. The Parenting Matters Initiative is a multi-year effort aimed at promoting good parenting practices through parent education, resource and referral, and social marketing

References

Benard, B. (1987, March). Protective factor research: what we can learn from resilient children. *Illinois Prevention Forum*, (73).

Benard, B. (1989, October). Working together: Principles of effective collaboration. *Illinois Prevention Forum*, 10(1).

Benard, B. (1992, Summer). Fostering resiliency in kids: protective factors in the family, school and community. *Illinois Prevention Forum*, 12(3).

Brewer, D., Hawkins, J. D., Catalano, R. F., & Neckerman, H. J. (1994). *Preventing serious, violent and chronic juvenile offending: a review of evaluations of selected strategies in childhood, adolescence and the community*. Draft prepared for the National Council on Crime and Delinquency. Seattle, WA: Developmental Research and Programs, Inc.

Cahill, M., Perry, J.,Wright, M., & Rice, A. (1993). *A documentation report on the New York City beacons initiative*. Report to the Annie E. Casey Foundation. New York: The Youth Development Institute, Fund for the City of New York

Canada, G. (1995). *Fist stick knife gun: A personal history of violence in America*. Boston: Beacon Press.

Carnegie Council on Adolescent Development. (1992). *A matter of time: Risk and opportunity in the nonschool hours*. New York: Carnegie Corporation of New York.

Coleman Children & Youth Services. (1995). *Report card on San Francisco's parks*. San Francisco: Coleman Advocates.

Coleman, J. (1987). Families and schools. *Educational Researcher*, *16*(6), 32–38.

Czikszentmihalyi, M. (1982). The value of sports. In J. T. Partington, T. Orlick & J. H. Samela (Eds.), *Sport in perspective*, (pp. 122–127). Ottawa: Coaching Association of Canada.

Eccles, J. S., Midgley, C., Wigfield, A., Buchanan, C. M., Reuman, D., Flanagan, C., & MacIver, D. (1993). Development during adolescence: The impact of state-environment fit on young adolescents' experiences in schools and in families. *American Psychologist*, *48*(2) 90–101.

Fox, J. A. & Newman, S. A. (1998). Quality child care and after-school programs powerful weapons against crime. Washington, DC: Fight Crime: Invest in Kids.

Fox, J. A. & Newman, S. A. (1997). After-school crime or after-school programs: Tuning in to the prime time for violent juvenile crime and implications for national policy. A Report to the United States Attorney General. Washington, DC: Fight Crime: Invest in Kids.

Gabarino, J. (1989). Preventing child maltreatment. In R. Price (Ed.), *Prevention in mental health: Research, policy and practice* (pp. 63–108). Beverly Hills, CA: Sage.

Gambone, M. A. & Arbreton, A. J. (1997). *Safe havens: The contributions of youth organizations to healthy adolescent development*. Philadelphia: Public/Private Ventures.

Hawkins, J. D, Catalano, R. F., & Miller, J. Y. (1992). Risk and protective factors for alcohol and other drug problems in adolescence and early adulthood: Implications for substance abuse prevention. *Psychological Bulletin, 112*(1), 64–105.

Jones, M. A. & Offord, D. R. (1989). Reduction of antisocial behavior in poor children by nonschool skill development. *Journal of Child Psychology and Psychiatry and Allied Disciplines, 30*, 737–750.

Karoly, L., Greenwood, P. W., Everingham, S. S., Houbé, J., Kilburn, M. R., Rydell, C. P., Sanders, M., & Chiesa, J. (1998). Investing in our children: What we know and don't know about the costs and benefits of early childhood interventions. Santa Monica, CA: Rand.

Kimball-Baker, K. & Roehlkepartain, E. C. (1998, Summer). Are Americans afraid of teens? *Assets,* 6–8.

Lewthwaite, R. & Piparo, A. (1993). Goal orientation in youth competitive athletes: Physical achievement, social-relational and experiential concerns. *Journal of Research in Personality, 27*, 103–117.

Lupher, E. (1996). *Public funding of youth sports and recreation in Detroit, Hamtramck and Highland Park: Report #316.* Detroit: Citizens Research Council of Michigan.

McLaughlin, M. W., Irby, M. A., & Langman, J. (1994). *Urban sanctuaries: Neighborhood organizations in the lives and futures of inner-city youth.* San Francisco: Jossey-Bass.

Marshall, J. Jr. & Wheeler, L. (1996). *Street soldier: One man's struggle to save a generation one life at a time.* New York: Delacorte Press.

Miller, A. & Ohlin, L. (1985). *Delinquency and community: Creating opportunities and controls.* Beverly Hills, CA: Sage.

Moore, J. & Brown, J. (1998). *Community use of schools process evaluation.* Detroit: Moore & Associates, Inc.

Neithercut, M. E. (1993). *Status of Detroit area youth.* Detroit: Wayne State University.

O'Hare, W. P. (Ed.). (1997). *City kids count: Data on the well-being of children in large cities.* Baltimore: Annie E. Casey Foundation.

Rauner, D. M., Stanton, L., & Wynn, J. (1994). *Sports and recreation for Chicago youth.* Chicago: The Chapin Hall Center for Children.

Skillman Foundation. (1995). *Re-Creating recreation in Detroit, Hamtramck and Highland Park: The youth sports and recreation initiative.* Detroit: Author.

Schorr, L. B. & Schorr, D. (1988). *Within our reach: Breaking the cycle of disadvantage*. New York: Doubleday

Seefeldt, V. (Ed.). (1994). *Reinvesting in communities: Sports, recreation and youth development in Detroit, Hamtramck and Highland Park, phase I, an assessment of needs*. Detroit, MI: The Skillman Foundation.

Seefeldt, V. (Ed.). (1995.) *An extended assessment of needs for the provision of sports, recreation and youth development in the cities of Detroit, Hamtramck and Highland Park*. Detroit, MI: The Skillman Foundation

Sickmund, M., Snyder, H. N., Poe-Yamagata, E. (1997). *Juvenile offenders and victims: 1997 update on violence*. Washington, DC: Office of Juvenile Justice and Delinquency Prevention.

Skillman Foundation. (1993). *Sports, recreation and youth development initiative: A concept paper*. Detroit, MI: Author.

Smith, C. A., Lizotte, A. J., Thornberry, T. P., & Krohn, M. D. (1995). Resilience to delinquency. In John Hagan (Ed.), *Delinquency and disrepute in the life course* (pp. 217–247). Greenwich, CT: JAI Press.

Tierney, J. P., Grossman, J. B., & Resch, N. L. (1995). *Making a difference: An impact study of Big Brothers/Big Sisters*. Philadelphia: Public/Private Ventures.

United Community Services. (1987). *Looking at leisure: A study of the negative aspects*. Detroit: United Community Services.

United Community Services. (1989). *The social and economic status of young black males and the impact on the formation of Detroit area families*. Detroit: Author.

United Way for Southeastern Michigan. (1993) *A closer look: An assessment of major local issues affecting metropolitan Detroit*. Detroit, MI: Author.

University Cultural Center Association and Zachary & Associates. (1991). *Lower Woodward Corridor: Facilities and programs analysis*. Detroit: Community Foundation for Southeastern Michigan and Ford Foundation.

Werner, E. & Smith, R. (1989). *Vulnerable but invincible: A longitudinal study of resilient children and youth*. New York: Adams, Bannister and Cox.

Wynn, J., Costello, J., Halpern, R., & Richman, H. (1994). *Children, families, and communities: A new approach to social services*. Chicago: The Chapin Hall Center for Children at the University of Chicago.

10

Youth and Community Development: How After-School Programming Can Make a Difference

Steven J. Danish

I hope you have gotten a sense of the possible from these chapters. We *can* promote development in youth and in their communities. The chapters in this book describe the state of affairs with regard to after-school programming; creative programs that have been implemented after school, some on a small scale, others approaching a citywide scale; and the actions communities must take if they are to better respond to their youth. In this chapter I will develop a number of themes alluded to or discussed directly in this book, which must be addressed if we are to succeed. My focus will be on the highlighting the importance of after-school programming for the community and its youth and delineating why, how, and under what conditions these programs work.

What is Youth Development?

There are a lot of people, programs, foundations, federal offices, and agencies devoting time, resources, and money to "help" the youth of our nation. What are their goals and how effective have they been? The main focus of these groups is to reduce the likelihood that youth will compromise their health or the well-being of their community by using drugs and alcohol, engaging in premature and unsafe sexual activity that may result in pregnancy or diseases such as AIDS, dropping out of school, committing violent or delinquent acts, and/or a number of other health-compromising behaviors. The most common approach used to prevent such behaviors can best be summarized by the slogan adopted by Nancy Reagan during her husband's presidency: "Just Say No." Prevention programs generally have as their goal to reduce the incidents of the various health-compromising behaviors [Perry & Jessor, 1985] by teaching what has become known as refusal skills. The projected outcome is a reduction in behaviors such as drug and alcohol use, school dropouts, violence, out-of-wedlock pregnancies, and STDs.

This goal is not so easy to assess, and it is even more difficult to attribute success to the prevention programs. We can see the difficulties if we look at the statistics related to crime in our country. Crime rates are dropping significantly, and everyone is trying to take credit for the drop. Among those who believe they have influenced the crime rate are advocates of longer jail time, supporters of community policing, developers of new technology, legislators who pass laws increasing the number of police on our streets, prevention programmers who implement violence prevention programs, and even proponents of gun ownership. Some demographers contend that the real reason has little to do with any of these factors and more to do with the aging of our population. Who is right? No one knows for sure, and we will probably never be certain.

The confusion surrounding this situation may be best understood by the following fable: Two strangers are sitting next to each other on a train trip from New York to Chicago. They strike up a conversation. One individual asks the other what she does. The first person responds that she is a scientist working on a cure for diabetes and has almost succeeded. The second person comments how wonderful that is and how proud she should be of her work. The scientist then asks the other individual what he does. The other individual responds that he works for the railroad and his job entails keeping the elephants off the tracks. The scientist is incredulous. "What elephants?" she responds, "There are no elephants on the tracks and there never are!" The other individual confidently responds, "See what a good job I am doing?" If having elephants on the tracks is an extremely rare occurrence, should this individual be given credit for succeeding? If, in the future, a circus train breaks down and all the animals must be removed, should this individual be blamed if elephants must be removed from the car via the tracks?

What is clear is that prevention programs directed at youth, regardless of how effective these programs are, will never totally eliminate their involvement in health-compromising behaviors. Too often what we are teaching are only partial mediators of the outcome we wish to achieve. In other words, if we are teaching violence prevention, we may teach self-control and conflict resolution very effectively, but that does not necessarily result in reducing violent or delinquent acts, because there are other variables that contribute to an adolescent's decision to commit a violent act such as a lack of future orientation, the inability to forgive, or some intrapsychic problem.

Another problem with the prevention approach has to do with how prevention programs are conceived of and subsequently funded. The different federal agencies treat the different health-compromising behaviors as separate problems and only focus on ones under their specific jurisdiction. For example, health-compromising behaviors that relate to mental health problems (really mental illness) are under the purview of the National Institute of Mental Health Prevention Branch; violence-related behaviors come under the purview of the Justice Department's Safe Street Initiative. For drug and alcohol problems, the funding source will either be the National Institute of Drug Abuse or the National Institute for Alcohol Abuse and Alcoholism. The reduction of welfare rolls will be funded by the Department of Health and Human Services, and the prevention of school dropouts will be funded by the Department of Education. It is as if money and resources are being funneled into big silos, each of which is independent of the others.

Despite the different purposes of the agencies, the interventions are likely to be very similar because the risk factors for the different behaviors are similar. In a longitudinal study of middle school students, a strong relationship among drug use, unsafe sexual activity, violent behavior, school attendance, and school disciplinary problems was found. Correlations among these behaviors were statistically significant and had an average value of .30 [Farrell et al. 1992]. In other words, youth who had problems in one of these areas were likely to experience problems in other areas. The result was a "lifestyle syndrome" of health-compromising behaviors. Perhaps more importantly, youth involved in one of these behaviors were likely to be involved in one or more of the other behaviors *and* it was unclear which behavior occurred first and how the cycle developed.

Unfortunately, there is little or no communication among the agencies, and when different agencies award money to the same city, the same adolescent is likely to be in several prevention programs simultaneously that are directed at different problems. It as if these different agencies are fighting over program ownership in the same way that different branches of the armed services fight over different weapons systems. Since the programs are so similar, and the target may be the same adolescent, the agencies tend to be less efficient and much less cost-effective than they should be. [Danish, 1995].

However, the most serious problem with prevention approaches is that they have little or nothing to do with youth development. Adolescence is a time when youth are seeking a sense of industry and competence. When and if they learn to avoid health-compromising behaviors, what have they learned about what *to do*? In other words, learning to say "no" or what to avoid does not teach adolescents how to be competent. We define competence as the ability to do life planning, be self-reliant, and be able to seek help from others [Danish et al. 1984]. Nor does learning to say "no" teach adolescents the life skills that enable them to know how to think about and develop confidence in their future, as well as how to acquire a sense of personal control over themselves and their environment so that they can make better decisions and ultimately become better citizens.

In 1989, the Task Force on Education of Young Adolescents sponsored by the Carnegie Council on Adolescent Development [1989] identified five desired adolescent development outcomes: (a) processing information from multiple sources and communicating clearly; (b) being en route to a lifetime of meaningful work by learning how to learn and therefore being able to adapt to different educational and working environments; (c) being a good citizen by participating in community activities and feeling concern for, and connection to, the well-being of others; (d) being a caring and ethical individual by acting on one's convictions about right and wrong; and (e) being a healthy person [Task Force on Education of Young Adolescents, 1989]. In 1995, the Council's *Great Transitions Report* [1995] identified factors associated with personal and social development. The factors not mentioned in the first report included: (a) finding a valued place in a constructive group; (b) learning how to form close and lasting relationships; (c) feeling a sense of worth; (d) achieving a reliable basis for informed decision-making, especially on matters of large consequence; (e) being able to use available support systems; (f) having a positive future orientation; (g) learning respect [Carnegie Council 1995]. As noted in the chapter by Edmundson [this volume], some of the essential program characteristics of youth development programs are adult social support, sustained and comprehensive services, life skill development, community service, and the constructive use of time.

Recently, a number of groups have started to focus on interventions for adolescent development. Some of these developmentally-oriented intervention groups are CASEL (The Collaborative for the Advancement of Social and Emotional Learning), CEP (The Character Education Partnership), and the Life Skills Center.

CASEL is based on the work of Gardner's [1993] *Multiple Intelligences* and Goleman's [1995] *Emotional Intelligence*. Some of the skills seen as essential for social and emotional learning are the same as those identified by the Carnegie groups just described. CASEL's mission is to promote social and emotional learning (SEL) as an integral part of education in schools throughout the world. Its purpose is to encourage and support the creation of safe, caring learning environments that build social, cognitive, and emotional skills. Two of its goals are to increase the awareness of educators, trainers of school-based professionals, the scientific community, policymakers, and the public regarding the need for, and the effects of, systematic efforts to promote the social and emotional learning of children and adolescents; and to facilitate the implementation, ongoing evaluation, and refinement of comprehensive SEL programs, beginning in preschool and continuing through high school. The group, founded in 1994, has worked to establish standards for implementing SEL programs by developing a school self-assessment procedure; to identify model SEL programs and practices and guidelines for educators wanting to implement SEL programs; and to provide training opportunities to educators interested in SEL programs [Elias et al. 1997].

Although our focus in this book is on after-school programming, some of the programs and guidelines identified by CASEL are quite relevant, if appropriately adapted for the differences in setting.

The Character Education Partnership (CEP) is a nonpartisan coalition of organizations dedicated to developing moral character and civic virtue as a means of promoting a more compassionate and responsible society. Their goals are to provide authoritative leadership for character education, assist local communities in initiating, improving and sustaining character education, and influence teacher education programs to make character education an integral part of the training of teachers and other educational professionals [CEP 1996].

What constitutes character education differs across different school and communities. One of the clearest statements resulted from the 1992 Aspen Declaration on Character Education which states in part: "Effective character education is based on core ethical values which form the foundation of democratic society, in particular, respect, responsibility, trustworthiness, caring, justice and fairness, and civic virtue and citizenship [CEP 1996, p. 35]." Other qualities highlighted by CEP are honesty, integrity, civility, courage, loyalty, self-discipline, kindness, perseverance, work ethic and truth.

The *Character Assessment and Program Evaluation Bibliographic Index*, located on the CEP website at www.character.org [CEP 2000], contains over 200 references about instruments and program evaluations useful in assessing character education programs. Each reference contains contact information, an abstract, and a list of instruments used in the study. A separate table within the Index lists available instruments with ratings for administration and scoring, reliability, and validity.

The Life Skills Center was founded by the author in 1992 at Virginia Commonwealth University. Its mission is to develop, implement, and evaluate life skill programs for children, adolescents, and adults. Life skills are defined as those skills that enable youth to succeed in the different environments in which they live, such as school, home and in their neighborhoods. Life skills can be behavioral (communicating effectively with peers and adults) or cognitive (making effective decisions); interpersonal (being assertive) or intrapersonal (setting goals). Environments vary from individual to individual, thus the definition of what it means to succeed will differ across individuals, as well as across environments. Individuals in the same environment are likely to be dissimilar from each other as a result of the life skills they have already mastered, their other resources, and their opportunities, real or perceived. For this reason, the needed life skills are likely to be different for individuals of different ages, ethnic and/or racial groups, or economic status. While it is necessary to be sensitive to these differences, it is also important to recognize that individuals can often effectively apply life skills learned in one environment to other environments as appropriate [Danish 1995].

The Center has developed both school-based and after-school programs that teach adolescents how to think about and develop confidence about their future, as well as to acquire a sense of personal control over themselves and their environment so that they can make better decisions and ultimately become better citizens. To teach students to be self-directing, we must empower them. Empowering them involves enhancing their well-being by promoting healthy choices, including teaching them how to set personal goals, how to achieve these goals in the immediate future, and to believe in their future [Danish 1999]. Additional information about the Center and its programs is available from the author.

The Technology of Youth Development Programs

Programs that focus on enhancing or promoting development can teach knowledge, attitudes and/or values, and skills. The choice about what to teach will be influenced by two factors: the ease with which the material can be taught, and the likelihood that behavior will be changed as a result of what is taught.

1. *Teaching Information.* Implementing programs designed to impart facts or information is the easiest to teach, but the least likely to produce behavior change. Information describes *what* to do, but not *how* to do it. The research is replete with studies indicating people know what to do, but often don't do it. For example, across a number of studies, individuals surveyed know they should eat healthfully, exercise, not engage in unprotected sex, and not use illegal drugs, yet there is a discrepancy between the numbers who know what they "should" do and those who do it. Some lack motivation, others lack skills. It is simplistic to assume that we can and will do everything we know we should. It is equally naive to assume we can do everything we should do, even when we want to.

    Information-based programs that have been successful, such as encouraging drivers and passengers to wear seat belts, are usually single issue programs using the media to disseminate information. They tend to be very visible, expensive programs that require a lengthy period of time to change behavior. However, despite their lack of effectiveness, they are usually the method of choice for programs directed at adolescents because they are the easiest to implement.

2. *Teaching Attitudes and/or Values.* At the other extreme, programs that teach attitudes and values are the hardest to teach but most likely to result in the development of new attitudes and values. Programs that teach character traits and what is referred to as social and emotional intelligence are examples of attitude and value-oriented programs. Unfortunately, such qualities cannot be taught through lectures or books, although these methods are often tried. Nor are they usually successfully taught through circumscribed intervention programs such as having a "character education" activity each week in school. Learning the values and character traits necessary to be a competent adolescent is most likely to occur when the individual is continuously

exposed and taught these qualities by individuals of social influence–parents and other adults such as teachers and religious and community leaders during childhood and early adolescence, and peers during later adolescence.

My comments about teaching character or social and emotional intelligence are not meant to disparage programs designed to teach these traits and/or behaviors. I believe that when such programs are successful they are actually teaching skills. Beland [1999] and Elias et al. [1997] seem to concur. Lickona [1991] describes character as "knowing the good, desiring the good, and doing the good [p. 51]." I would contend that many of the circumscribed programs are teaching "how to do good" without really teaching participants to "know and want good." To know and want good is not so easily learned and probably cannot be taught in school, only reinforced. If the "doing good" activity is repeated continually, it *may* become a habit but will not be transferable to other situations unless the rationale for doing it is understood and the behavior specifically taught. More will be said about the process of making what is learned portable later in this chapter.

3. *Teaching Skills.* Skills are in the middle in terms of the ease with which the material can be taught, and the likelihood that behavior will be changed as a result of what is taught. Skills are taught differently than knowledge, attitudes or values. Just as learning to drive a car, dance, or play a sport cannot occur solely through listening to a tape or reading a book, skills for living cannot be taught in a passive manner. A Chinese proverb states: "I listen—and forget. I see—and remember. I do—and understand." When learning skills, the skill is first named and described and a rationale for its use is given. The skill is demonstrated so that the individual can observe correct and incorrect use of the skill. Finally, there is extensive supervised practice of the skill with continuous feedback [Danish & Hale 1981].

These three technologies are not mutually exclusive. Effective youth development programs can and should incorporate all three. Perhaps we can learn something about the optimal model of youth development from those who have studied and worked with youth who have achieved world-class talent in areas such as the sciences, the arts, or sports.

B. S. Bloom [1985] and his colleagues followed 120 individuals who had achieved world-class success in one of these areas. He adapted a previously-developed model of learning that divided learning into three phases: romance, precision, and integration. During the romance phase, development is multifaceted and characterized by play, exploration, and fun. It is a time when youth develop a love for learning. Youth learn that hard work and fun are not incompatible. The need to have high expectations for yourself is communicated to you through the expectations that parents, teachers, and the community in general have for you. Benard [1991] has identified high expectations as a critical component of resilient youth. It is during this period that both character education, social-emotional learning, and life skill acquisition would be taught.

The romance phase is followed by a focus on precision. This is a period of systematic learning and skill development. Skills are learned but not necessarily demonstrated very effectively. It is not until the integration phase that the individual experiences the behavior as part of him/herself. It would be interesting to explore how such a framework, which has been so successful with adolescents who have world-class talent, can be applied to adolescents on a larger scale.

Expanding our Understanding of Education

School is a "have to" rather than a "want to" for too many youth. They don't care to learn the three Rs despite our best efforts to convince them of the importance of education and how it will better prepare them for the future. Instead, they often ignore what we teach, because as Millstein [1993] contends, knowledge is important to adolescents only if they believe it is relevant for their future.

However, it is not just the content of the teaching that is irrelevant to many youth, it is the setting where it is delivered and the manner it is taught. A myth that continues to be perpetuated, even by some involved in youth programming, is that school-based programs are where "education" takes place and after-school programs are where the focus is on "fun." I am very uncomfortable with this dichotomy on several grounds. First, it assumes that learning takes place only in a school house or room. One need only to read the chapters in this volume by Blumenkrantz, C. Gullotta, Porter, and Stemmermann to realize the learning that can occur after school in communities, as part of arts programs, at festivals, and in the outdoors. Second, the dichotomy assumes that education cannot be fun. The comments from the girls in Stemmermann's chapter are indicative of how much fun they are having while they learn. Also, the chapters by M. Bloom and Blumenkrantz, and Petitpas and Champagne, describe the important role of play in self-learning. Third, it assumes that the three Rs, as represented by "cultural literacy" [Hirsch, 1988], is the epitome of learning. As Hirsch noted: "This book (Cultural Literacy) focuses sharply on the background knowledge for functional literacy and effective national communication [1988, p. xi]." Beginning in the 1980s, Hirsch's perspective was that 5,000 essential names, phrases, dates, and concepts constituted the definition of an educated person. Critics of the educational establishment have used Hirsch's concept to go beyond trying to understand why "Johnny can't read" and have jumped headlong into a return to the "basics"—trying to decipher what students don't know about math, history, geography, chemistry, biology, and government, and teaching them the basic facts of each. States and the federal government have become so intent on testing students' knowledge of these facts, that little else seems to matter. Teachers report "teaching to the test." Schools themselves are now even graded on how well students know these facts and worry that they may lose their accreditation if too many students do badly on these tests.

No one denies the importance of this information, but to equate having this knowledge with having a passport for future success is being simplistic. Much of this knowledge is clearly necessary, but it is not sufficient. If the schools view their mission as confined to teaching this information, they will fail our students and our society badly. What is being overlooked or ignored is that without the concomitant life skills, this knowledge by itself provides little more than a head start in winning Trivial Pursuit, "Jeopardy," or "College Bowl"; it is not the equivalent, nor anything close, to a passport for success.

Where will students learn the proper work ethic and the other myriad of skills and attributes so necessary for success, if they are not taught at home or school? As Comer [1988] has so aptly stated, schools must recognize that social and personal development are as important as academic development; and, in fact, changes in students' personal behavior are likely to affect their academic performance. Unfortunately, despite the efforts of CASEL, the CEP, or life skills programs like GOAL, too many schools are choosing to eliminate such "frills" and place their total emphasis on developing standards of learning based on acquiring cultural literacy. However, it is not only life skills or character education-oriented programs that are being eliminated. It is art, music, physical education, and anything else that will not serve to enhance test scores on the assessments being developed by states to measure what they believe should be the standards of learning. For these reasons, we must look elsewhere for opportunities to teach youth how to succeed in life. One of the best settings for teaching these life skills and other attributes is after-school.

The rationale for educating students after-school is an elementary one. *We all learn best when we are in an environment where we want to be.* How many youngsters do we know who cannot remember the gist of a story or who cannot repeat a mathematical or chemistry formula but are able to write poetry, learn the lines of a play in which they are participating or a series of complicated football plays, or work with others to solve a practical logistics problem requiring an understanding of mathematics and physics? For many youth, their preferred environment is a playground, gymnasium, stage, art studio, or the outdoors. It is where they are open to learning and often to new experiences.

Unfortunately, those involved in after-school programs have set their sights too low. We are prone to thinking that after-school settings are merely places where we supervise free-play activities and keep youth out of trouble during the dangerous period when juvenile crime is at its highest. It is true that research has indicated that youth involved in after-school programming are less likely to put themselves at risk for involvement in drugs, premature and unprotected sex, sexually transmitted diseases, dropping out of school, or engaging in delinquent or violent acts, and that communities are at less risk for vandalism and crime, violence, and gang activity. The results of this research are probably a major reason why both the public and private sectors have chosen to fund programs such as Midnight Basketball.

Making our cities safer is an admirable goal and something we all want, but it will not be ensured simply by keeping youth off the street. And that is the problem. When our goal is to keep youth off the street and occupied during 3 P.M. to 8 P.M., we are not directing our efforts at enhancing youth development. Although there may be overlap, these two goals are not equivalent. We must focus our efforts on designing creative educationally-relevant programming.

Ensuring Effective After-School Programming

What I am proposing is that we consider after-school activities such as sport as they did around the turn of the century—as a "training ground for life." For example, it was assumed that through sports, children and adolescents would learn good sportsmanship and other values and skills that would serve them well as they prepared for the rest of their lives. At the same time, these activities were viewed as a means of social control over children. It was believed that youth could be taught to accept the prevailing norms and use their free time constructively.

Using after-school programs as a "training ground" will not be easy. There are lots of barriers to developing such programming—the lack of staff and adequate training for these staff, the lack of volunteers and training for volunteers, the inability to retain volunteers, insufficient equipment, inadequate facilities, and lack of access to the facilities because of inadequate transportation among others. Edmundson [this volume] has delineated some of the problems in detail and Fukuzawa [this volume] has described how one city has dealt with these problems. They are not minor problems, but until we present a compelling case for what we can do during the after-school hours, we should not expect things to change.

Clearly, if we are focusing on providing "fun" and not "education," our chances of receiving support for our efforts are limited. However, if we make the case and can demonstrate the viability of after-school experiences as educational, we improve our chances tremendously. What can be learned in after-school settings and how do we design effective programs?

Potential Outcomes of After-School Programming

M. Bloom [this volume] has laid out a number of potential outcomes. The area that I found most intriguing was the competency area: "the ability to work well, play well, love well, think well, and serve well (p. 14)." I would add the concept of "be well" to the list. Too often social scientists use words like health, development, resilience, competence, and the like indiscriminately, using definitions loosely adapted from other social scientists. Bloom has been much more specific. He has provided some operational clarity that can guide program development, implementation, and evaluation if specific criteria for defining "well" are developed. When we can show changes in developmental terms among the targeted youth in some of these behaviors and in the communities in which they live, we will be making the kind of difference that really means something.

Designing Programs that Work

As someone who has spent much of his career developing and implementing programs, I am prone to putting too much emphasis on the program as the key to success. There are barriers in the community that mediate against successful programs. The public institution traditionally responsible for providing after-school activities, the parks and recreation departments, are under-financed and supported. As Fukuzawa [this volume] and Edmundson [this volume] point out, they are inappropriately or under-maintained and staffed. Because they are usually the first budget item cut, they now have to compete for private dollars with private youth-serving agencies. The problem with the schools, the other public institution, has been previously discussed. Furthermore, the schools are reluctant to extend their operating hours to accommodate after-school activities.

Although there are a large number of youth-serving agencies in most cities, they are fragmented, decentralized, and competitive with each other for funding and turf. The number of staff is inadequate, pay is low, training is scarce, recruiting and retaining volunteers is difficult, many youth are either unserved or underserved, and the quality of programming is uneven [Edmundson & Dithmer 1997; Reid & Tremblay 1994]. What is perhaps the biggest problem is the lack of a community infrastructure to remedy the situation.

It is within this context that a program must be designed. Traditional programs will probably not be effective. Any new program must have some or all of the following characteristics:

- Modular. It must have building blocks that can be used for training, teaching, and learning by youth workers and the youth with whom they work. A multicomponent program can be built from these modules, although each should be able to be used independently.

- Flexibility. If we are to attract and retain current and existing youth worker volunteers and attract and retain current and existing participants in a wide variety of activities, this program will have to be flexible so it can be customized to the audience. Although there will be differences in what is taught depending on the activity (i.e., sports, the arts), there should be a common core.

- Cost and time effectiveness. Keeping the participant's interest and not overwhelming the youth worker with too much material is critical. Once we have everyone's interest, we can expand the program. Therefore, we have to build a system which is time-modular so programs can fit the time constraints. Training of youth workers must be viewed as a process of learning over time.

- Multimedia. Delivering the training and developing program materials in multiple formats, including training manuals, volunteer manuals, hand outs, videos, etc is needed.

- Consistency. In determining critical elements for a program, there must be a consistency of viewpoint and philosophy.
- Teachable. The program has to be capable of being taught by different people at different times in different settings and capable of being learned in the same versatile fashion. This is especially important if we expect community ownership of the program.
- Transportable/Replicable. What is developed must be transportable across communities and organizations and replicable within various activities, settings, and neighborhoods;
- Adaptable. The program must be sufficiently robust to be applied in different settings in which there may be differences in the community's level of resources.
- Measurable. The program must contain multiple levels of assessment and evaluation, many of which can be embedded in the delivery of the program.

In addition to these general guidelines, it is necessary to consider how to recruit and retain youth workers, who are seriously underpaid, as well as volunteers. What seems to be missing is how to create a training program that provides something positive for the youth worker, and especially the volunteer. When the adult workers and volunteers benefit, they become more skillful and more likely to enjoy what they are doing. As a result, they tend to treat the youth they work with respect and the expectation that they will be responsible and succeed. When volunteers are used, we cannot expect them to have the needed expertise for some of the activities. By providing useful training, and using an educational pyramid model of training [Seidman & Rappaport 1974], we can expand community capacity.

As part of the recruitment strategies, we must focus on attracting more women (especially as athletic coaches), people of color, particularly men in the cities, and college students participating in service activities. However, recruiting youth workers and volunteers is only half of the problem. We must work to expand the number of youth participating. Special attention must be given to attract the unserved and underserved, especially girls and youth with disabilities, to sport activities. The chapter by Edmundson details these issues.

Delivering the after-school program itself requires special attention as well. Too often, program developers assume incorrectly that programs developed for schools are easily transferred to after-school settings. In schools, students are fairly attentive and well-behaved because of the school rules and consequences for not adhering to them. In after-school settings, participants must enjoy the material or they don't pay attention, are disruptive, or just leave. After-school leaders must command respect, know the material exceptionally well, be informative without lecturing, and facilitate participation among the youth.

Transferring What is Learned in After-School Programs to Other Domains

Although I am a strong advocate for after-school programming for youth, I believe that involving youth in after-school programs, whether it is sports, the arts, outdoor adventure, county fairs, or rites of passage programs, without having a specific life-skills component sends the wrong message, especially when it is done by organizations that have a youth's welfare as a major concern. I am afraid that such programs reinforce the belief that if youth become better athletes, singers, actors, or whatever the goal of the after-school program is, their world and that of their family's will be a better place. For the overwhelming majority, this belief is not true. There is nothing about a ball or a sport venue, a play or song, a mountain or water rapid that teaches a youth how to live life successfully.

What is true is that when life skills and the activities in which youth are involved are taught together, *and* the avenues to transfer skills from the structured activity to other areas of life such as school, home, neighborhood, and eventually the workplace are known, the effect can be very powerful.

However, the process of transferring what is learned to other domains is not easy. As De Coubertin, the founder of the Olympic movement, noted in 1918 about the process of transferring what is learned in sport:

Sport plants in the body seeds of physio-psychological qualities such as coolness, confidence, decision etc. These qualities may remain localized around the exercise which brought them into being; this often happens — it even happens most often. How many daredevil cyclists there are who once they leave their machines are hesitant at every crossroads of existence, how many swimmers who are brave in the water but frightened by the waves of human existence, how many fencers who cannot apply to life's battles the quick eye and nice timing which they show on the boards! The educator's task is to make the seed bear fruit throughout the organism, to transpose it from a particular circumstance to a whole array of circumstances, from a special category of activities to all the individual's actions. [De Coubertin 1918/1966].

What steps must be taken to enhance the likelihood that what is learned in an after-school activity can be transferred to other domains? First, participants must understand what they have learned about themselves from the after-school activity and how this self-learning has value in other settings. Simply telling participants is not likely to be convincing as it is very possible that they will be concerned only about doing well in the activity and miss the opportunity to gain maximum benefit from the experience. As I noted in the Athletic Footwear Association report [AFA 1990], "When knowing oneself becomes as important as proving oneself, sport becomes an essential element in personal growth and self expression" [p. 6].

Second, participants must know not only what they have learned but understand how it was learned and in what context. Without such information, transferring what was learned will be difficult, if not impossible. Discussions with parents and friends on such issues as what participants learned from their successes and failures in the activity, how these experiences have helped them develop, and how this learning can be applied to areas outside of the activity, such as in school or maybe even a future career, will be a valuable exercise. Using individuals who are role models to the participants as examples of "success stories" may also be useful.

Third, participants who are exceptionally anxious in a new setting because of the unfamiliarity of the setting will have considerable difficulty applying what has been learned in a new setting. In such situations, leaders must assist the participants to facilitate the transfer.

Fourth, some participants accrue much of their sense of identity from the activity and have little interest in exploring other options or lack the confidence that they can succeed in other settings. As a result, they may either have insufficient motivation to invest energy in applying what was learned in other contexts or settings, or be afraid to take the risk of failing at a new task and choose not to try. Having the support of family and friends may help participants be more likely to try something new.

Leaders will play an important role in this process. Addressing the issue directly and developing plans to facilitate the transfer of what has been learned will be necessary.

A Brief Description of an After-School Sports and Life Skill Program

SUPER (Sports United to Promote Education and Recreation) Program is a sport-based life skill intervention program designed to teach sport and life skills developed by the Life Skills Center. For many youth, as they become adolescents, their interest and involvement in sport increases and so does their concern about their performance and competency. Sport then becomes a readily accessible metaphor and example of personal competence and, as a result, an effective analogy for teaching skills for successful living.

For example, Kleiber and Kirshnit [1991] observed that sport may be a forum, and perhaps even a structured test, for learning responsibility, conformity, persistence, risk taking, courage, and self-control among other attributes. They note that although adolescents see these attributes as important, they are also viewed as elusive.

The goals of the SUPER Program are for each participant to leave the program with the understanding that: (1) there are effective and accessible role models; (2) physical *and* mental skills are important for both sports and life; (3) it is important to set and attain goals in sports; (4) it is important to set and attain goals in life; and (5) roadblocks to goals can be overcome [Danish & Nellen 1997].

SUPER is a 30-hour, 10-session program. Sessions are taught like sports clinics, with participants involved in three sets of activities: learning the physical skills related to a specific sport; learning life skills related to sports in general; and playing the sport. Sometimes the students learn several sports within a SUPER program; other times the focus is on one sport. Both leaders and participants are given manuals to facilitate dissemination. Some of the life skills we have developed for our clinics are: learning how to learn; communicating with others; being your own coach; giving and receiving feedback; becoming part of a team; increasing focus and concentration; dreaming about your future; turning dreams into reachable goals; developing plans to reach goals; identifying roadblocks to goal attainment; overcoming roadblocks; learning to rebound from temporary setbacks; creating your own supportive system ("dream team"); identifying and building on your strengths; and learning how to win, lose, and respect your opponent.

We have developed training material for the coaches, both for teaching life skills and for teaching sports skills. In addition to directly having a life skills segment of the clinic, we have developed a sport observation system that is integrated with the sport instruction. Coaches are told that when they instruct, demonstrate, and conduct practices, they need to focus on *how* youth are participating as opposed to just *how well* they are performing and participating.

Understanding "how" provides information on the mental skills that the participants have in dealing with coaching may be indicative of how they will respond to other forms of instruction, such as school and job training. Observing "how" participants react gives the leader answers to such questions as: (a) Are the students attentive when given instructions or observing demonstration? (b) Do they become frustrated with themselves when they cannot perform the activity to their expectations, and does this frustration impede or enhance later efforts? (c) Are they first to initiate questions when they do not understand something being taught or do they wait quietly for someone else to talk first? (d) Do they initiate conversation with group members, or do they wait for someone else to talk to them first? (e) How do they react when they have a good performance? A bad performance? (f) How do they react when others have a good performance? A bad performance? (g) How do they react when someone gives them praise? Criticism? (h) Do they give up when they can't do as well as they would like, or as well as others, or do they continue to practice in a determined manner to learn the skill? (i) Do they compete or cooperate with the other youth [Danish et al. 1996]?

We ask the SUPER coaches to speak to the participants about what they have observed and help the youth explore what this means to them. We expect that the coaches will spend several minutes with each individual to discuss the "hows" of their performance (separate from the "how wells") during each session of the sport clinics. Additionally, at the end of the program we provide "report cards" to participants, detailing their strengths and weaknesses in both areas.

To date, we have been piloting SUPER Programs [Danish 1999]. The first program was a basketball program conducted with 75 urban and suburban middle school girls. The coaches were an intercollegiate women's basketball team who were enrolled in a service-learning course. Following a period of training for student-athletes, during which they learned how to teach life skills, there were 11 clinic sessions in which the student-athletes taught basketball and life skills and supervised basketball games. Each component was half an hour long. The girls (approximately 10 per team) had the same two coaches each week for the 11 weeks and thus had benefit of some adult role models. During one week, the girls observed a practice and had an opportunity to speak to the different players after the practice. The girls and a parent were given free tickets to each game, and after several of these games, there was "pizza get-together" for the girls, parent, and players. Some six months after the program ended, a number of the student-athletes were still in contact with girls from their team and had attended some of their games and other school-related activities, and had even spent time in the girls' homes. Both players and middle school participants reported benefiting significantly from the experience.

The Importance of Evaluation

Federal agencies, private foundations, and state and local governments are all looking to adopt programs that work. Programs that meet the criteria of being a "best or exemplary practice" are ones that have either been formally evaluated as evidenced by peer-reviewed empirical findings and/or are considered effective as evidenced by a significant consensus of experts, evaluators, or policy makers. Evaluating youth development programs first requires identifying the potential outcomes of program participation for the youth involved. These outcomes have been previously described. Equally important is ensuring that the program has been implemented as planned or what is known as program integrity or fidelity. This aspect of evaluation has been too often overlooked [Dane & Schneider 1998; Meyer, Miller & Herman, 1993].

There are several kinds of fidelity issues. The first has to do with program or curriculum development. One needs to ascertain whether the curriculum is designed to meet the stated objectives or outcomes. Programs may be interesting and fun but not focused on teaching aspects of youth development. A determination of whether the dosage is sufficient and the methodology consistent with the stated goals must be made? Teaching new skills, for example, is not the same as teaching information. An hour session on a topic may not be intensive or extensive enough for learning to take place.

The second integrity issue has to do with program implementation. Some of the questions that must be addressed are: did the intervention agents receive training; were the trainers able to teach the program to the intervention agents effectively; did the intervention agents understand the content of the program; and could they teach the program effectively? Supervision while the intervention agents are teaching the program should also be included. Finally, if it is important to verify program integrity, trained observers can serve as raters of program integrity.

The third fidelity issue has to do with setting. As we have discussed, a program developed and found to be effective for schools may not be effective in after-school settings. Further, if the personnel in the setting are unsupportive of the program, it will not succeed.

The likelihood of having a successful program is enhanced through the provision of training manuals, program material, and the training and supervision of the intervention agents. The development of an Operations Manual facilitates the implementation process, as it pertains to the settings where the intervention takes place.

Once it has been determined that a program has fidelity, then evaluation of the program outcomes can take place. Have the participants learned the program material? Has it affected their behavior? The answer to these two questions is partially dependent on how well the proposed outcomes are to be measured. Measurement problems often interfere with determining whether a program has been effective. Does the measurement methodology provide evaluators with an opportunity to see whether the projected behavior has changed in the expected way? If not, the design and implementation of the youth development intervention may be for naught.

Determining what was learned and how it affected behavior must be asked separately, although policymakers are usually concerned only about the latter question and eschew all the other questions and issues of fidelity. However, behavior and/or attitude change that takes place when there are unresolved questions about program fidelity are often indications that the program itself may not be the reason for those changes.

As important as program integrity is for determining program outcomes, there is a downside for adhering too strictly to program procedures. Adapting to the needs of new communities enables these sites to assume some ownership of program and increases the likelihood of acceptance by the intervention agents and participants alike. Dane and Schneider [1998] address the issue of balancing the need for program integrity and program flexibility, and along with Meyer et al. [1993], conclude that if programs are able to identify their essence (the essential components), then program modifications can be made on other components to accommodate local needs. Distinguishing essential from nonessential components is aided by the development of material that highlights the critical features of a program.

Where Do We Go From Here?

It is evident that youth development programming, as opposed to prevention programming, is still in its infancy. This is especially true when we focus on after-school settings. Despite the efforts to support after-school programs, what is missing is support for programs that focus on youth development, as we have defined it in this volume— support for the development of effective programs, not just the implementation of existing or new programs that may or may not work, and subjecting these new efforts to see if they reach the "best practices" standard.

What follows are some simple ways to build on the momentum developed in this volume to move the youth development field toward its goals. First, the different youth development programs that focus on the development and implementation of after-school efforts should establish a communication network to share ideas, resources, research results, and perhaps programmatic models and curricula. Although there are often a lot of "turf wars" among programs, the problems we face in this area are too big for one perspective to resolve. Collaboration is critical. The development of a web site that would include program information, a practice digest, sharing of methodologies, and information about workshops would be valuable. Conducting training and implementation workshops would also be valuable. Too often, potential consumers of programs learn *what* is being done in the area of programming but not *how* it is done.

The title of this book, *Developing Competent Youth and Strong Communities Through After-School Programming*, was chosen carefully. If we are to assist in the development both of our youth and our communities, we will have to recognize that their futures are intertwined. In other words, if it truly "takes a village to raise a child," it also requires strong and effective children to build a competent community. One of our best tools is the after-school programs we develop.

References

Athletic Footwear Association (1990). *American youth and sports participation*. N. Palm Beach, FL: Author.

Beland, K. (1999). The social and emotional learning connection. *Character Educator*, 7(2), 4–5.

Benard, B. (1991). *Fostering resiliency in kids: Protective factors in the family, school, and community*. Portland, Oregon: Western Regional Center for Drug-Free Schools and Communities Far West Laboratory.

Bloom, B. S. (1985). *Developing talent in young people*. New York: Ballantine.

Carnegie Council. (1995). *Great transitions: Preparing adolescents for a new century*. New York: Carnegie Corporation.

Character Education Partnership (1996). *Character education in U.S. schools: The new consensus*. Unpublished report.

Character Education Partnership (2000). *Character Assessment and Program Evaluation Bibliographic Index*. [Online]. Available: http://www.character.org.

Comer, J. (1988). Educating poor minority children. *Scientific American, 250*(5), 42– 48.

Dane, A. V. & Schneider, B. H. (1998). Program integrity in primary and early secondary prevention: Are implementation effects out of control? *Clinical Psychology Review, 18*, 23–45.

Danish, S. (1999). *SUPER (Sports United to Promote Education and Recreation) program: Leader manual and student activity book*. Richmond, VA: Life Skills Center, Virginia Commonwealth University.

Danish, S. (1995). Reflections on the status and future of community psychology. *Community Psychologist, 28*(3), 16–18.

Danish, S., D'Augelli, A., & Ginsberg, M. (1984). Life development intervention: Promotion of mental health through the development of competence. In S. Brown and R. Lent (Eds.), *Handbook of Counseling Psychology* (pp. 520–544). New York: John Wiley & Sons.

Danish, S. & Hale, B. (1981). Toward an understanding of the practice of sport psychology. *Journal of Sport Psychology, 3*, 90–99.

Danish, S. & Nellen, V. (1997). New roles for sport psychologists: Teaching life skills through sport to at-risk youth. *Quest, 49*(1), 100–113.

Danish, S., Nellen, V., & Owens, S. (1996). Community-based life skills programs: Using sports to teach life skills to adolescents. In J. Van Raalte & B. Brewer (Eds.), *Exploring Sports and Exercise Psychology* (pp. 205–225). Washington: APA Books.

De Coubertin, P. (1966). What we can now ask of sport. In J. Dixon (Trans.), *The Olympic Idea: Discoveries and Essays*. Kolm: Carl Diem Institut. (Original work published 1918).

Edmundson, K. & Dithmer, B. (1997). *Developing opportunities for participation in structured activities for children and youth.* Unpublished report to The Robert Wood Johnson Foundation.

Elias, M., Frey, K., Greenberg, M., Haynes, N., Kessler, R., Schwab-Stone, M., Shriver, T., Weissberg, R., and Zins, J. (1997). *Promoting social and emotional learning: Guidelines for educators* (Appendix B). Alexandria, VA: Association for Supervision and Curriculum Development.

Farrell, A., Danish, S., & Howard, C. (1992). Relationship between drug use and other problem behaviors in urban adolescents. *Journal of Consulting and Clinical Psychology, 60*(5), 705–712.

Gardner, H. (1993). *Multiple intelligences: The theory in practice.* New York: Basic Books Inc.

Goleman, D. (1995). *Emotional intelligence: Why it can matter more than IQ.* New York: Bantam Books.

Hirsch, E. Jr. (1988). *Cultural Literacy.* New York: Vintage.

Kleiber, D. & Kirshnit, C. (1991). Sport involvement and identity formation. In L. Diamant (Ed.), *Mind-body maturity: Psychological approaches to sports, exercise, and fitness* (pp. 193–211). New York: Hemisphere Publishing Corporation.

Lickona, T. (1991). *Education for character: How our schools can teach respect and responsibility.* New York: Bantam Books.

Meyer, A., Miller, S., & Herman, M. (1993). Balancing the priorities of evaluation with the priorities of the setting: A focus on positive youth development programs in school settings. *Journal of Primary Prevention, 12*(4).

Millstein, S. (1993). A view of health from the adolescent's perspective. In S. Millstein, A. Petersen, & E. Nightingale (Eds.), *Promoting the health of adolescents* (97–118). New York: Oxford.

Perry, C. & Jessor, R. (1985). The concept of health promotion and the prevention of adolescent drug abuse. *Health Education Quarterly, 12*(2), 169–184.

Reid, I. & Tremblay, M. (1994). *Canadian youth: Does activity reduce risk.* Unpublished report to The Inter-Provincial Sport and Recreation Council.

Seidman, E. & Rappaport, J. (1974). The educational pyramid: A paradigm for training, research, and manpower utilization in community psychology. *American Journal of Community Psychology, 2,* 119–130.

Task Force on Education of Young Adolescents (1989). *Turning points: Preparing American youth for the 21st century*. New York: Carnegie Corporation.

About the Contributors

Janice Antonellis, MA, is a training consultant with the Center for Ventures in Girls' Education in Wellesley, Massachusetts. She works primarily with parents and other educators, and conducts a workshop called "Raising Courageous Daughters." She is the mother of two adolescent daughters, and has also coordinated a program for adolescent girls called the Girls Adventure Project.

Martin Bloom, PhD, received his doctorate from the University of Michigan and a certificate in social study (social work) from the University of Edinburgh, U.K. He has no pretense of being an athlete, although he swims almost daily. He has written a number of books and papers, concentrating on primary prevention, the evaluation of practice, and on human behavior and development. He teaches social work at the University of Connecticut.

David G. Blumenkrantz, PhD, is founder and president of the Center for the Advancement of Youth, Family & Community Service, Inc., in Glastonbury, Connecticut, whose focus is on building community through the re-creation of contemporary rites of passage. He received his doctorate degree in community psychology and social policy from The Union Institute. He has been a visiting fellow at the Bush Center for Social Policy and Child Development at Yale University. Dr. Blumenkrantz has served in a variety of administrative capacities in public and private human service agencies. He is the creator of the national model primary prevention initiative, the Rite of Passage Experience, ROPE. He is presently an adjunct professor in the psychology department at Central Connecticut State University.

Delight E. Champagne, PhD, has been a professor in the psychology department at Springfield College for 15 years, where she has coordinated the graduate program in student personnel and taught courses in counseling, young adult development, and career development. Prior to her work at Springfield College, she was an elementary school teacher and Director of Adult Education in Stafford, Connecticut. She has been a career consultant with the LPGA, the U.S. Olympic Committee, and adult education programs in Connecticut. She coauthored a book on career planning for athletes and authored a number of professional articles related to the developmental issues of athletes and adults.

Steven J. Danish, PhD, is the director of the Life Skills Center and professor of psychology, preventive medicine, and community health at Virginia Commonwealth University. He is a fellow of the American Psychological Association, the American Psychological Society, and the Association for the Advancement of Applied Sport Psychology (AASP) and is past president of the Society of Community Research and Action (a Division of APA) and served on the Executive Committee of AAASP. He has written over 80 articles and eight books in the areas of counseling, community and life-span developmental psychology; health and nutrition, substance abuse prevention; and sports psychology. He is the developer of the Going for the Goal Program, which was a winner of the Lela Rowland Prevention Award from the National Mental Health Association, honored by the U.S. Department of Health and Human Services as part of its Freedom from Fear Campaign, and received an honorable mention by the Points of Light Foundation. He was also involved in the development and implementation of the Career Assistance Program for Athletes (CAPA) for the United States Olympic Committee, the Youth Education through Sports (YES) Program for the NCAA, the life skills component for The First Tee, and the COACH Program sponsored by the NFL.

Kathryn L. Edmundson has a consulting practice assisting foundations, nonprofits and corporations to develop new initiatives and revitalize existing ones—through mapping analysis; new program development; fundraising, strategic communications, organization development, and technical assistance. She has expertise in a range of areas—arts, education, youth services, family services for people with disabilities, community development, leadership development, strategic communications. Formerly, she worked at The Rockefeller Foundation, New York University, and CBS as CBS Foundation President.

David Fukuzawa, MDiv, MSA, is currently a program officer with the Skillman Foundation, a private grantmaking organization in the Metropolitan Detroit area. Prior to the Foundation, he served as the director of the Human Needs Division of New Detroit, Inc., the nation's first urban coalition. His background also includes 10 years of youth work, inner-city ministry, and work in human and civil rights. He was the founding director of the Asian American Center for Justice, headquartered in Southfield. His bachelors degree is fromYale University. He holds two masters degrees from Catholic Theological Union in Chicago and Central Michigan University.

Chris Gullotta, BA, Certified Prevention Specialist, has worked with youth and their families for over a quarter of a century. She is presently the Youth Program Director for Glastonbury's Youth and Family Services. Last year she received the Connecticut Youth Services Association Award for her efforts in the field of prevention. She developed the Creative Experiences Program for her agency and has assisted other communities in developing similar programs. Ms. Gullotta frequently teaches in the STEP program at the University of Connecticut School of Social Work.

Thomas P. Gullotta, MA, MSW, is CEO of Child and Family Agency and is a member of the psychology and education departments at Eastern Connecticut State University. He is the senior author of the fourth edition of *The Adolescent Experience* and is the founding editor of the *Journal of Primary Prevention*. He is the senior book series editor for *Issues in Children's and Families' Lives*. In addition, he serves as the monograph series editor for *Prevention in Practice*. Tom holds editorial appointments on the *Journal of Early Adolescence, Journal of Adolescent Research, Adolescence*, and the *Journal of Educational and Psychological Consultation*. He serves as vice-chairman for children and prevention on the Board of the National Mental Health Association and works frequently as a consultant for several branches of the U.S. Federal Government. He has published extensively on adolescents and primary prevention.

Albert Petitpas, EdD, is a professor in the psychology department at Springfield College, Massachusetts, where he directs the graduate training program in Athletic Counseling. He is a fellow and certified consultant of the Association for the Advancement of Applied Sport Psychology. He research and applied work focus on developmental concerns of athletes, such as managing transitions and coping with injuries. He has provided consulting services to a wide range of sport organizations including the U.S. Ski Team, the Career Assistance Program for Athletes of the U.S. Olympic Committee, the National Football Foundation's Play It Smart Program, and the First Tee.

Robert W. Plant, PhD, is currently the superintendent of Riverview Children's Hospital. Prior to this he was the director of clinical services at Child and Family Agency of Southeastern Connecticut and a practitioner in private practice. He was educated under fellowships from the National Institute of Mental Health and the National Institute of Drug Abuse. He received his doctorate in clinical psychology from the University of Rochester and was a clinical and research fellow at Yale University Medical School. He is a frequent lecturer on psychotherapy and has published numerous articles on motivation for treatment, substance abuse, family support services, and a variety of clinical and practice issues.

Maureen K. Porter, PhD, is assistant professor of education and anthropology at the school of education, University of Pittsburgh. She holds adjunct positions in the anthropology department and women's studies program, and is a senior associate at the Institute for International Studies in Education and a center associate with the Learning and Research Development Center. She has studied at the University of Wisconsin-Madison and at the University of Freiburg im br. in Germany, and earned masters and doctoral degrees at Stanford University. Her interest in community festivals, and particularly in county fairs, springs from her many years of participation as a 4-H'er. She has worked in many areas of community-building and ritual studies, but is continually drawn to small, community-run celebrations. Recent honors include giving the keynote on community development at the Ohio Appalachian Conference and speaking on regional development in Augsburg, Germany. She is active as a consultant, scrapbooker, ice-cream quality control specialist, and young mother.

Joann Stemmermann, EdM, is executive director of the Center for Ventures in Girls' Education. She is also a project associate for the Harvard Outward Bound Project. She is an instructor in education at the Harvard Graduate School of Education. She created the Connecting With Courage Program at Thompson Island Outward Bound Education Center.

PROMOTING POSITIVE OUTCOMES IN CHILDREN AND YOUTH

Edited by Arthur J. Reynolds, Herbert J. Walberg, and Roger P. Weissberg

This book, the first volume in the Issues in Children's and Families' Lives series, focuses on practical solutions to the problems facing children and youth today—especially those living in urban areas. Specifically, these solutions include early childhood education, parenting programs, life skills training, school-family partnerships, school reforms, and job training. The chapters describe interventions that enhance the prospects of children and youths from early childhood to the beginning of adulthood.

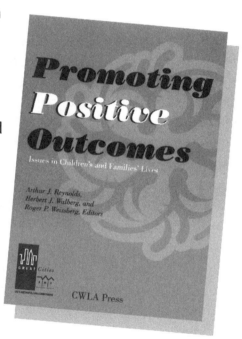

1999/0-87868-759-9/#7599 . . . . **$39.95**

THE PROMOTION OF WELLNESS IN CHILDREN AND ADOLESCENTS

Edited by Dante Cicchetti, Julian Rappaport,
Irwin Sandler, Roger P. Weissberg

A tribute to Emory L. Cowen

What can be done at the beginning and throughout a child's life to maximize the likelihood that he or she will develop in a healthy way? That question serves as the foundation for this book. The theory, research, and programs in this book go significantly beyond the more traditional mental health focus of diagnosis and repair of disorders. Rather, the vast possibilities in fostering positive development, even in the absence of risk or disorder, are proffered. This volume is a lasting tribute to Emory L. Cowen's contributions to fostering the well-being of children. In a fitting ending, Cowen presents his vision of the future of wellness enhancement of all children and adolescents.

2000/0-87868-791-2/#7912 . . . . $28.95